MICHAEL STIPE

MICHAEL STIPE

THE BIOGRAPHY

ROB JOVANOVIC

PORTRAIT

Visit the Portrait website!

Portrait publishes a wide range of non-fiction, including biography, history, science, music, popular culture and sport.

Visit our website to:
- read descriptions of our popular titles
- buy our books over the internet
- take advantage of our special offers
- enter our monthly competition
- learn more about your favourite Portrait authors

VISIT OUR WEBSITE AT: www.portraitbooks.com

First published in 2006 by **Portrait**
an imprint of
Piatkus Books Ltd
5 Windmill Street
London W1T 2JA
e-mail: info@piatkus.co.uk

This edition published 2007

The moral right of the author has been asserted

A catalogue record for this book is available from the British Library

ISBN 978 0 7499 5147 4

Text design by Paul Saunders
Edited by Penny Phillips

This book has been printed on paper manufactured with respect for the environment using wood from managed sustainable resources

Typeset by Palimpsest Book Production Limited, Stirlingshire
Printed and bound in Great Britain by Clays Ltd, St Ives plc

Sources

ALTERNATIVE PRESS, Associated Press, *Atlanta Journal* (Bo Emerson), *Billboard*, *Bucketful Of Brains* (Stuart Batsford, Marcus Gray, Jon Storey), *Details* (Chris Heath), *The Face* (Sheryl Garratt), *the Guardian* (Adam Sweeting), *Guitar World*, *Hot Press* (Mike Edgar), *Magnet*, *Melody Maker* (Harold DeMuir, Allan Jones, David Stubbs), *Mojo* (Keith Cameron), *Musician* (Bill Flanagan, Vic Garbarini, Mark Rowland), *New Musical Express* (Jack Barron, Barney Hoskyns, Gavin Martin, Terry Staunton), *New York Times*, *Observer* (Jon Savage), *OOR* (Erik van den Berg), *Option* (Mark Kemp), *Q* (David Cavanagh, Adrian Deevoy, Tom Doyle, Nick Duerden, Andy Gill, John Harris, Michael Odell, Matt Snow), *Record Collector*, *Rolling Stone* (David Fricke, Chris Heath), *Select* (Jeff Giles), *Spin*, *Sounds* (Sandy Robertson, Roy Wilkinson), *Tasty World*, *The Times* (Sean O'Hagan), *Trouser Press*, *Uncut* (David Stubbs, Adam Sweeting, Jon Wilde), *Vox* (Steve Mallins), *Washington Post*, *Word*.

Contents

Introduction

When L. P. Hartley wrote that 'the past is a foreign country; they do things differently there,' he was absolutely right. Even the recent past can seem like a century ago, when the whole pace of life was different and the way things were done was a world away from how they're done today. It was 'only' back in the early 1990s that I was working as an organic research chemist. In my spare time I'd just begun contributing to a series of music fanzines. When I look back it really *was* like a different country: everyone I knew was slimmer than today (including myself), the clothes and haircuts we had then seem foreign now, and we didn't use computers to make the fanzines – it was really a cut-and-paste environment, using scissors and glue. The internet was unheard of and, for the most part, my then favourite band, R.E.M., was still unheard of by the general public. Sure, *NME* readers knew who they were, but before *Out of Time* was released in 1991 the average person in the street would not have been able to tell you who Michael Stipe was.

Today, of course, the situation is very different. Stipe is now one of the most recognisable faces in world music and I'm writing this on a computer. In between then and now R.E.M. became the best band in the world and then the biggest band in the world, and then slipped back to a more manageable level where they stand today as one of the most respected bands in the world.

Having followed the band over two decades, I've witnessed their rise and slight fall with interest. As a former member of the R.E.M. fan club I've been lucky enough to see the band at close quarters giving intimate performances to small numbers of fans, even when they were selling 10 million copies of every album they released. Unlike some other R.E.M. biographers I've made several trips to Athens, Georgia, and been on the receiving end of some wonderful southern hospitality, including being granted the use of the R.E.M. office archives to research the band. I've also been lucky enough to meet and talk to the band members over a number of years. A nicer globetrotting bunch you're unlikely to meet.

Michael Stipe comes across as an average person in an unusual position. He handles it very well, and while some try to paint him as some mystical messiah, he's merely a pop star who's pretty good at what he does – but because he's someone who likes a good laugh he'll throw a curve ball to the press once in a while to keep things interesting. He isn't someone to idolise, but he is interesting enough to spend time researching a book on.

Along the way I've had much help as usual, so I'd like to thank: my wife Carolyn, ex-partner-in-crime Tim Abbott, Gino Farabella, Graham Palmer, Peter Buck, Mike Mills, Kevin O'Neil, Amy Hairston, David Bell and Chris Bilheimer at the R.E.M. office, Louise Gallacher, Alison Jolley, Tom Smith, Linda Hopper, Michael Lachowski, Laura Levine, Ken Stringfellow, Scott McCaughey, Kathleen O'Brien, Neil Phillips, Jason Gross, Denise Abbott, Dean Brush, Paul Butchart, Chris Edwards, Mitch Easter, Terry Allen, Steve Wynn and of course Alice Davis, the picture of patience, Alison Sturgeon and everyone else at Piatkus Books.

Rob Jovanovic
Burton Joyce
England
2006

Chapter One

Where's the War?

1979 and 2004

'Two years ago we were in France with Bert, who is our attorney. Bert doesn't know any foreign languages, but he's very strident and he tries to communicate himself. What's a good word to describe Bert? Verbose. He's very verbose. He was looking for the train station in Paris and he went around all day asking people, "*Où est la guerre*?" As you know, in French train station is "*gare*". "*Guerre*" means war. So Bert's going around asking everyone, "Where's the war?"'

— MICHAEL STIPE

MICHAEL STIPE ISN'T PSYCHIC. Like millions of other teenagers he had dreams that he could be a rock star, but deep down he never really thought it would happen, and not on the scale that it did. When he was walking through Athens, Georgia, to the Wuxtry record store with his two sisters, he couldn't have predicted the chain of events that was about to ripple away from a chance meeting. Stipe almost didn't move to Athens, and Peter Buck – who he was about to meet at Wuxtry – had travelled around before landing, by chance, in this quiet college town.

Wuxtry Records was much more than just a small chain of record stores. Its branches in the southern US cities of Atlanta and Athens proved to be a fertile breeding ground where music fans could meet and discuss and listen to music that wasn't necessarily being played on the radio. In 1978, 22-year-old Peter Buck – a Californian by birth – moved from the Atlanta branch to one of the two branches in Athens. He later took over at the store on the corner of College Avenue and Clayton Street, which was as much a comic-book store as it was a record shop. For Buck, a massive music collector himself, it was the dream job.

Athens, with its population of around 40,000 (of which half comprised the student body), had a burgeoning music scene that belied its size. As the 1970s drew to a close, an increasing number of clubs and bars were starting to allow bands to play, but you could still count them on the fingers of one hand. What helped make Athens such a hotbed of activity was the profusion of house parties and outdoor events at which bands could play, even if they'd formed only that week. The small-town atmosphere (even though Athens is technically classed as a city) meant that everyone knew everyone else. At weekends, large groups of revellers would roll from party to party, seeking out the houses and gardens that had free beer kegs and a band on an improvised stage – or simply playing in the living room. Athens's heritage meant that a surplus of large houses around the downtown area had been converted to student rentals.

One local scenester famously quipped that an Athens party wasn't complete until two girls were fighting and a guy showed up wearing a dress. After Buck and Stipe had met at Wuxtry, they too could be found at all manner of parties any day of the week. As the hot muggy Georgia summer approached, the party season really took off. Everyone wanted to be outdoors, so the parties just followed. The student radio WUOG did numerous outside broadcasts, bands played outside, parties spilled into the surrounding countryside.

As well as a plethora of outdoor parties, Athens's favourable weather led to another popular late-night and early-morning pursuit: skinny-dipping at the local ponds and water-filled quarries. Often as a club closed for the evening or a party ran out of beer, the whole troupe would decamp to a secluded body of water deep in the Georgian undergrowth, where the sweaty dance-soaked revellers would continue to party, often naked, under the moonlight. There were drawbacks, though: bugs, muddy embankments and the occasional local or law-enforcement officer with a torch had to be contended with. It's surprising that no one was ever reported getting hurt – or worse – as the heady mixture of alcohol and swimming was not the wisest of combinations. For those not willing to travel too far for a quick dip, there was always the option of crashing the private pools of several apartment blocks around town.

Athens didn't just turn into party central overnight; several key moments broke the ice and helped forge the route. A bunch of five hip kids in wacky outfits and with a small handful of wacky songs, calling themselves the B-52's, played a house party in February 1977, which many locals saw as the ice-breaker to everyone else's thinking they too could form a band. The other big factor in helping to start things – or allowing things to happen – was the University of Georgia (UGA) art department. This forward-thinking department actively encouraged all sorts of experimental art, which spilled over into music.

Before then, Athens had been a pretty unremarkable southern town. Between the start of the 20th century and the Second World War, the number of inhabitants doubled from 10,000 to 20,000. Having in the previous century boasted only small mills, during the 1950s and 1960s Athens saw an influx of outside investment that swelled the town to almost the size it is today. The university rapidly expanded too, quickly becoming Athens's largest employer.

Before the mid-1970s, it was bands like Sea Level and singers like Randall Bramblett that were Athens's contribution to the world of music. Almost no one remembers them now. Athens was the site of the 'world's largest streak' at UGA in 1974 as the area's liberal nature hit the news. Later in the year the future members of the B-52's – Fred Schneider, Kate Pierson, Keith Strickland and Ricky and Cindy Wilson – met. Punk was about to hit the USA and slowly seep its way south, allowing bands like the B-52's to jump on stage with no training and just have a go at being a band. The first B-52's 'show' was a rambling affair. Using as their stage a large wooden table that could have given way at any moment, they played each song for six or seven minutes while everyone danced like crazy, then took a break and rejoined the party themselves. A little while later they clambered back on the table and got everyone dancing again. When they'd exhausted their short repertoire of songs they went back to the beginning and played them all again.

This style of guerrilla gigging became legendary. And a lot of the party-goers decided they could form their own bands too. People's living rooms were soon too small to hold the numbers of people wanting to cram into these shows. It was OK in the summer, as everyone would just spill out into gardens and on to the street, but in the winter that wasn't so much fun. Local bars and clubs gradually came around to seeing the potential of having these unorthodox bands – after all, they weren't playing the usual southern boogie or Allman Brothers covers – play at their venues. But in the same way as they'd set up bands without a second thought, the party-goers decided they could set up their own clubs to host them as well.

The most famous of these was the 40 Watt Club. To put on a Halloween party, Curtis Crowe hired out a big old ballroom above some shops on College Avenue at the centre of town. Cheap and large, it fitted the bill perfectly. The drawback was that it had no electricity, so long extension leads were rolled out for the equipment and the whole space was lit by a – you guessed it – 40-watt light bulb. The night was a rousing success and the 40 Watt Club became a travelling road show setting up at various places around town.

Partying reached legendary levels in 1978 – so much so that a book, *Party Out of Bounds*, was written about the scene (by Rodger

Lyle Brown). Partying was a serious business too. Michael Lachowski set up the Athens Party Line, a phone number to call for a recording of where the best parties were that night. Everything was being done for fun; no one thought about making money from it. 'We were just a bunch of free-spirit artists and never really planned anything,' said the B-52's' Cindy Wilson. 'Whatever happened happened.' What did happen to the B-52's happened very quickly. Before the end of 1977 they had been invited to New York, where they played at the legendary Max's Kansas City. The following January they headlined the inaugural Atlanta Punk Festival, four months before their début single, 'Rock Lobster', was released.

While the B-52's were still in their embryonic stages, Peter Buck, then still in Atlanta, met a girl by the name of Kathleen O'Brien. Soon after moving to Athens, he found out that she had also moved there, to study at UGA. In Athens she was getting heavily involved in the increasingly influential WUOG radio station. By now Michael Stipe had been pestering Peter Buck to start a band with him. Buck could play a little bit of guitar, and Stipe could sing. But for a band they needed more. It was through Kathleen O'Brien that Stipe and Buck met a ready-made rhythm section, from Macon, Georgia, who had also just come to study in Athens. Bill Berry, a self-confessed wild child, played drums; his unlikely bass-playing partner was the geeky-looking Mike Mills. Like Stipe, the pair had enrolled at UGA in January 1979. By the end of their first year the quartet had agreed to form a band.

In early 1980 O'Brien influenced their collective futures even more when she asked them to play their début show for her birthday party. All very nervous about playing before an audience, they nevertheless agreed to do it. So on 5 April 1980, in a deconsecrated church, the future R.E.M. readied themselves for their first show. Michael Stipe was especially nervous, downing his fair share of alcoholic Dutch courage before they began. Had he been psychic he would probably have been even more nervous: he was about to take the first step on the long ladder of becoming the front man for the biggest band in the world.

★ ★ ★

Fast-forward a quarter of a century. It's October 2004 and President George W. Bush is at the end of his campaign to win a second term in office. Some say he didn't really win the first time around and shouldn't even be here, but since the terrorist attacks of 11 September 2001 and the war in Iraq those opinions have been pushed well into the background. The mood in America is polarised. After a universal coming-together following the al-Qaeda atrocities the country is split over the war in Iraq. Entertainers from the world of music and film are getting involved as never before. Michael Stipe and R.E.M. are at the centre of the campaign to remove Bush from the White House.

On the 'Vote for Change' tour, R.E.M. were working along-side James Taylor, the Dixie Chicks, Bruce Springsteen, Bright Eyes, John Fogerty, Pearl Jam, Jackson Browne and many others. The tour would play shows in 11 'swing states' during October, right before the November election. Bruce Springsteen had written a long letter to the *New York Times* explaining why he wanted change and why it was so important for people to get out and vote. The anti-Bush/-war lobby also included Sean 'Puffy' Combs, Willie Nelson, Sean Penn, Johnny Depp, Michael Moore (of course), Leonardo DiCaprio, Tim Robbins and Jon Bon Jovi. All had been outraged when in July 2004 Linda Ronstadt was physically removed from one of her own shows in Las Vegas.

The singer had been expressing her support for Michael Moore and his controversial anti-Bush film *Fahrenheit 9/11* throughout her summer dates. But at the Aladdin Casino show in Las Vegas, things got out of hand. At the end of her show, Ronstadt dedicated the Eagles' 'Desperado' to Michael Moore – and the room erupted. The casino management stepped in and Ronstadt was escorted to her tour bus, without even being allowed to collect her personal belongings from her room. In the prickly political times it seemed the right of free speech was being taken away unless you agreed with the status quo. Even the reporting of this incident caused eyebrows to be raised.

The Associated Press said, 'Ronstadt's comments drew loud boos, and some of the 4,500 people in attendance stormed out of the theater. People also tore down concert posters and tossed cocktails into the air.' The local *Las Vegas Sun*, on the other hand, commented that 'the room erupted into equal parts boos and cheers'. America seemed to be at war with itself, and those with the ability to speak out felt they had to try to do something – and that included Michael Stipe.

'It was always embarrassing to me that when I was in a room with either Clinton or Gore, or for that matter the Dalai Lama, they've got to have better things to do than hanging around with pop stars,' said Michael Stipe. 'But I've got something they want, or something that can help with them in their mission.' As had the rest of the 'Vote for Change' tour. Republican politicians spotted this danger and started to attack the artists rather than their own political opponents. Boycotts were called for various films and albums. 'I felt like I couldn't have written the music I've written and been on stage singing about the things that I've sung about for the last 25 years and not take part in this particular election,' said Bruce Springsteen. Pearl Jam's Eddie Vedder added, 'At some point, you can't sit still, you can't spend your life, when people are getting killed, without asking serious questions about why.'

Ultimately George Bush won the race. When R.E.M. performed their first gig after the election, at New York's Madison Square Garden, Stipe had little to say. The band opened with 'It's The End Of The World As We Know It (And I Feel Fine)', which was usually their closing song. Stipe later said it had been 'a black week'. While the tour had not had the hoped-for overall effect, it had made a difference. A reported 21 million voters under the age of 30 took part in the election, an increase of 4.5 million over the 2000 election. What's more, the under-30 age group was the only one to give John Kerry a majority. Stipe hadn't managed to change the world, but he had made a difference. Isn't that really all that can be asked?

So what had happened in the intervening 25 years? How had a shy college kid come to tour the US in an attempt to bring down a government? Stipe now cuts a very distinctive figure in the entertainment world; his face is universally known. Most people in the Western world can name one R.E.M. song, or at least hum it. 'I can go to Korean neighbourhoods and be fairly anonymous, but just about anywhere else that's no longer the case,' he says. 'But, at the end of the day, I cut myself shaving just like everybody else. You can't let something as abstract as fame rule the important decisions and priorities that you choose in your life, and if you do you're kind of a fool.'

Stipe is a rare performer in that he appeals to both genders, all ages, all colours and to a lesser extent all nationalities and all religions. That's one of the reasons R.E.M. have sold 50 million albums. As an articulate, thoughtful singer he's easily labelled a spokesperson for a generation – but which one? He appeals to teenagers, 20-somethings, 30-somethings . . . the list goes on. In 2010 Stipe will be 50.

While battling against overexposure and a slight loss of critical acclaim, Stipe and R.E.M. have become a soundtrack to your life. There is much speculation about Stipe, the most closely analysed of the band, much of it wide of the mark. 'There's a headlong rush to make Michael the genius weirdo,' says R.E.M. adviser Bertis Downs. 'Yes, he's a very complicated guy. He's also a very talented guy who is very warm and caring.' Not surprisingly, when you look closely, Stipe is just as anyone taken from the street would be if they were thrust into the homes of millions of people and every nuance and comment they ever made was magnified out of all proportion.

Stipe brings many things to R.E.M: artiness, mysticism, lyrical obliqueness, ambiguity, a striking visual presence and the indefinable 'front-man appeal'. The 'Vote for Change' tour was just one side of a complicated performer who is equally at home talking about politics, the environment, art, music, photography or film. Let's see what he has to say.

Chapter Two

No Place Like Home

1960 to 1978

'You can travel around the world eight and a half times and always find out, click your heels together, there's no place like home.'

— MICHAEL STIPE

JOHN MICHAEL STIPE, to give him his full name, was born in Decatur, Georgia, on 4 January 1960. The Stipe family already had a daughter, Cyndy; a second girl would follow John Michael and be named Lynda. John would soon be called by only his middle name, Michael. His parents had led a travelling existence for a while, as his father was an aircraft pilot in the US Army; it was during a rare stop that Michael was born, in the American South. Before having children his father had been active in the Korean War, and later he would serve overseas again as the Vietnam War escalated. All the time he was away, Michael's mother, Maryanne, would hold the family together. She'd sit the children down with their tea to see if they could spot their father on the nightly television news reports about the conflict. Because of Stipe senior's position, during Michael's formative years the family were constantly moving between army bases.

Whether Michael's father was at home or abroad the family was an extremely close one. Because they moved so frequently, Stipe never really had a chance to make friends outside the army bases, though his parents did try to foster links with local communities in the US and Europe. But just when it seemed he had settled in somewhere, he knew that the family would be off and travelling again. This constant upheaval instilled a 'family first, friends second' outlook, since his family was the only constant in his life. Stipe came to accept that he would make friends only to have to up sticks and leave them behind; as a child he never knew anything else. As an adult he has exhibited the same rootlessness, often leaving people to wonder whether he finds it hard to stay close to anyone.

The strong family bonds formed during Michael's youth have continued to be his personal strength throughout his adult life. He's been extremely protective of his family and their privacy. To this day almost nothing has emerged about his parents' lives before he was born; even their names have been closely guarded secrets. Sister Cyndy grew up to become a care worker, while Lynda has had a slightly more public profile, having played in a number of bands herself. Michael still spends as much time as possible with his parents, and often flies them out to R.E.M. shows around the world.

Michael's earliest days in Georgia also brought him into close contact with his paternal grandfather, who was a Methodist preacher. Stipe later revealed that his own name had been chosen partly because of his grandfather's work. 'Methodism was started by John Wesley, who was, in his way, a really radical guy,' says Stipe. 'He believed in a lot of individual responsibility. It's not the kind of religion that's right around your throat. I was named after him. It wasn't like a fundamentalist, born-again Baptist thing. The Methodist Church doesn't try to dictate every single aspect of your life.' Religion has not, however, ever seemed to play a prominent role in Michael's life. What did emerge from his relationship with his grandfather was a set of strong memories of his grandfather at work. As with other southern American rock performers with links to Biblepreaching, the ebb and flow of the service easily translated to that of a rock performance.

'My grandfather wasn't a pulpit-pounder,' says Stipe, 'although I do remember him doing that from time to time and it making a big impression on me. The excitement from that, for a kid, can be really overpowering. I don't know what the right word is, it was more than just a "kick" or a "thrill" – it was like "Wow!" It's such great theatre and can be so beautiful. I guess I just wanted to be part of that somehow, maybe not the religion, but just that feeling that my grandfather was giving off.'

Stipe's earliest childhood memory was of catching scarlet fever at the age of two. 'I was hallucinating and I was having my picture taken,' said Stipe. 'I had a Christmas sweater on and I was really miserable and there was this guy zooming in and out. To me that was weird, but I can remember people remarking that *I* was weird. I remember the photographer asking me to smile and me not being able to fathom smiling.'

Michael Stipe the young boy was very like any other. Hyperactive, he would run and run all day before collapsing from exhaustion and sleeping where he fell. He told the *New Musical Express* in 1994 that he had hypoglycaemia and had to eat a meal every three hours because his metabolism worked so fast. This excess of energy has helped to cement his reputation as a tireless worker throughout his life. Even now, when R.E.M. take a few months off Stipe can be found working on various non-music projects and jetting around the globe.

As a child he was protective of his two sisters, and in the course of his adult life people have remarked that he seems more comfortable in the presence of women. Growing up in largely female company – with his mother and sisters and a nanny – while his father was away presumably has a lot to do with it.

Very keen to explore, he was an avid collector of little boys' paraphernalia. Dead-snake and spider collections were some of his favourites. Among the former were copperheads and cotton-mouths, while the latter included black widows. They would be lugged along as the family moved around the southern army bases (a brief stint in Alabama was soon followed by a trip further west to Texas), as would his prized cow's skull. Dead animals weren't the norm, though, and the Stipe kids usually had pets. Michael's dog, Major, would accompany them around the world.

Over the years in the hundreds, if not thousands of interviews that Stipe has given, his openness about his own life has changed considerably. Early interviews portrayed him as incredibly shy (which he was), before he went through a phase of almost self-mythologising – no doubt something he did to keep himself interested during long spells of promotional work for the latest album, single or video. Now he seems to have matured and often goes back, or is led back by an interviewer, to statements he made long ago. He takes great pains to point out when something was just an off-the-cuff remark that was blown out of proportion, or else denies it and puts the record straight. An example is an early remark he made about having been an extremely sensitive and perceptive child. On an Australian talk show in 2003 he denied having been overly sensitive as a child, but did say, 'I had an incredibly happy childhood. But whenever something was going on in the world, certainly within my family and the adults were all a little bit frantic, I seemed to be the one that broke away from the sandpit and would walk over and tug on someone's shirt and say, "What's happening?"'

In late 1967 the Stipes had their furthest move to date when Michael's father was posted to West Germany. Michael has previously been quoted as saying he could remember every single day of his 18 months in Europe, and though he later said he'd been misquoted the experience certainly resonated with him for the rest of his life. The family lived on a base close to the Dutch border, and for Stipe it was a massive culture shock to go from the US South – all he had known for seven years – to Europe. He recounted the journey over during the Australian television interview: 'I remember being on the plane and throwing up and my mum telling my dad that I was going to throw up, and him saying, "Maryanne, stop saying that because he is going to do it." And of course I did. I used to vomit a lot actually when we travelled. Now that I think about it, we had a signal where I would say "Stop" in the car, and they learned to stop immediately.' Michael has random memories from his time in West Germany: of a gypsy camp near the army base; a frozen railway line near which he would play; and a trip to Holland to see some flowers.

In 1968 Stipe senior took a tour of duty in South-East Asia. It was obviously a worrying time for the family, Mrs Stipe being left to cope with three young children. 'I remember eating French fries,' Stipe says, 'and getting ketchup all over my lap because I was watching *The Flintstones* and they would interrupt the show to show these soldiers running through North Vietnam. Pretty wild for an eight-year-old. My mother would say, "Now watch for your father." We would of course sit there and go, "I think I saw him," over and over again. At that time, transcontinental phone calls were not possible, certainly not from Vietnam. The letters that he would write and pictures that he would send were coming from this very faraway place. But I think it was a way of not only making us realise where he was, but also recognising the situation, keeping us close to him through those periods.'

Watching *The Flintstones* is characteristic of the young Michael Stipe, and he has always been a big cartoon fan. As an adult he had tattoos done of Krazy Kat, and the packaging for R.E.M.'s *Monster* album included the character Migraine Boy. In his childhood his favourite cartoon was Mighty Mouse, so his dad nicknamed Michael 'Mr Mouse'. Stipe senior has been described by Michael as a 'Math wizard', and he actually tried to explain the Vietnam War to his son with algebra. Whether or not this was completely serious is unknown, but the elder Stipe evidently possesses a very dry sense of humour. Michael Stipe once said that it could sometimes take years before someone figured out how funny something his father had said actually was. This wry mischievousness is something he has clearly passed on to his son.

It's not surprising that when Michael later began writing songs the war had some influence on him; what *is* perhaps surprising is that he seems to have written only two directly about it – 'Orange Crush' and 'Body Count' – the second of which was never even recorded in a studio. When Stipe senior thankfully returned to Europe in one piece, unlike so many of his countrymen, he rarely spoke about his experiences to his family. Michael knows little about what he went through or what he saw in Vietnam – or in Korea for that matter. 'There's a part of his life that I know nothing about,' says Michael. 'I really would never have given him any credit for it; he has the ability to pick this machine up off the ground and fly it around, in the worst circumstances, with people firing at you, and all these incredible fucking things. That's amazing to me. Helicopters scare the life out of me.'

★　★　★

The Stipes always made sure they would spend Christmas together, and even when Michael was a jet-setting megastar he would always ensure that the family was together for the holidays. These family gatherings were clearly very important to him, and older interviews have him claiming to remember every Christmas present he ever received from the age of seven upwards. Later he denied this, saying he was misquoted. 'There are a lot of misquotes in music journalism, more so than even in the American news media, which is hard to imagine,' he explained. 'In certain parts of the world, but certainly in the UK, they tend to take one little thing and turn it into an entire story. You know, I'm sentimental. I tread that line carefully, I think, as a lyricist and as an artist, being a man in the late-20th century and now the 21st century, showing insecurity and showing sentimentality and showing vulnerability particularly is not something that people are that used to. Anyway, back to Christmas. We do all of the Christmas things. We sit around, we have a big dinner, we trim the tree, and my parents go to a sunrise service, we open presents.'

As far as music went, before he was a teenager Michael didn't have any strong leanings in that direction. He recalls a certain Mr Pemberton who owned the local record store in Texas. 'He was really old and looked really mean,' laughs Stipe. 'But he was really nice, and he used to give me and my sister the singles he didn't need any more, the ones that wouldn't sell.' Before going to Europe Stipe also took part in his first musical performance at school. The song he performed was 'Dizzy' (originally by Tommy Roe). 'They ran out of organs so I had to play the accordion,' says Stipe. 'Me and this other guy named Michael, who had ringworm and a burr haircut. Neither of us could sing, so we convinced the teacher to let us yell out beatnik phrases like "Cool Daddy-o"!' This accordion story has been exaggerated over the years, by Stipe and by journalists, to the point where he was a child prodigy and played to very high levels. No doubt Stipe once made an off-the-cuff jokey comment which became distorted through a process of Chinese whispers. One of his first experiments – as it is for millions of children – was with a little tape recorder. 'The first recording I ever made was when I was 13,' he recalled. 'My sister had one of those secretary's type of tape recorders. One day, everyone was gone from the house. I locked myself in the den in the basement, turned the thing on "record" and screamed for ten minutes.'

In the early 1970s Michael's father was sent back to the USA, where he was stationed at Fort Hood in Texas, and the family moved to Copperas Cove, just over 100 miles south of Dallas. At the Copperas Cove Junior High School, which all three Stipe children attended, Michael helped his class win the prestigious Christmas Door Decorating Contest. In the mid-1990s, a local newspaper tracked down his seventh-grade maths teacher, Mary Shipley, and quizzed her on what Michael had been like as a student. 'Mike was a good student and did really well in class,' she recalled. 'I wish I had kept his old papers. Now I ask all of my students for their autographs, because you never know, there may be a future Michael Stipe in one of my classes!' Asked what was his worst memory from high school, Stipe replied simply, 'Grades 9 through 12'.

At school, Michael was most interested in fossils, geology and archaeology. These would continue to be at the forefront of his academic thinking right up to his enrolling at university, where he almost signed up for a geology course before deciding that the faculty building was too far away and opting for courses closer to his dorm. 'I liked the idea of stripped-down men and women with bandanas and cut-off shorts digging in a ditch until a dinosaur appeared,' said Stipe of his early enthusiasm.

It was back in the US that Stipe bought his first 7-inch single, Tammy Wynette's 'Skip A Rope', but at home his parents' musical favourites were less than inspirational in shaping his rock-music tastes. Stipe recalled that they mostly listened to Gershwin, Mancini, Wanda Jackson and the soundtrack to *Doctor Zhivago*. Such tunes were of course quite detached from the world of rock music in the early 1970s. Prog and glam rock had briefly come and made an impression, but a massive musical about-turn was about to be made in the middle of the decade. For Michael Stipe 1975 would prove a pivotal year. Meanwhile he was growing into a shy, introverted teenager – the polar opposite, in fact, of most of the pupils at what was a loud, outgoing kind of school.

The previous year, yet another move had taken the Stipe family to Collinsville, which was near East St Louis, just over the state line in Illinois. Stipe found it difficult to adapt at first. After attending Collinsville High for the final four years of his schooling, he began a series of after-school jobs to earn some spending money. Locals mischievously nicknamed him the 'Maybelline Cowboy' because he had long eyelashes, looked very much like his sister Lynda and had a Texan accent. One job was at the local Waffle

House, and a later one at a local bar called Sonny & Cher's, where he 'worked as a busboy in the discotheque; I carried ice around'.

Part of the money he earned was spent on his new obsession, photography. His father gave him a Nikon camera and he signed up for a photography course. Photography would play a big part in his life and thinking. It might now seem strange, given that we know him as a writer, but he preferred to keep a 'diary' by taking photographs of everything and everyone around him. Other funds went the way of a subscription to the influential New York magazine, the *Village Voice*, which Stipe claims to have come by 'accidentally'. 'Right about that time, middle to late 1975, they were talking about this thing that was going on in New York with Television and Patti Smith and the Ramones,' he said. 'I read about all of those bands before I ever heard them, and it just sounded so amazing.'

Ever since the Velvet Underground had been recording music that tapped into the hearts and minds of loners, outsiders, rebels and the disaffected in the late-1960s, New York had cultivated an undercurrent of musical poets and radical outcasts. In this atmosphere of rebellion a young woman by the name of Patti Smith enlisted the help of ex-Velvet John Cale to produce her début album, *Horses*.

Stipe had been listening to some pretty middle-of-the-road material, even by mid-1970s standards. Elton John, David Essex and some run-of-the-mill heavy metal were not exactly the genre-changing stuff of lore, but Stipe gradually began to suspect that there was more going on below the surface of popular music. In the monthly music magazines that were mailed to the Midwest from New York, he read more about bands such as Television and the Ramones and saw photos of gigs by Patti Smith. Everything in these pages seemed alien to him, but at the same time was exciting. The only problem was that where Stipe lived, getting anything to listen to by these bands was just about impossible. It wasn't until Patti Smith's *Horses* was released that he had a chance to hear what the fuss was really all about.

So in November 1975, Stipe circled the date when the local

army base's PX store was getting a delivery and skipped the last period of school to go and buy *Horses* right away. What happened next has become the stuff of Stipean legend. 'I had been waiting for weeks for its release,' he says. 'I then went to work at the Waffle House, second shift, till 11 p.m. I drove home and sat in the living room, in the dark, with the headphones on. I was so hungry so I got this giant bowl of cherries out of the Frigidaire and sat on the couch all night till morning when I had to go back to school. I couldn't stop listening to it. I had these crappy headphones on, and I sat up all night listening to Patti Smith and eating this bowl of cherries going, "Oh shit", "Holy fuck", and then I was sick. I was very impressionable, very gullible. I heard *Horses* and it gave me, you know, I had this secret and I was afraid to tell anyone about it. I didn't think anybody would accept it. It gave me incredible strength and I knew immediately that that's what I wanted to do. I decided that morning that I was going to dedicate my life to being in a band. I don't know, it was a very naïve decision to make that I was going to dedicate my life to being in a band. I didn't even know that I could sing at that point. But I could.'

'I was a teenager in the '70s, so I watched Don Kirshner's *Rock Concert* [TV programme], which was pretty raw, wild, and very diverse in terms of what they presented,' recalled Stipe. 'They had a knack for presenting people that weren't nationally known acts, like Bad Company and David Bowie. They were both mind-blowing at the time, but it was presenting a universe that I knew very little about. If I had been aware of it, it would only have been through record covers and magazines, so TV takes something that's two-dimensional, and even though it's still two-dimensional, it's moving. That's the power of television. You're seeing these people actually walk and move their hands around, and you get a better idea of who and what they are.'

In a loud and sometimes oppressive high-school atmosphere, Stipe turned his life around from being a painfully shy loner to becoming an extrovert wannabe rock star. In the process he went from having a pudding-bowl haircut to sporting a curly, semi-afro, all the time wearing a pair of large-framed spectacles. Through 1976 he continued to read about and listen to the bands coming from the east, and by the end of the year he was keen to adopt the punk anyone-can-form-a-band attitude.

He also took inspiration from closer to home. He had become friends with classmate Melanie Carr, who in 1977 started singing with a local covers band. Stipe was still working after school at the local Waffle House, and he and Carr would debate music for hours while he was supposed to be working. 'Michael would serve me tea and talk for hours about how we'd be big rock stars someday,' Carr told the *Waterfront Times*. 'I don't remember there ever being a point where I suddenly said "I want to be a singer",' recalled Stipe. 'I always used to hum along with records. I think one reason I wanted to be a singer was my friend [Melanie Carr] sang in a band and I felt left out. If she could do it, why couldn't I?'

At the same time as making this new discovery, Stipe was having conflicting thoughts about his sexuality.

The Stipe hormones must have been racing during 1976–77. Aged 16 and 17, he was figuring out what he wanted to do with his life, getting into music and photography, working after hours to fund these joint passions, trying to get into a band and wrestling with the idea of his own sexuality. 'Between the ages of 16 and 19, I really had no idea where my desires lay,' he explains. 'That was when I was like, "What the fuck am I?" I read Rimbaud's entire works when I was 16 and that was a good thing to read at a time of really confused sexuality. That was the other thing that punk rock was kind of good for. It was different from the macho posing of the music at that time.'

The death of 'the King' on 16 August 1977 made a strong impression on Michael – though he has never really confessed to being a big Elvis fan. Almost a decade later R.E.M. would record a song called 'Just A Touch', which was directly about Stipe's experiences of the day Presley died. Ironically, Stipe was due to work at Sonny & Cher's, and the act booked to play at the club that night was an Elvis impersonator! Maybe in hindsight it would have been a good idea to cancel the act, but it went ahead anyway, whether in good taste or not. Stipe's co-workers found out about Presley's death in a variety of ways – by word of mouth, by reading about it in the paper or by hearing about it on the news – all of which Stipe included in the lyric. The poster advertising the show said 'Is it Elvis or just a touch?' and this gave Stipe his song title. He also referred to women mourning in black, and to the fact that nobody found the impersonator's act very funny. The most telling line in the song came when Stipe credited Elvis with setting the pace and said that now Stipe himself would have to carry on in his place. Teenage fantasy or telling insight?

In 1978, in a short space of time Stipe went through a whole series of rites of passage. He was going to have to grow up in a hurry. He finally started singing in a band, he graduated from high school and enrolled at university, his parents moved away and he lived on his own for the first time, and he was involved in a car accident. Quite a heavy load for Stipe to carry.

Stipe finally found a band to sing with, after doing what many hopefuls have done down the years – responding to an advertisement. He couldn't play any instruments so he would have to be a singer, despite the fact he'd never really sung. Inspired by seeing Melanie Carr get on stage and front a band, he grabbed his chance when he saw a poster seeking a singer to join a punk covers band. It was exactly the kind of opening he'd been looking for. The band was called Bad Habits and the advert had been posted by guitarist Joe Haynes, who had similar musical tastes to Stipe.

Stipe went along for an audition and was immediately given the job. 'That was the first time I ever learned the words to a song and sang them into a microphone,' admitted Stipe. 'We did cover songs from the '60s, a few new-wave covers, and a few originals. The most interesting thing about the band was meeting Joe Haynes. He played guitar. He was the first person I met who was already listening to the music I had just started discovering.' Joe Haynes's remembrances of Michael Stipe were very different from those of Stipe's schoolmates. Far from being a potential rock star, in Haynes's opinion Stipe was almost an anti-rock star. 'He doesn't like the limelight, and couldn't begin to spend a million dollars,' Haynes told a St Louis newspaper. 'He lives a pretty simple life and requires few things.'

Bad Habits practised a lot, but didn't get many bookings. By now Stipe was about to graduate from Collinsville High, and at the end of the year the band had the chance to play at a prep-rally at school. But, depending on who tells the story, they missed out either because the school thought they weren't good enough or because the event ran out of time. Either way, Stipe was hopping mad about it and kicked up a fuss. This was a very different Michael Stipe from the one who had been shy and introverted a couple of years before. Now he was as loud and brash as the rest of the older school population; his final high-school yearbook entry attests to this. Stipe was voted the member of the year most likely to be a 'future rock star' – something that baffled the young singer. He didn't think that his idea of being a rock star was the same as his classmates'. 'I have never thought of myself as a very cool person,' he said in 2003. 'I think a lot of people that wind up being public figures, there might be some degree of insecurity that leads you to desire that kind of attention. I consider myself to still be kind of a nerd and not particularly talented, attractive, interesting, intelligent or anything else. I used to wonder why my friends hung out with me. Then, you know, of course a little bit later in life I figured out that I do have qualities that are worthwhile. The degree to which I apply myself as an artist, as a songwriter, is at the very least absolutely sincere and giving everything that I can. And that counts for something.'

Stipe's graduation photograph has been used on R.E.M. items and famously on the *Eponymous* compilation album sleeve with the banner headline 'They airbrushed my face', which Stipe says the school did to remove his acne from the photo. The summer after graduation saw Stipe party, party, party. He spent many weekends at the Varsity Theater, where he attended numerous performances of the *Rocky Horror Picture Show*. The show ran all summer long and was described as 'one part freak show, one part festival'. As is customary, the audience would dress up as characters from the show for each performance, and Stipe could regularly be seen attending as 'Frank N Furter' in black fishnet stockings, red corset, satin pants and silver platform shoes. A few photos of him in this outfit still circulate, but Mike Mills once said, 'Good luck finding any photos from his *Rocky Horror* days; he's had them all destroyed. Sometimes people send them and he destroys them.'

At the end of the summer Stipe had to make a big decision about his future. The family was moving back to Georgia – to Watkinsville, to be precise, a few miles south of a sleepy college town called Athens. Stipe senior was retiring from the army and wanted to settle down back in his home state. Michael, however, wanted to stay in Illinois, enrol at university and continue with Bad Habits. He was accepted at nearby Southern Illinois University, Edwardsville (SIUE), to study art and painting. Michael's parents had always been very supportive of their children's choices in life, and that was no different now. 'They were scared for me to start with but saw my commitment and were then supportive,' says Stipe. 'But once I decide to do something I'm not one to back off or give in. They were encouraging throughout.' Michael's decision to stay in Illinois also impacted on younger sister Lynda, who had followed Michael's musical lead and got into punk and new-wave bands. Later she would co-write with Michael and form bands of her own. But for now her means of transport had just been cut off.

Collinsville is split from St Louis by the mighty Mississippi river, and Stipe skipped over the water to test out what he thought would be the model of cool urban living. He moved to nearby Woodriver, where he shared a house with three members of another local band called Bevision (Matt Cahill, Dave and Steve Diesel). It's a time of his life about which he has never really opened up, apart from to comment on the hardships of being a student. 'I was having a blast in St Louis,' he recalled in 1984. 'I thought it was so urban and so punk rock, whatever. I was living with this band, and we were eating spaghetti and butter every night because we couldn't afford anything else, and they lived in this industrial waste site, and you know it was an exciting and wonderful time.' By now he was starting to see bands first-hand, and during his months in Woodriver he caught shows by the likes of the Ramones, Wire and the Jam.

During their entire lifespan, despite putting in many hours of practice Bad Habits only ever played two or three shows. The high point of their short-lived career was when they opened for Dave Edmunds's and Nick Lowe's Rockpile at a local venue called Mississippi Nights. Stipe did have just about enough money to keep and run a car, but that autumn he was involved in an accident. Over the years the descriptions of this crash have changed, but according to various versions it was 'probably' a foggy night and a deer 'may have been' involved. What is sure is that Stipe hit the steering wheel face first and was left with a distinctive scar between his eyebrows. 'I remember that time slowed down to nothing and I said, "Oh shit!" But it took, like, ten minutes for me to say it, and my voice was slowed down like in the movies to "Oooooooohhhhh sssshhhhhiiittttt".' According to Marcus Gray in *It Crawled from the South*, Stipe was upset by having broken up with a girlfriend too, and soon after the crash he decided that enough was enough. He quit SIUE before the first term was up, packed up his belongings at the Woodriver house and disbanded Bad Habits. At one point he'd hoped that St Louis was going to be the next musical hotbed in America, but it wasn't to be. Instead he was going back to his parents in Georgia, and to the university there at Athens, a place Stipe considered to be a backwoods, hippy enclave. Certainly not a hip, up-and-coming musical and artistic centre that would soon be known the world over. If he'd been paying closer attention to his copies of the *Village Voice*, he'd already have known that a band called the B-52's had broken out of Athens and made a name for themselves at the hip venues of the Big Apple. Had he known about that, he might not have been so reluctant to leave his friends in the Midwest behind and head back south to the state of his birth.

Chapter Three

Everybody's Walking Up and Saying, 'Hey' to Me

1978 to 1980

'Woke up this morning, put on my shoes, walked into the bathroom, and I scrub my eyes. Walk on down the street, got happy feet, everybody's walking up and saying, "Hey" to me.'

— MICHAEL STIPE

WHATEVER THE REASONS – financial, girlfriend-related, connected with the band or family-orientated, Michael Stipe found himself living in Watkinsville, Georgia. Located a few miles south of Athens, Watkinsville was a sleepy little place with a post office and little else. By going from the outskirts of a major city to the outskirts of a college town virtually in the middle of nowhere, Stipe found the carpet pulled from under his feet. After taking years to gain the confidence and swagger to front a band before a live audience, he was back to being an unknown shadow with no friends around. He slipped into life as an uncomfortable, shy teenager once again.

After dropping out of SIUE and moving to Georgia just before Christmas, Stipe signed up to start at UGA on 4 January 1979, which happened to be his 19th birthday. Initially he enrolled on a communications course, later switching to art; he dropped his geology leanings only because the building was too long a walk from the centre of Athens. For the first semesters he had to attend evening classes in order to gain enough credits for the major courses he wanted to study. Because the UGA campus was right in the heart of town, it influenced almost everything around it. Music, art, parties, friendships and employment were all centred around the campus on Broad Street.

By 1980 Athens had a total population of around 40,000, of whom more than half were students. And since in addition so many local people worked at the university, college life rather dominated the 'Classic City' as it's known. UGA's many dormitories housed much of the student body, but the town was also student-friendly: the architecture of many of the big houses, designed in the typical southern stereotype – looking like ex-plantation mansions or something from *The Addams Family* – made them perfect to be split into rooms and apartments and rented out to students.

Though the town had been home to more traditional southern music for many years, it was 1977 that became Athens's musical year zero as far as outside attention was concerned. On Valentine's Day, three boys and two girls were talked into playing a few songs at a house party. Fred Schneider and Kate Pierson had moved to Athens to attend UGA, while Ricky and Cindy Wilson and Keith Strickland were Athens locals. They called themselves the B-52's, and the original songs they performed that night included 'Planet Claire', 'Rock Lobster' and 'Killer B's', a trio of danceable, retro tunes with an undeniable kitsch factor which started a buzz that would soon make them stars. By the end of the night, the party-goers were so taken with the band that they insisted they play all of their songs again.

That summer the quintet were sneaked into the UGA broadcast studio with some friends, who secretly recorded videos of 'Hot Lava', 'Hero Worship', 'Strobe Light' and 'Devils In My Car'. In typically exuberant fashion they didn't go about this quietly, having arrived at the college with an entourage of outrageously dressed friends and go-go dancers.

Murray Attaway (future member of Guadalcanal Diary) and Curtis Crowe had been friends in Marietta, Georgia, before moving to Athens. Crowe really made his mark on the Athens scene by forming a band called Pylon; he also helped set up the legendary roving venue the 40 Watt Club, which survived around town for the next three decades.

Pylon were another art-school project, and after playing their first show at a party in March 1979, they immediately garnered a cult following in Athens with their hypnotic beats and danceable tunes. That was all most people wanted from a new band – to be able to dance to it and to have a good time. No one cared too much whether the musicians were particularly proficient or whether the lyrics made any sense. Before long everyone and their dog seemed to be starting a band. Along with the B-52's and Pylon, there were the Tone Tones, the Method Actors and a little later the Side Effects. What all these bands had in common was that they were the antithesis of the usual southern bands, which were all 'boogie-woogie' and long guitar solos.

As Michael Stipe began exploring Athens, he found the local branch of Wuxtry Records. It had a pretty good selection of discs by the kinds of bands he liked, which weren't always available in the usual chain stores. Stipe would go shopping with Lynda and Cyndy, but people who didn't know them simply thought he had two good-looking girlfriends. That's exactly what Peter Buck thought when the trio began shopping at Wuxtry, where he was a sales clerk. 'He [Stipe] had pretty good taste musically and he always came in with his two sisters and they were pretty,' recalls Buck. 'I thought, God, this guy's got two great-looking girlfriends. He must be pretty hip. So from that mistaken impression we introduced ourselves and started talking.'

The tall, slim Buck was well known around town for his encyclopaedic knowledge of music and massive record collection. He also knew his customers well enough to hold back new stock for those he thought would appreciate it more – and naturally he'd try to keep back what he thought was the best for himself. Over a period of weeks, Stipe began to visit Wuxtry more often, and Buck became one of his few Athens friends. The two of them would talk about music, and after a while Stipe revealed that he'd been in a band before and would like to start another. Buck, however, wasn't interested and so Stipe looked elsewhere.

Peter Buck, four years Stipe's senior, had been born in Berkeley, California, and had a younger brother, Ken. As becomes apparent for all of R.E.M., the band members' families moved around quite a lot during the boys' formative years. When Buck was six the family moved north to Richmond, California; a couple of years later they went east to Indiana, and a couple more years later headed south to Roswell, Georgia, a suburb of Atlanta. Buck had been a record hound since the age of six when he'd been given a bunch of 7-inch singles for his birthday. Since then he'd spent almost every penny he came across on adding to an impressive collection of vinyl. By the time he reached his teens in Georgia, he'd progressed to hunting down then virtually unknown bands like the Velvet Underground, while also reading anything and everything he could find about music in general.

He was now old enough to go to gigs, and he once told a newspaper that 'The number-one experience in my life was seeing the New York Dolls in Atlanta. The thing that was so important about them was that they weren't stars and didn't go through that whole solo trip. They staggered around and missed chords but the magic was there. They were the one band that influenced me the most. The thing they proved was that you can be great without anyone thinking that you were great.' Like Michael Stipe, he bought *Horses* as soon as it was released; he then went a stage further by styling his whole look on Patti Smith. 'I bought it the day it came out because I liked the way she looked,' said Buck. 'It was real arty, and it was kind of, what is this? I wore Patti Smith jackets, I even had the barber give me a Patti Smith haircut. I don't think Georgia was ready for men to dress like their favourite woman artist.' Stipe, meanwhile had long curly hair in a fringe at the front, as was the fashion for post-punks and new-wavers alike. It was also good for him to hide behind.

Buck enrolled at the local Emory University, started hanging out and trying to play a little bit of guitar and landed his dream job at Doo-Dah's record store. Here he met a local high-school student called Kathleen O'Brien, who would later play a big part in the R.E.M. story in Athens. University life didn't really suit Buck; in April 1976 he walked out of college and hitchhiked to California. After a few months' washing dishes and cleaning toilets, he returned to Georgia to work at a record distribution depot, before landing another record-store opportunity. After popping in to the Decatur branch of a small chain called Wuxtry Records and speaking to the owner, he was dispatched, in January 1978, to work at one of two branches in Athens, 60 miles down the road. As luck would have it his brother Ken was already studying at UGA, and Peter moved in with him in a house on Lexington Highway. He initially worked at the Baxter Street store before moving to the College Avenue branch in the centre of town.

Later in the year the Buck brothers moved into a strange place to live, a deconsecrated church at 394 Oconee Street. St Mary's Episcopal was something of an Athens landmark and had been called the 'birthplace of Athens'. The church was built by the mill workers of the Athens Manufacturing Company around 1870 and was regularly filled until the 1880s when the mill closed and attendance dropped off. The American Red Cross used the church around the Second World War, but by the 1960s it was falling into ruin. It was given a new lease of life when a local developer built a two-storey 'box' inside the main church structure and fitted it out as a series of apartments. The main volume of the church, the altar area and 40-foot-high ceiling could be accessed through the back of a cupboard in the new build. It made a perfect venue for holding parties – the altar could even be used as a stage. This was how the church still stood in 1979, some 11 years after its redevelopment, when Peter and Ken Buck moved in.

The apartments were being rented out by Wuxtry owner Dan Wall, and he needed to fill all the rooms of this one in order to make it financially viable. Peter and Ken took a room each, but still two more people were required. Kathleen O'Brien heard about the vacancy, met Peter at Wuxtry and agreed to take a room, as did another girl, Robyn Bragg. Myths and stories about who lived at the church and when and what happened have understandably morphed over the years. Michael Stipe claimed once that 13 people lived there at one time; previous residents included the exquisitely named Purple Hayes. With the exterior masonry literally falling away, poor plumbing and little or no heating in the living areas, it wasn't as romantic a setting as some reports have made out. 'It was really wretched,' said Peter Buck. 'College students are the last people left with that streak of romanticism to think it would be cool to live in a church.'

Soon after the Bucks moved in, Peter asked Michael Stipe if he'd like to take one of the rooms instead of having to commute to college from Watkinsville every day. Stipe said yes and moved in in late summer 1979. The friendship was strengthening, and now they'd talk about music well into the early hours. Sharing living accommodation also meant that Stipe thought he should come clean to Buck about his private life. 'When Peter and I moved in together we spent a lot of time in his bedroom late at night, and we were drinking and I was doing a lot of drugs,' said Stipe. 'The first week we moved in I said, "Peter, if you ever think that I'm coming on to you, I'm not. I don't want you as anything but a friend, so don't be freaked out by that."'

Stipe also continued trying to get Buck to join him in forming a band. Buck still wasn't interested, but Stipe was persistent and eventually after more late-night discussions Buck said he'd give it a go. 'I had to coerce Peter into doing stuff,' recalled Stipe. 'He had this feeling that everyone in rock bands were egotistical assholes. Plus, he couldn't play guitar to save his life.' By the end of August they had set up a primitive rehearsal room in the vastness of the church. With Stipe singing, Buck would thrash away at his guitar and Dan Wall would join in on both bass and saxophone. A passing friend known only as 'Tim' also stepped in to play drums for a handful of jam sessions. However, no one felt it was going well enough to take it any further; Dan Wall moved back to Atlanta and Tim drifted off too.

Buck and Stipe were left to try out a few things on their own. Buck would assemble some rudimentary chord sequences, and Stipe started writing a few sparse lyrics so that he could sing along to Buck's playing. In this hotchpotch manner they pieced together a handful of original tunes, but they were far from polished. 'When I started writing with Michael it was obvious that he was a very oblique writer,' says Buck. 'I liked the fact that there wasn't a whole lot of explanation. The first songs we wrote were all straightforward, starting on an A-chord.' Stipe felt, and Buck agreed, that the actual words didn't really matter; what was more important was that they made the right sound to go along with the music. While the pair messed around at the church they often had a small audience of friends hanging about on the ancient pews. Kathleen O'Brien took a special interest in what they were doing, and thought she knew someone who could help out. At the WUOG radio station she had met a guy from Macon who played drums. His name was Bill Berry.

Unbeknown to Buck and Stipe, Mike Mills and Bill Berry had also enrolled at UGA in January 1979 and had been around town ever since, without their paths crossing. Both were two years older than Stipe, two years younger than Buck. The pair had been friends since meeting down in Macon, Georgia, years before. Berry had been born in Duluth, Minnesota, one of five children; Mills had just one brother and had been born in California before moving to Georgia at an early age – first to Atlanta, then in 1971 to Macon. Berry's first musical adventures started when he was given a ukulele, while Mills was surrounded by music from an early age: both parents sang – his father was a tenor – and his mother also played piano.

Berry's peripatetic early years took him from Minnesota to Wisconsin, then to two different places in Ohio. It was in Sandusky, Ohio, that he took the opportunity of missing some school lessons to play drums in the school band; it was this that started his career as a drummer. Three years later he was moving south, with a newly acquired drum kit, to Macon, Georgia. Like Michael Stipe he thought moving to Georgia was a horrible prospect, and his friends put on a 'pity party' for their departing friend. In Georgia he wound up at the same school as Mike Mills, and in time they played in the high-school marching band together – with Mills on sousaphone! 'We weren't friends at first because Bill ran with a rowdy crowd,' said Mills in a later interview. 'He didn't like me because I was a nerd and I didn't like him because he was an asshole, so it was a real shock on both our parts when we got together.'

The pair finally met up one weekend when they were both independently invited to a mutual friend's jam session. Despite early reservations, they hit it off and were to become firm friends. The bands they played in together came thick and fast. First was an unnamed lounge trio (with a teacher from school) that played at weddings, then Shadowfax – a covers band in 1974–75 – followed by the Backdoor Band and finally the Frustrations. The last of these had the biggest effect on their musical development, being a punk band with Ian Copeland. Copeland had come over to the Paragon booking agency (where Berry worked part-time) from England, with a case full of brand-new punk singles which had yet to reach Georgia. These new sounds blew the minds of Berry and Mills, renewing their enthusiasm for storming the music business – which, after years of playing the covers circuit, they'd both thought about abandoning. The Frustrations also worked up some original punk-flavoured tunes including 'Action' and 'Narrator' which would later be played live by R.E.M.

When the pair graduated from high school they both chose UGA and moved to Athens. Mills moved into the Myers Hall dorm, Berry into the Reed Hall dorm. Berry decided that the locals of Athens should be educated in the new ways of punk, and could often be seen hauling his stereo speakers on to his window ledge, from where he would blast out his punk singles collection to anyone in earshot, whether they liked it or not.

Mike Mills had yet to decide what he wanted to do; he thought in the long run it might be English literature. Bill Berry had vague thoughts of studying law, to try to get some involvement in the music industry as a career, the main problem being that he just didn't go to class. He partied and enjoyed the freedom of being away from home a little too much, although he did find the time to get involved with the WUOG radio station and to play in a band made up of the station's staff, called the WUOGerz.

It was through WUOG that Berry met Kathleen O'Brien, who DJ'd at the station. One night at a party in town she introduced Berry to Buck and Stipe. According to Stipe, he immediately liked Berry's eyebrows and thought he was pretty cool. The church-dwelling pair mentioned to Berry that they needed a drummer; Berry was receptive to the idea but only if his bass-playing friend (Mike Mills) could join too. Stipe and Buck arranged to meet Berry and Mills later that week, at a local club called Tyrone's.

Michael Stipe's first impressions of Mike Mills were not as favourable as those he'd had on meeting Bill Berry. Stipe's immediate response was, 'No fucking way! He was wearing bellbottoms and a stupid haircut. But it was a bargain: if we take Bill we [have to] take Mike.' Despite his reservations Stipe agreed that the four should meet up at the church and see what happened. This was early autumn 1979, but things took a while to come together properly. There was much partying to do, and despite wanting to form a band, the three musicians weren't in a rush to do so. In the meantime, Stipe was talked into fronting an Athens cover band (covering Tom Petty, Elvis, and so on) by the name of Gangster. Gangster actually earned a good wage whenever they played, which Stipe later maintained was the only reason he sang with them, a claim that may or may not be true.

Stipe would scour the local classifieds to see who was looking for a singer. He tried out with a couple of bands, but it was Derek Nunnally's Gangster he hit it off with. The band couldn't have been further from Stipe's punk ideals, playing the cheesy gangster roles to the bitter end. They dressed in gangster 'zoot suits', changed their stage names (Stipe was christened Michael Valentine after the famous St Valentine's Day massacre), and rehearsed at the 'the Gangster hideaway' which was actually Nunnally's parents' garage in Munroe, a few miles outside Athens.

Emerging bands and wild parties were becoming an increasing staple of Athens nightlife. Athens parties soon gained a notoriety all of their own. The hipsters around town were constantly trying to put on a better gathering than the one before, the more outrageous the better. Having fun was all that mattered to anyone. If bands played, no one really cared what they sounded like so long as you could dance to them. No one was thinking about making a serious career in music; it was just a way of having fun and entertaining your friends. As the number of bands grew, so did the number of clubs that would allow them to play. A simple case of supply and demand.

One club that saw the potential of all the new bands around town was Tyrone's. Tyrone's was set up in an old railway ware-house at the east end of town on Foundry Street, not far from Oconee Street. As other clubs around the South would do later, it started, on Halloween 1979, a so-called New Wave Nite. Pylon and the Method Actors played that night, at what was to become Athens's most important new music showcase. When the club closed for the night, most of the occupants simply crossed Broad

Street and went down the hill to the church on Oconee Street, where the party continued till morning. Carol Levy was there that evening and was introduced to Michael Stipe. She was a big music and photography fan, and the two hit it off immediately.

As Christmas approached Buck, Berry, Mills and Stipe agreed to meet early in the new year and try again to get a band going. On New Year's Eve, Kathleen O'Brien arranged a party at the church – and all hell broke loose. Stipe was falling-down drunk and decided it would be a great idea to trash all the festive decorations; this then deteriorated into a food fight with Peter Buck and Stipe's two sisters. O'Brien was less than impressed and refused to speak to Cyndy and Lynda for many months. 'I ended up being the only girl living there for a while,' says O'Brien. 'We had a New Year's party with bands, but I don't remember who. I do remember that I had ham and turkey and little biscuits for party food. And I remember this huge food fight ensuing. What was I thinking?! There were people dancing and food was getting ground into the carpet.'

Just when it seemed as though the prospective band quartet would never meet up, Berry and Buck ran into each other at Tyrone's and agreed it was now or never. Berry and Mills borrowed some drums and a bass respectively and went over to the church. The cold January day wasn't the best for playing together in an unheated church for the first time. Mills ended up playing guitar because he was better than Buck; as their breath rose in front of their faces he tried to play wearing gloves because he was so cold. Berry and Mills presented some of the songs they'd written together back in Macon, while Buck and Stipe showed them the songs they'd worked on the previous autumn. Initial thoughts included one of getting a little keyboard for Buck to play, because of his lack of ability on the guitar, but that idea was tossed out as they decided to keep the band as vocals, guitar, bass and drums. Mills and Berry formed a solid rhythm section, having played together for around five years, so it seemed best to keep them together as the engine of the band.

The initial experiment was promising enough for them to meet again – and then again and again. By February they were working on some new songs and spending more time jamming at the church than they did in class. Kathleen O'Brien was keeping an ear to proceedings and, with her 20th birthday approaching on 5 April, she asked if they would be willing to play at the party she was planning to hold in the church.

O'Brien had also tendered the idea to a couple of other new bands, and after a bit of persuading she got her flatmates to agree. 'I knew they had a real chemistry,' says O'Brien. 'I had been listening to them practise for months and months. They didn't even have a band name yet. They had written names all over the walls, but none of them was really taking. We wanted to have another couple of bands to play, too. The Side Effects agreed, and Turtle Bay. And all their friends came. So it just turned into this big thing. It was one of those rock-the-house parties. It was pretty much like that at every house party.'

O'Brien had asked the Side Effects to play on 29 February, the night of a John Cale show in Athens. After the gig O'Brien and Paul Butchart went on to a birthday party for O'Brien's fellow WUOG DJ Kurt Wood. Like the Stipe/Mills/Buck/Berry band, Butchart's band didn't have a name, had never played live and had been together for only a couple of months. They were nervous about the prospect, but agreed to do it.

A few weeks later, during spring break, a road trip was arranged to New York in a little van. The travellers included Butchart, Peter Buck, Stipe and a couple of girls. Butchart knew Buck from the Wuxtry and Stipe from the Steak and Ale Restaurant where they both worked. The long weekend in the Big Apple was spent with them all sleeping in the van, parked up in Columbus Circle, with no way of taking a shower or having a wash. Somehow they managed to blag their way into a party, where they met the legendary music writer Lester Bangs; R.E.M. would later write a song about this event. One night Buck disappeared, and later he told Butchart he'd gone back home with a girl, but only so he could get a shower at her apartment.

With five weeks until their first public performance, the band got serious about working up some new songs of their own. They were nothing if not prolific, and soon had about a dozen original tunes and some classic covers nailed down to fill out a set for the party. No one was willing to take the lead, though, and suggestions would usually be met with silent nods of the head from the other three. The increased band activity had the predicted consequences on the members' education: Mills spent so little time at UGA that he unofficially moved into the church and slept on a couch, while Berry was asked to leave UGA after his grades and attendance slipped to an unacceptable level.

'As soon as the university asked me to discontinue my affiliation with them, I got a job at the Holiday Inn as morning busboy,' explained Berry. 'That really sucked. Here I was staying at the church and I had to get up at four in the morning to get the breakfast buffet set up. There would be parties still going on at the church and I would be dressed up in these brown polyester pants and Peter and Michael would be sitting there, wasted, drinking beer and laughing at me, saying, "See ya Bill. Heh, heh, heh."' Berry wouldn't have to worry about the ridicule for too long.

Chapter Four

Don't Worry About School

1980 to 1981

'Drive carefully. Wear your seat belts. Don't drink and drive at the same time. Don't worry about school. And call your parents before the weekend.'

— MICHAEL STIPE

ON FRIDAY 4 APRIL 1980 a trio of bands began hauling their equipment into the church at 394 Oconee Street. Luckily it wasn't as difficult a job as some had suspected. Most visitors had to go through the living quarters, into Kathleen O'Brien's bedroom and through the little doorway at the back of one of her closets, out into the chapel behind. There, dusty rotten floorboards and peeling masonry awaited them. An old back door allowed the bands to set up rather more easily. Mike Mills and Bill Berry greeted the Men in Trees and the Side Effects as they set up and ran through their sets. Earlier in the day, Michael Stipe and Peter Buck had been interviewed on WUOG and invited listeners to suggest names for their new band. They had previously scrawled a list of possibilities on the walls inside the church; the rejected names have become legendary: Cans of Piss, Negro Eyes, Negro Wives, Third Wave, the Male Nurses, Africans in Bondage, Slut Bank. Contrary to popular opinion, however, they did not call themselves Twisted Kites for this first show, but remained nameless. Someone did add 'Twisted Kites' to some posters put up around town by the Side Effects, but not to many.

Only 120 to 150 invitations had been sent out for the party, but after the WUOG publicity the numbers were bound to swell. Friends from UGA made up the majority of those invited. Linda Hopper had met Michael Stipe at UGA. 'I spotted Michael because he looked really bizarre,' said Hopper. 'His hair was really blond, bleached, and very long and curly, and he always wore sunglasses – a totally cool look. It wasn't hard to find others like you. I met Michael Stipe in my art class. He was new to town, and I could tell by looking at him that he was interesting. I sat down next to him and said, "I've got some friends I think you'd like." We've been best friends ever since.' A small group soon formed in the art department who would sit around in class talking about music for hours. Stipe's art-class buddies now jokingly called his haircut the 'reverse ponytail' as it was now so long at the front and short at the back. He also wore badly ripped jeans, quite a radical sight for Georgia in 1980.

Stipe's art teacher was James Herbert, and he influenced Stipe on all aspects of his general thinking. Herbert had originally been going to join the Peace Corps in Peru in the early 1960s, but when that fell through he took a teaching job at UGA. Not being from the South he intended to stay for no more than two years, but he's been there ever since. He was much more than 'just' a lecturer. He was a progressive painter and filmmaker too, and he later encouraged Stipe's liberal art-school leanings which helped push the singer towards more innovative approaches. But at the time Stipe didn't make much of an impression in Herbert's classes. 'I was able to convince my teachers that what I was doing was worthwhile,' Stipe admitted, 'when I wasn't really doing anything.'

Scott Belville, who also taught Stipe in the art department, recalled him as being above the other students in both ability and insight. It was Belville who took Stipe on a field trip to meet religious artist Howard Finster, another big inspiration to Stipe.

★   ★   ★

Saturday night on 5 April 1980 was a rainy one in Athens, Georgia. But the poor weather did little to stop hordes of party-goers from converging on St Mary's. As more and more people continued to cram into the church, they helped themselves to the contents of five kegs of beer provided by Kathleen O'Brien. The bands themselves also drank a fair share, to build up some Dutch courage for what was fast becoming a big event rather then a low-key birthday party. Michael Stipe's band formed a huddle to try to gee one another up. 'We were scared shitless,' recalled Bill Berry. Talk turned to the fact that it wasn't too late to back out, but calmer heads prevailed and they agreed they had to go for it now. Stipe and company were the final band to play. By that time about 500 people had taken up position in every nook and cranny that afforded any kind of vantage point. People outside scaled the walls to peer in through the broken church windows, while the already creaky wooden floor threatened to give in at any moment. A handful of people did indeed suddenly see their feet disappear below, but no one was seriously injured.

Finally Stipe, Buck, Berry and Mills squeezed through the crowd and shuffled on to the stage. Perhaps it was some kind of destiny that led Michael Stipe to play his first gig with what would become R.E.M. in a church. Some of his grandfather's preacher-man charisma had certainly rubbed off on the singer. No one can now be sure what the first song was – after all, it was a good party and memories were hazy the next morning, never mind many years later. The second song was the Sex Pistols' punk anthem 'God Save The Queen'. Once that was over, the nerves evaporated and the band took off. The first set began with a host of cover versions to make sure the crowd were up and dancing. The songs chosen covered classics and some then obscure cult tunes. Popular consensus has it that at some point during the night they played 'I Can't Control Myself' (the Troggs), 'Needles And Pins' (the Searchers), 'Hippy Hippy Shake' (the Swinging Blue Jeans), 'There She Goes Again' (Velvet Underground), 'Shakin' All Over' (Johnny

Kidd & the Pirates), 'Secret Agent Man' (Johnny Rivers), 'With A Girl Like You' (the Troggs) and '(I'm Not Your) Steppin' Stone' (the Monkees).

Exactly which original tunes were played is harder to pin down. People at the party had never heard them before, so didn't know what the songs were called. On the basis of later interviews with the band and recordings of R.E.M.'s earliest shows (no recording of the first show was ever made), it's probable that 'Permanent Vacation', 'All The Right Friends', 'Narrator', 'Just A Touch', 'Baby I', 'Action', 'Dangerous Times', 'Different Girl' and 'Mystery To Me' were played during their début. All these new songs were played at a furious tempo, just as the covers were, and at least one eyewitness pointed out that all the songs sounded as if they could be cover versions, such was their catchiness. The band had a distinctly garage-rock sound, due to a combination of the church's acoustics, the band's level of ability and the drawbacks of their simple equipment. After a short break, and to a thundering ovation, the band returned for a shorter second set of covers, including the Modern Lovers' 'Roadrunner' – which went on for about ten minutes!

Everyone in the audience was amazed by the performance, quite taken aback. Michael Stipe was transformed from quiet, shy student into a whirlwind of onstage energy and confidence – a conversion that everyone agreed was a revelation. Stipe danced around the tiny stage like a madman, doing what he later described as 'letting his backbone slip' to become a whirling mass of hair and flailing arms. He was energetic and eccentric in a way that was so uncool it was cool. He was a weird cross between Little Richard and Mick Jagger, Elvis and Joe Cocker. He did on stage exactly what he felt he could never do in real life. But for the most part, this historic first show passed him by. 'I just got incredibly drunk and don't remember much of it, which shows how seriously we took our début day,' he said. 'From what I've heard I spent half the night on the floor on my stomach. I don't remember.'

By the end of the night, most people had drunk enough to be sure they wouldn't remember much the next day. The five kegs of beer had been drained; people had passed out and paired off into the night. When Paul Butchart came to return the van he'd borrowed to move his equipment, he found some underwear which years later turned out to have been Peter Buck's. As for the performance, 'Michael Stipe's band' caused a tremor of gossip around town about how good they were. For the next week people would come up to them and say they'd really enjoyed the party and hoped the band would continue. Stipe was impressed and excited by the reaction that one party show had managed to stir up. One of these newly converted fans was Mike Hobbs, who also happened to help book bands for Tyrone's. He contacted Stipe and said he'd like them to open a show for Atlanta band the Brains when they played Tyrone's in a month's time. The deal-clincher was that they'd get $100 for their time. That one performance must have made quite an impact for them now to be offered a paying show, even though they still didn't have a name.

Though riding a wave of euphoria after their début, the quartet were still grounded enough to realise they would need to play another practice show before facing a club audience. With this in mind they arranged to play at the tiny 11:11 Kaffee Klub, which could cram in a maximum of 150 people. Before the show they decided they had to give themselves a name. The list on the church wall was abandoned; Michael Stipe sat opening a dictionary at random pages to see what entries came up. One of them was 'R.E.M.' The band didn't read on to see what it stood for, they just liked the fact that it was three letters; as far as they were concerned it didn't mean anything. 'We wanted something vague enough so that we couldn't be easily categorised,' said Stipe. 'Three letters is fairly vague. We didn't really think of the connotation it indicated of rapid eye movement.' They also didn't wait to find out if it had been used before. In fact there had been several bands using similar names over the years. A band called R.E.M. came from Austin, Texas, while there was Rapid Eye Movement from Washington, DC, and another called REM from the UK.

So on Saturday 19 April the new R.E.M. prepared for their second performance at the tiny venue. The show didn't start until after 1.30 a.m., and it caught the attention of a passing police car. Although it was classed as a private party, the Kaffee Klub owners required a licence to sell alcohol – something they didn't have. The officers closed the show mid-performance. Stipe had again woven a spell over the crowd, and when the police insisted on taking photos of everyone present no one seemed to care. On the contrary, in fact, many of the revellers posed for the police in ever more outrageous stances.

Like Mike Hobbs at the band's début, one particular member of the audience at this abbreviated show would be influential in R.E.M.'s future. This time it was UGA law student Bertis Downs. After the performance he sought out Stipe and gushed that R.E.M. were going to be bigger than the Beatles. He had another chance to reinforce this opinion on 6 May when R.E.M. opened for the Brains on Tyrone's ever more popular New Wave Nite. Not only was it R.E.M.'s first paying gig, but they received their first newspaper write-up in UGA's *Red & Black* student paper with a headline that said it all: 'Underdog R.E.M. upstages the Brains.' R.E.M.'s cult status in Athens was now well and truly cemented.

Stipe was proving to be quite an enigmatic and engaging front man. Far from being the shy boy he was off stage, he was happy to regale the audience with anecdotes and to ad-lib new lines to cover versions and original songs alike. 'I was a phenomenal contradiction,' Stipe told *Mojo*. 'This gargantuan ambition but embodied in someone who could barely finish a sentence. Who could barely hold a conversation with someone without shrinking into the couch. And yet I would get on stage and something else would happen.' Tyrone's management were so happy with R.E.M.'s performance and the crowd's reaction that they immediately booked the band to headline New Wave Nite the following week.

Already the band was in great demand. Further shows at Tyrone's sandwiched a performance at UGA ('Stipe was unstoppable' crowed the *Red & Black*) before on 30 May the band played a support slot at the 40 Watt Club – just their seventh show, eight weeks after their church début. After being 'lost' for over a quarter of a century a recording of part of this show miraculously surfaced in 2005, sending fans around the world into a frenzy and becoming the earliest known recording of the band (beating the previous earliest known concert tape by several weeks).

Of course the tape is historic in many ways. A snapshot of the band in its very earliest stages, it provides an unexpected chance to hear what they sounded like, and in particular Michael Stipe's vocal style. It also showcases the most primitive of their self-penned compositions, many of which, dropped from their set list within the next few months, would otherwise be forgotten for ever.

'Baby I' opened the set and demonstrated the band's confidence and ability right away. Unlike the other bands forming around town, R.E.M. could play their own material and cover versions pretty well. The sound was basic but the strong Berry–Mills rhythm section carried any shortcomings that might have been exposed by Peter Buck's jangly guitar work. The choice of covers does indeed make it difficult to discern which songs were originals and which weren't. The songs are played at breakneck speed and in rapid succession with little time for respite in between. Stipe's vocals ape all kinds of styles throughout the show, from Buddy Holly's 'hiccups' to Elvis Presley's low groans and everything in between. Stipe is truly a garage-band revelation. (He and Mills still needed some work on their harmonies though!) Even at this stage the band had gelled to the point where they could segue songs together seamlessly. The tape also highlights a trio of songs unknown elsewhere. Listed tentatively as 'Chappaquiddick' (with references to going into the water), 'Mediocrity' (a slower, bass-led song) and 'I've Got A Charm (I Wear Every Day)' (a semi-reggae number) they were obviously written and discarded in super-quick time, because they're not on the surviving concert tapes from later that summer. Of these early songs, 'All The Right Friends' would survive and be re-recorded and released by the band over 20 years later.

The band's instant popularity around Athens was greeted with suspicion by some of the other bands. Athens purists wanted things to be in the cause of 'art'; R.E.M.'s pop approach was seen as selling out. 'The thing about R.E.M. was at first they were so unlike all the rest of the bands,' explains photographer Terry Allen. 'Everybody was saying, "These guys are like a bar band or something," and everybody else was more of an art band, like Pylon. At the time R.E.M. weren't Athens-like.' Another criticism was that they played cover versions, a big no-no in the art scene. But R.E.M. carried on regardless.

The band soon started to spread its wings, with shows booked in Atlanta, as 6 June saw their first performance outside Athens. Kathleen O'Brien, who was now dating Bill, had a large car and offered to ferry them to Atlanta for the show, so they hauled amps, drums and everything else that would fit into the car and set off. Atlanta, just 85 miles along the road, was a metropolis by comparison yet failed to have any kind of music scene to match Athens. Athens was open to new ideas, and in its relatively small and tight-knit community things could crystallise and develop.

The first stop was at the Atlanta branch of Wuxtry Records. The band set up their kit in the middle of the shop and proprietor Mark Methe filmed the band using a video camera. The 'practice session' that followed included practically all the original material the band had written so far – such as 'Dangerous Times', 'Different Girl', 'Just A Touch' and 'Baby I' – though it's not known which other songs the band played. Methe later dubbed the video soundtrack on to cassette and put the 'good' tracks on to a tape (*R.E.M. Slurred*) which he copied for a handful of fans around town. Inevitably this low-fi recording made its way on to bootleg vinyl, and remains the earliest available 'studio' recording in circulation, made just two months into the band's career.

At the end of June the era of living in the church came to an end: the rental lease expired and everyone moved out. Bill Berry and Kathleen O'Brien moved into an apartment together while Peter Buck, Michael Stipe and Mike Mills rented a house. Over the summer Berry began taking over the booking of dates for the band, saying he didn't want his girlfriend to be his band's manager!

More shows followed in Athens and in Atlanta, this time at the newly opened 688 Club which would become a regular haunt for the band. They also opened for the English band Gang of Four, with whom they struck up a long-lasting friendship. Stipe in particular was taken with their lyrical approach and singing style.

Back in Athens, Stipe was making his mark off stage as well as on it. With bands springing up all over the place, Athens had more than its per-capita share of wannabe pop and rock stars. Many people in these new bands would act like stars after playing just a couple of shows. Right away they'd try to jump queues and expect to be let into clubs and shows for free. But right from the beginning Stipe was seen as being a little different from the norm. He'd stand in line at a club and patiently wait his turn while counting out his cents (literally) to get in.

During these early months of R.E.M.'s existence, the band made numerous important connections that they would carry with them for years. The next of these began with a chance meeting with a booking agent/record-store owner by the name of Jefferson Holt. In July 1980 Holt was managing a record shop called Schoolkids Records in Chapel Hill, North Carolina. He was also helping to book bands for local clubs. He really did meet up with R.E.M. almost by accident.

Pylon had been due to play at the Station (it *was* a disused railway station) in North Carolina, but they'd had to pull out. Holt needed a replacement band, and quickly. Though he had never been to Athens he was aware that the scene down there was developing into something interesting. He made a couple of calls and finally was put in touch with Bill Berry. Berry only too happily agreed to step in, so R.E.M. quickly found themselves with a trio of gigs – outside Georgia for the first time. Beginning what was to become years of trudging around the South to build up a following in small towns, they jumped into a van and drove the 300 miles determined to make a positive impression. They also had a secret weapon, a car full of girls (including Kathleen O'Brien and Linda Hopper), who drove behind to act as cheerleaders. The Ian Hunter look-alike behind the microphone did his usual crazy-man dance routines with his characteristically vigorous moves. With the girls at the front of the stage dancing up a storm, the rest of the audience were soon won over by R.E.M.'s energetic show. Holt was also blown away, and after a second night at the Station he drove with the band to Raleigh for the third show, at the Pier, for that club's own New Wave Nite.

For such a young band the number of gigs they were playing within a few months of forming was amazing. Throughout a hot and steamy Georgian summer they played almost every weekend. One show at the 40 Watt Club had a dance-floor temperature of 125 degrees! The money earned from all of these shows, though modest, was enough for the band to rent a practice space on Jackson Street. With college closed for the summer they had plenty of time to jam together and work on new songs. Mike Mills wrote one of the best early compositions with '(Don't Go Back To) Rockville'.

Michael Stipe was honing his song-writing skills extremely quickly. From a song like 'Body Count', which was pretty obvious with its message, he progressed to using lyrical ambiguity: by the time he penned 'Gardening At Night' a few months later he was demonstrating a completely different style of writing.

That autumn, with the Athens scene getting press across the South, Jefferson Holt decided that the 'Classic City' was the place to be and moved there. His initial plan was to open a record store called Foreign Legion. He regularly attended R.E.M. shows around town and became friends with the band, even helping out by taking money at the door on some occasions.

Michael Stipe was keeping himself extra busy. As well as pursuing the R.E.M. activities and full-time education at UGA, he had met up with Tom Smith and embarked on a serious of splinter projects. Smith was something of an Athens purist. He'd started out playing, and abusing, turntables, and various modes of percussion. In the early 1970s he'd taken an electronic music course, inspired by Lee 'Scratch' Perry, Richard Hell, Brian Eno and Faust. In 1979 he moved to Athens where he linked up with Mike Green to play as Prepared Party, an experiment in recorded sounds (shoes in a clothes dryer, short-wave transmissions) mixed with overdubbed bass guitar.

Like Stipe, Smith had met Carol Levy in 1979, and when he ran into her again in 1980 he asked if she'd like to join a band – and she said yes. Soon afterwards, Smith met Stipe outside the Cobb Institute. 'He just sort of wandered up; he had a bit of green dye in his hair,' recalls Smith. 'Vic Varney seemed to know him, and as they engaged in conversation I listened for clues. Michael's responses were agreeably oblique.' Soon Stipe also joined the loose ensemble that was going under the name Pre-Cave. He spent the summer of 1980 rehearsing and playing with R.E.M. as well as with Pre-Cave. Mike Green left to go to Paris, leaving Stipe (organ and backing vocals), Smith (bass, vocals and tape loops) and Levy (organ and backing vocals) to prepare for their début show on 28 July. When this fell through they changed their name to Nest (adj.), finally débuting at the 40 Watt Club in October.

A second gig on Valentine's Day 1981 didn't include Stipe, and by the third performance on 11 June the band had changed its name again, this time to Boat Of. Carol Levy is said to have played in a style reminiscent of the Slits, while Stipe produced some monotone vocals and plonked away at his keyboard. 'Boat Of primarily localized within the realm of performance,' says Tom Smith. 'A corrective affront not only to Athens but to contemporary scenes in general.'

Stipe's final appearance with the group was at Tyrone's in July 1981. By then Smith had ventured to see R.E.M. play, but was far from impressed. 'I was utterly appalled by their set,' says Smith. 'Of course, mine was a minority opinion. We wanted everyone, save Limbo District, to die. We found all the other groups insipid beyond reckoning. In hindsight, I probably made too much of it. Twenty-six years on, people claim to have attended our gigs, cite performance specifics I can't even begin to remember. I find this oddly comforting.' A two-disc compilation of Smith's early bands was issued in 2006 by Smack Shire records. Stipe continued to help the band and is credited with lighting design and choreography for later shows up to 1982. Boat Of folded after Carol Levy's tragic death in 1983.

It was for one of these shows that Michael Stipe helped his sister Lynda start a band for the first time. 'My brother needed an opening band for one of his splinter groups,' says Lynda Stipe. 'Me and [Linda] Hopper were friends so we were like, "We could do that!" I'd been farting around on bass and started writing. I think we opened with four songs at the original 40 Watt Club. Everybody played something. And everybody was into everybody else's band, which seems to be happening again now. Just hanging out with the Side Effects and other people that played around town. It was really, really forward-moving and optimistic. It didn't matter if you could play or not.' Lynda and Linda called their band Oh-OK. Michael Stipe wrote lyrics for one of their 1981 songs, 'Jumping'.

A quieter autumn for R.E.M. on the gigging front was boosted in early December when Bill Berry landed the group their biggest show to date. The Police were then one of the world's biggest bands and they were touring to promote their third album *Zenyatta Mondatta*. Berry's friend from Macon, Ian Copeland, was the link. He'd now set up his own booking agency, and of course his brother Stewart was the Police's drummer. After Berry sent some positive reviews and live tapes to Copeland he agreed to book them as the opening act when the Police played Atlanta. The result was R.E.M.'s playing before 4,000 fans, to complete a memorable first year of gigging.

Two days later, on Monday 8 December, the mood changed with the news that John Lennon had been shot dead in New York. Almost worse was the news that his murderer, Mark Chapman, had attended high school over in Atlanta. News of the shooting spread across Athens as people were still in clubs and bars late that night. At the 40 Watt the music was stopped for the murder to be announced, and people spilled out on to the street, many in tears. It was a sad end to an otherwise triumphant year.

Michael Stipe woke up to the new year knowing that it would be an important 12 months for both himself as a lyric writer and the band as a whole. Their ability to win over fans in small live settings was now beyond doubt, but they needed a stronger set of original songs and would soon need to test some of them out in a studio setting. During 1981 the band would drop almost all the early songs written to date and replace them with more mature compositions. These new songs featured lyrics by Michael Stipe that would enthral and confuse listeners in equal measure.

On stage Stipe would continue ad-libbing lyrics and telling stories during interludes between songs. This helped to make an R.E.M. show one that wasn't just a by-the-numbers routine. Each time you saw the band you knew you'd be experiencing something different from the last time. Athens, Atlanta and North Carolina were becoming the band's main stamping grounds. A typical weekend trip initially began on Friday afternoon and would see the band return on a Monday. Then it became Thursday until Monday, which later stretched to Thursday until Tuesday. By then they would all have been ousted from UGA and finding it hard to hang on to regular day jobs. Usually they'd sleep in the van; occasionally a friendly fan would put them up on a couch or floor. Michael Stipe recalled one night after a show when they were allowed to stay after the club had cleared. 'We couldn't afford a hotel room. So we slept on the stage and woke up with some mice running around our heads,' he laughed – though it probably wasn't so funny at the time.

Bill Berry continued to keep enthusiasm for the band going as he arranged more local gigs. Local photographer Terry Allen would often be at the clubs around town with his camera and managed to catch the early R.E.M. shows in some detail. 'I had a buddy that was a business partner of mine and when we were in college we did sorority and fraternity party pictures,' he said. 'We were like the two guys in town that everybody knew who had a dark room and had cameras, and we were always there at the shows, so whenever something came along that needed photographic work we were available to do it. The thing about Tyrone's was that it was hard to force yourself to take pictures at those shows because it was so much fun. You just wanted to drink beer and dance because that's what everybody else was doing. Who wants to be taking pictures? Now of course I wish I'd done it a lot more!'

Athens scenester Lance Smith told writer Denise Sullivan for her book *Talk About the Passion* that the running joke around town was 'Who's going to be Michael Stipe's new best friend this week?' It seems Stipe would be inseparable from someone for a couple of weeks, then never be seen with them again. This somewhat confusing persona bled through into his song-writing. The latest batch of new songs included 'Shaking Through', 'Sitting Still' and the incredibly catchy 'Radio Free Europe'.

For this last song the writing process was a wholly collaborative effort, something that would continue throughout the band's career. Mike Mills arrived at practice one day with a chord sequence for the others to work with, Bill Berry added the verse section and Peter Buck consulted his notebook before coming up with the title 'Radio Free Europe', which he'd had sitting around for while. When Stipe arrived at Jackson Street the others played the new composition to him and suggested he use the phrase 'radio free Europe'. He immediately started singing some words and within two hours the song was finished.

In February, the time seemed right to break new ground by going into a studio, which for Stipe was a potentially terrifying ordeal. When playing live he was always careful to ensure that his vocals blended deep into the sound mix; he didn't want his voice in the studio to come out too loud and clear. Despite writing what some fans would later pore over as profound lyrics, he wanted to make sure that exactly what he was singing stayed semi-hidden in the murky depths.

The studio they chose to try out in was the relatively unknown facility of Joe Perry's Bombay Studios in Smyrna, Georgia. With a little naïvety on their part, the band wanted to try to push through as many as eight songs in a single day, one day being all they could afford. Michael Stipe was very self-conscious about his voice and was almost visibly cringing when he heard it played back into the control room. He told Perry to keep it as low in the mix as possible and not to let it stand out at all. Perry wasn't in a position to finance a single for the band and neither were they themselves, so the tapes made that day were shelved.

A few weeks later the band were ready to try again, at a different studio. By this time they had played a stream of new gigs and saved up some money. Joe Perry later commented that he thought the Bombay demos were great, but the band disagreed and wanted to try somewhere else. By now they had a new manager/booking agent in the shape of Jefferson Holt. His record store in Athens had closed and he was unofficially working for the band. To raise money for the next recording session they'd played shows across several states. Holt had even gone so far as to design a little poster to send ahead to advertise the band before they reached town. On these posters he'd had printed the words 'Rapid Eye Movement Tour 1981'. Stipe was upset and berated Holt for using the words *rapid eye movement*, a phrase that was not meant to have anything to do with the band's name. Despite this *faux pas* Holt continued to do an otherwise sterling job for the band and the shows went well, earning enough money for the next session. It wasn't easy work, though: they'd play a show, then pile back into their van and drive overnight to the next town. With all the equipment they had just about enough room for four to sleep in the back while the fifth person drove. At the end of the mini-tour Bill Berry asked Holt if he wanted to manage the band on a full-time basis. He did.

Holt immediately set to work looking for a cheap, but efficient, studio for the next session. He called an old friend from North Carolina, Peter Holsapple, who suggested Mitch Easter's Drive-In Studio – so called because it was literally in his parents' garage. The band pulled up on Easter's drive a couple of days later; it was the start of a long working relationship.

'My first impression was that Michael looked like Ian Hunter,' recalls Easter. 'He was wearing sunglasses due to a case of "pink-eye", and had blond curly hair back then. I'd had a call about doing a session, and back then bands sometimes stayed at my house. They got in town the night before we were going to record, and we stayed up a while and played some records. I realised then that I had seen Jefferson Holt out at the clubs before. They were all easy to hang out with. Regular band guys.'

This time R.E.M. wanted to just try three songs ('Radio Free Europe', 'Sitting Still' and 'White Tornado'). Easter easily slotted into their work pattern and helped provide all manner of extra gimmicks and sounds to the mix. 'We didn't just put on guitars and tambourines,' says Easter. 'There was also plenty of backwards reverb, tape loops, household items-as-instruments, and radio static thrown in too.'

Easter worked on the songs on and off for six weeks, then in early May sent a cassette of the finished tracks to the band. They were pleased enough with the results to compile a tape they christened the *Cassette Set*, of which they made 100 copies. Instinctively taking on the art duties, Michael Stipe designed an inlay card for the set. The package he put together was instantly confusing to most people who received a copy: only the band's first names were mentioned and there were no contact details; it was just a mystery package that landed on desks around the South and beyond. To top it all, on the outside of the sealed cassette was a 'Careful – Do Not Open!' sticker. Those brave enough to ignore this warning found a cassette, together with hand-coloured photos which had been clipped into little pieces and inserted inside. The band had spent a night at Jefferson's apartment, cutting up photos taken by Terry Allen and Carol Levy and sealing up tapes.

The cassettes were sent to newspapers, magazines, clubs and record labels. Of course they never got any feedback because no one knew where or how to get in touch with them. Most of the tapes were most likely destroyed soon afterwards; any that survived now fetch a small fortune on the very rare occasion that one comes up for sale.

Atlanta native Johnny Hibbert had wanted to start his own record label for some time, but had yet to find the right band for the task. He'd travelled back and forth watching a number of bands, but it wasn't until he saw an R.E.M. show at Tyrone's that he knew the band he wanted. He instantly offered to pay for studio time for the band to record a single, and to finance the record and its distribution.

As they were pretty happy with the songs already done at the Drive-In, they had only to return there to add some overdubs to the tracks they already had. Debate raged over what should be the A-side, with 'Radio Free Europe' winning over 'Sitting Still'. Johnny Hibbert took the tapes to Nashville to be mastered, while the band went to New York to play for the first time, supporting the Gang of Four. The mastering didn't go too well, however, and the energy of the original tapes was lost in translation.

Again Michael Stipe took over the packaging for the record. His murky photograph on the front cover was a typically obscure image. He asked Terry Allen to print copies of his photo shoot. 'Michael brought those negatives over to our place,' says Allen. 'He said, "Can you make a print of these?" I said, "What, you want a picture of this blur?" He said, "Yeah." So I said, "I've got a picture that's probably better than this that you could use," but he said, "No, I want this blur!"'

Hibbert pressed 1,000 copies of the single and, as they had with the cassette, the band themselves set about posting review copies to anyone and everyone. A further 6,000 copies were then pressed, this time with the label's address printed – the only way to differentiate between the two, which can now fetch significantly different prices.

Despite the band's disappointment over the mastering of the record, it got rave reviews across the board. The *New York Rocker* said, 'Their ringing guitars and effortless rhythms are indeed a pleasure to behold, and "Sitting Still" carries an air of adolescent yearning that reminds me of Scotland's Orange Juice. Highly recommended.' The *NME* added, 'They echo classic sounds and remind you of things you can't exactly place, but never descend to imitation. The guitar pulls like a Siren's song and the singer's voice is as comforting and intimate as that of an old friend. Innocent charm and magic at work.' By December the record was being placed in end-of-year 'best of' lists. The *Village Voice* voted it 'Best Independent Single of the Year', while the lofty *New York Times* featured it among its 'Ten Best Singles'.

Over the summer of 1981 Michael Stipe continued to experiment with more art forms. Having already tried photography, music and painting he decided to enrol at a dance class at UGA. Stipe was an enthusiastic if not terribly controlled dancer. He was hyper as ever, so that his teacher, Danna Frangione, had trouble keeping his legs still. Frangione also taught another of UGA's famous alumni, US football player Herschel Walker. She died of cancer in 2002 at the young age of 50.

After drifting away from Boat Of, Stipe hooked up with Lee Self to form Tanzplagen (German for 'dance troubles'), playing a couple of shows and even recording a single at Bombay Studios. While Stipe hacked away at his keyboard again, he and Self (guitar and bass) shared vocal duties and drafted in the girls from Oh-OK to help out. Neil McArthur (bass) and Dave Pierce (drums) fleshed out the sound. In the studio they put down versions of 'Treason' (a prototype Paisley Underground guitar track), written and sung by Self, and 'Meeting', a Self–Stipe composition which saw Michael and Lynda Stipe share vocal duties on a slow-burner not a million miles away from *Murmur*-era R.E.M.

Yet another Stipe experiment was his one-man show '1066 Gaggle O'Sound' which made its one and only live appearance in May 1981. This multimedia event was named after Stipe's favourite year in history. Pre-recorded tape loops, slide projections and live 'music' from Stipe's Farfisa organ gave an alternative embodiment of an early Velvet Underground show.

As ever, R.E.M. continued to forge forward, playing as many shows as they could get bookings for and working on yet more new material. New songs like 'Stumble', 'Ages Of You' and '1,000,000' further demonstrated Stipe's move towards mysterious lyrics which were often completely unintelligible.

Despite the murmurings of some critical acclaim, it was still a low-paid road that the band were travelling on. 'Bill and I learned how to live on potatoes and rice,' said Peter Buck. 'We'd steal butter and ketchup from McDonald's. On the road, we'd get invited to parties and then we'd raid the fridge. We came back from one tour and found that we'd only made $37, so three of us got evicted. We said, "What are we going to do?" So we got back in the van and went back on tour.

'The whole idea was to walk on and do like a 50-minute set

that was like a hurricane blowing off the stage. We wanted to present those people with something that was just undeniable. By the time we were finished we wanted them to think that everything else was irrelevant. I just loved that challenge. And we did it every night in all those bars. We must have played 200 bars, all over the South. We'd go in and there'd be maybe 30 people if we were headlining on maybe a cheap drink night, because we always tried to play cheap drink nights as that would draw them in. By the end of the set, we'd always be able to say, "See? Now tell your damned friends about us!"'

Chapter Five

The Only Person Who
Had a Key

1982 to 1983

'The last time I saw Howard Finster he had a bucket of water. There was this box full of kittens that was stuck inside one of his buildings that he'd kept padlocked and the only person who had a key was him. These kittens were inside this box and were about two weeks old. Howard had this air-compressor hose and he was showing me how to make flying saucer noises by sticking the air-compressor hose into a bucket of water and by using your thumb over the air-compressor hose you could make different flying-saucer noises with it. You can also use it to clean out the cobwebs around the workhouse and if you're inventive with your air-compressor hose you can unlock the padlock, go into the workroom and open up the box of kittens and wake them up with it.'

— MICHAEL STIPE

LIFE IN ATHENS, GEORGIA, changed considerably for many of its bands during 1982. The Method Actors and Love Tractor released their début LPs, R.E.M. recorded a five-track EP which gained national attention, but the Side Effects broke up and, most shocking of all, early in the new year Tyrone's burned down. On 8 January, just before six in the morning, a ceiling-mounted heater developed an electrical fault which started the fire. The building was empty at the time, so the fire spread rapidly and by the time the fire department arrived it was out of control. Even more devastating was the lack of insurance, which meant the club couldn't be replaced and was gone for ever. One slightly amusing sidebar to this story occurred when co-owner Chris Edwards was allowed to survey the damage: he found a box of paperwork which contained a collection of unpaid bar tabs, including those of the four members of R.E.M. Apparently Michael Stipe still owed for Tyrone's for a few bottles of Beck's and Budweiser.

Several Athens bands played benefit shows to help out Tyrone's ex-employees, but the loss of the club left a big hole in the town's social life. Many members of various bands now lived on Barber Street, a short walk from the downtown area. By 1982 so many musicians were living there that Barber Street was nicknamed the 'Street of Stars'. Linda Hopper lived at number 169, which was the centre of the social scene; Michael Stipe seems to have been around there a lot. Peter Buck and his girlfriend Ann lived a couple of doors down, while Mike Mills lived across the street with girl-friend Lauren Hall.

Along at number 181 the men of the street formed an ad-hoc drinking society called the Men's Club. It was very much a tongue-in-cheek endeavour, where local men would gather to drink beer and Scotch, smoke cigars and partake in drunken games and dares. It was formed partly as a sarcastic reaction to a group of girls who'd founded what they called the Cackle Club, which was an excuse to have a good girls' night in. One night Kathleen O'Brien decided she wanted to join in at the Men's Club – only to be physically carried out kicking and screaming. The door was barricaded, and the men went back to teeing golf balls off each other and drunkenly attempting human pyramids.

Across from number 169 Barber Street was a drive-in car wash and a site of dumped old cars. A group of down-and-outs started sleeping in the cars overnight; the stars of the street dubbed them the Barber Street Motor Club. Michael Stipe would sometimes wave at them as he walked past, and got to know one or two of them as they settled in for the night with a brown paper bag concealing a bottle of their favourite tipple. One morning as he and a friend were walking past one of the cars they saw its occupant passed out across the front seats. That evening, passing again, they noticed that the guy hadn't moved all day. It was only late that night when the police arrived that they realised the poor man had died.

Stipe would often make friends with the various eccentrics around town; he was seen by many as pretty eccentric himself. For example, shortly before Christmas one year he was noticed scrabbling through a skip of garbage outside Belt's department store. He commented to a passer-by that he'd found some metal grating which he thought might be useful one day. That type of actual eccentricity that was hard to fake and wasn't the expected behaviour of a cool up-and-coming rock star. He didn't do this because he thought someone was watching, it wasn't a show to an audience, it was just Michael being Michael.

R.E.M. now had more new songs they wanted to record. Mitch Easter was the obvious choice, so they drove to North Carolina with a half-dozen tracks to try out. By early March Mitch Easter had recorded and mixed five songs for use on an EP, as things for the band started hotting up. On 12 March Jay Boberg, the vice-president of IRS Records, saw them play at the Beat Exchange in New Orleans.

The band had considered the option of forming their own label on which to issue the new EP tracks, so they could keep their own house in order. This wasn't, however, for lack of record-label interest: they'd been getting letters and proposals for quite some time. But they wanted to do things their own way and didn't think a label would give them enough artistic freedom. Jay Boberg managed to convince them otherwise. But Boberg himself had taken some convincing to get involved in the first place. The president of IRS Records was actually Miles Copeland, Ian Copeland's brother. Ian had been impressing on his brother how good he thought R.E.M. were and how big they were going to become.

Boberg was impressed enough to approach the band, even though the show he witnessed was to only a tiny number of people and not one of the band's best performances. The next day he told Miles Copeland that he thought IRS should sign R.E.M. 'We had some other labels looking at us, but we wanted to go with someone who was our size,' said Stipe. 'Any label that would sign the Cramps, you've got to have some respect for. I think the Cramps are geniuses, and for someone to pick up on that is really cool.'

Bertis Downs, who had been advising the band on legal matters as a friend, was now asked to come and work for the band full time. He worked on the negotiations with IRS before the contracts were signed in May. The deal was for five albums, plus the already recorded EP, and IRS paid them $25,000 in advance. It wasn't a fortune but it was enough to live on for a while, and the band were safe in the knowledge that they could carry on doing things their own way. Now that Michael Stipe could see that R.E.M. would be going places, he attended UGA's art department for the last time as a student. After deciding that R.E.M. was the way forward, he took his parents out for dinner at a Mexican restaurant to tell them his news. Though obviously worried about their son's future they were highly supportive of his decision.

A couple of overdubbing sessions later, the EP was ready to go. 'At the time the EP was recorded we were going through a lot of changes,' said Peter Buck. 'The band was changing very radically, and that was kind of a period of experimentation. We went to the studio and messed around a lot. I would say, "What's a tape loop?" Mitch would show us what a tape loop was, and I'd say, "Let's put it in a song." There's everything on those cuts. I'd put ten guitars down and compress it to one track and Mitch would dig it and say, "This is fun!" He was having a great time.'

The EP was named *Chronic Town*, after the alternative title *Pretty*

Good for a Lizard was thrown out at the last moment. 'It doesn't have any symbolic meaning as far as that goes,' explained Stipe. 'We were just sitting around trying to figure out a name. It doesn't have anything to do with anything like specific personal problems. We threw out a bunch of things and then decided on that one.'

At IRS's request, R.E.M. spent much of the summer on the west coast, staying around the corner from the label's Los Angeles headquarters. *Chronic Town* was released in August, and a live performance of 'Wolves, Lower' was filmed at Club Lingerie to act as a promo video for the EP – the band's first venture into film.

Stipe wanted a gargoyle image from Notre Dame in Paris to be on the front cover of the record, and the rest of the band liked the idea. They saw Stipe as the arty one, and were more than happy to sit back and let him take on that aspect of the band's work. Stipe would become very forthright in every aspect of the band's image, from record-sleeve designs to posters, flyers and T-shirts. If he didn't like it, it wasn't used and IRS had to accommodate this.

Chronic Town was a critical success, thanks in large part to the jangle of Peter Buck's Rickenbacker drives and the infectious melody of 'Wolves, Lower' in particular. Also, unlike many other early R.E.M. recordings, on this EP Michael Stipe's vocal is pretty clear in the mix – not that it gives any real idea of what he's actually singing about. 'Carnival of Sorts' and '1,000,000' were murkier and gave clues as to where the band would be heading when they recorded their first album.

Though the reviews were mostly positive, Stipe had to defend his singing style on more than one occasion. 'Our feelings are that the vocals should be used as another instrument,' he explained. 'If the words are to be understood they have to be dug for.' Before long Stipe would have legions of fans first trying to decipher what the words were and then trying to figure out what they actually meant. Often they weren't proper words at all and didn't really mean anything. Stipe was frequently misconstrued – but he didn't mind, as he would soon find himself at the centre of attention surrounding the band. The sound of R.E.M. was quickly defined by Stipe's voice: as soon as you heard it, you knew it was R.E.M. you were listening to. And so, right from these early days, Stipe became the focal point of the group – to a large portion of the press he *was* R.E.M. Luckily for the others, they could get on with their lives and pretty much be left alone while everything was centred on Stipe. So rather than be jealous of all the attention he was getting they were actually quite happy about it.

To promote the EP, R.E.M. spent the rest of the year on the road, plying back and forth across the country and visiting for the first time the major north-eastern cities – Boston, Pittsburgh and Hartford to name just three. Stipe was growing more confident as a front man, and was happy to keep ad-libbing and trying out new things on stage. By October the band were back on the east coast, where they played the Pier in North Carolina. Mitch Easter attended the show and was called on stage to play extra guitar for most of the night. Stipe was clearly in his element now. During the encore he called members of the crowd on to the stage to sing lines of Buddy Holly's 'Rave On'. Next he commanded that everyone lie down, face to the floor. Everyone did. The adrenalin was coursing though Stipe's veins; the feeling of having a real power over so many people was exhilarating. He repeated the up-down routine a couple of times, then stage-dived into the crowd.

By the end of the year the EP had been a resounding success, propelled mainly by massive airplay across the college radio network, and the band were more confident than ever. 'I've never been so surprised in my life by any project I've taken on,' beamed an ecstatic Michael Stipe. 'I've never carried through on any one project as long as I have on this one. We've never really had any grand plan, or any plan at all, frankly. We're probably the most haphazard group of people who've ever been put together to do any certain thing!'

★　★　★

For R.E.M.'s début album they had to undergo their first battle of wills with IRS. The complete artistic freedom didn't mean that IRS would stand back from making 'suggestions' as they saw fit. They wanted the band to use a name producer for the album, and suggested pop maestro Stephen Hague (OMD, Pet Shop Boys, Robbie Williams). Not really having anything to lose, the band went along for a trial – but the session just didn't work out and they insisted to IRS that they wanted Mitch Easter once again. IRS offered a compromise: they would bankroll sessions with Easter, but the band would have to use a 24-track studio, not Easter's own 16-track facility. Easter suggested the Reflection Sound Studios in Charlotte, North Carolina, and drafted in an old friend, Don Dixon, to help out, as he himself had never worked in such a large commercial setting before.

Through January and February 1983 the group worked at Reflection in sporadic bursts of two days here and three days there. The sessions gained momentum, and a total of three weeks was all they needed to record, overdub and mix 19 different songs, 12 of which would make the début album, *Murmur*. Dixon and Easter complemented each other and the band perfectly. They just let the band follow their own path, helping out only when required. In particular, Easter was the best producer around for the job of keeping Michael Stipe happy in the studio. If the singer wanted to do something unusual, Easter would humour him and go along with it for the ride. Often it worked out really well.

The band revamped 'Radio Free Europe' and added most of the new songs they'd been playing live for the previous few months. Stipe's vocals, while on the whole quite difficult to make out, did engage the listener in many different ways. The opening to 'Pilgrimage' has him echoing away in the distance, in 'Laughing' there's a real nasal quality to his singing, 'Talk About The Passion' sees him slip in a little bit of French, while 'Perfect Circle' was the band's prettiest song to date with Stipe displaying a subtle side to his voice. The subject matter of the lyrics on *Murmur* is varied and quite baffling. This would be a stigma against which Stipe would battle for the next decade. A recurring theme that does emerge is one of communication, or more specifically problems with communication – quite ironic for someone who enrolled at UGA for a communications course. 'Laughing' and 'Sitting Still' both touch on this, but it's '9-9' that really goes overboard, with just about the only clear line being about 'conversation fear'. In a seemingly perverse moment the band decided to call the album *Murmur*. Critics joked that it could easily have been called *Mumble*, while Stipe explained that the title was chosen because it's one of the seven easiest words to say in the English language.

The album cover showed a disused railway station covered in a weed-like growth called kudzu, which added to the sense of myth surrounding the record. On the back cover was a gloomy picture taken by Sandi Phipps of a railway bridge just outside Athens. She also supplied portraits of the band, in which none of them looks as if he wanted to be there. Overall no one could really make out what Stipe was singing, what was on the cover, or what 'R.E.M.' stood for. But the music was good. To help out frustrated listeners, IRS requested that the album include a lyric sheet. Michael Stipe wasn't so keen on the idea. He went away, typed out his favourite lines from each song, rearranged them into a mini-story and sent it to the label. Needless to say IRS dropped the idea.

While R.E.M. had been working on *Murmur*, *People* magazine had sent a reporter to write about the Athens scene; it was the first time a major national magazine had taken notice of what was going on down in Georgia. In hindsight many locals now look back on this event as the end of the Athens scene as they knew it. The ever widening publicity brought to Athens a wave of musicians and artists wanting to join this movement and take advantage of it at the same time. Soon the locals were bemoaning the fact that when they went to a show they hardly knew anyone else in the audience, whereas a year or so before everyone had known everyone else.

Things got worse just before *Murmur* was released. On their way back from a cinema trip to Atlanta, a car full of UGA students, including Carol Levy and Limbo District keyboardist Larry Marcus, was hit from behind. Levy and Marcus were both killed. The whole of Athens was devastated. R.E.M. were out on tour at the time and heard the news through the grapevine. The loss would deeply affect Michael Stipe, who would later write 'Camera' about his lost friend, and mention finding out about her death in a song called 'South Central Rain'.

The tour R.E.M. were then undertaking was with the Beat. 'Touring with the English Beat was exciting,' said Stipe. 'We were playing places that were mostly all-age shows, and that is very hard to do. I think I can speak for all of us and say that we felt a certain camaraderie with them.' While they were touring, the album was well received in the USA – partly because it was priced a full $3 below the average album price; it wasn't released in the UK until August. When it did reach England as an import *The Times* was generous with its praise, calling Michael Stipe 'the best country pop singer to emerge from Georgia since Gram Parsons'. The *NME* also picked up on Stipe's vocals: 'Whether it's through clear enunciation or a breathless, jumbled voice, Stipe always suggests a lot more than he says. His lines send out ripples of meaning that won't stop.'

More great support from college radio helped sales of the album as it flew from the shelves. Thirty thousand copies were sold in the first two weeks, and sales reached the 85,000 mark by June. Sales were further helped by the release of 'Radio Free Europe' as an IRS single. Michael Stipe took a photograph of a childhood rag doll for the single's cover and suggested that the band make an unconventional promotion video to go with it. He didn't want to be direct about expressing himself, either through video or on record. This shyness was seen as being mystery, something Stipe did nothing to correct. In fact he probably even played on it, and sometimes exaggerated it, especially during the 1980s. The video he suggested for 'Radio Free Europe' was a case in point. It was the complete antithesis of the fodder doled out by the fledgling MTV network, which was being overrun by bright and colourful English bands and Michael Jackson. This video would do nothing to give R.E.M. any mainstream appeal but did everything to increase the air of haziness around the band.

Stipe took the band to Paradise Gardens in Georgia, which was an unusual labyrinth of crude sculptures and walkways owned by the Reverend Howard Finster. Stipe had visited the Reverend before on recommendation of some art-class teachers and thought it would be perfect for the shoot. Directed by Arthur Pierson, the film shows Jefferson Holt in an office where he gives Bill Berry a small package. A close-to-the-ground camera then moves over a kudzu-covered landscape – similar to that on the *Murmur* cover – before we see Berry at Paradise Gardens in a pair of outlandish white cowboy boots. He picks his way through the sculptures, meets a pink-shirted Peter Buck and continues his walk. We first see Michael Stipe from behind, walking through an archway, looking like a foppish literature student with open-necked shirt and glasses. The camera follows his route as he meets Mike Mills and, after some more kudzu shots, the four band members arrive at Howard Finster. The Reverend opens the box and takes out a small doll (the same one as on the single's cover) and places it on a sloping plank of wood. The doll flip-flops down the plank as the video ends. As the picture fades out, 'R.E.M.' is displayed on the screen.

By the middle of 1983 R.E.M. shows were often attracting the very same frat-boy element that had shunned them in their early days. Previously, the 'Jocks' would chase Stipe down the street, hurl abuse and aim an occasional punch or kick at him. Now these people were slowly becoming fans and going to the shows – something that took a lot of getting used to for the band and for Stipe in particular. During what seemed to be becoming a never-ending tour, the band washed up at an air-force base in Wichita Falls for a show. Whoever had booked R.E.M. hadn't really thought it through. Their brand of mysterious college rock wasn't what a bunch of drunken servicemen wanted to hear.

Right away the crowd were heckling the band and screaming for 'Rock and roll!'. As it became apparent that R.E.M.'s usual selection of material didn't fit in with the audience's 'requests', the band switched to playing a series of tried and trusted covers that they'd regularly performed in earlier shows. So 'Route 66', 'Secret Agent Man' and '(I'm Not Your) Stepping Stone' were dusted off. But this still wasn't what the increasingly aggressive crowd wanted to hear. Luckily for R.E.M., members of the military police were standing by to make sure things didn't get too out of hand – but the band did start getting pelted with fruit and plastic cups. Peter Buck eventually lost his patience and screamed at someone in the front row to tell him what they meant by 'rock and roll'. Def Leppard, came the reply, or Lynyrd Skynryd. Michael Stipe knew a little about the mentality of forces personnel, having lived on various bases during his childhood. 'The thing about that show is that these guys would not get really violent, because they'd be arrested by the military police,' Stipe recalled. 'But they had this mock violence and mock threatening, and that was more threatening to me than just having them come up and smash our heads in. That's what drove Peter and me to kiss and rub butts together in the middle of "Radio Free Europe"!' When notes started being thrown on the stage, saying things like 'Die Faggots!' and 'You're gonna get it after the show', the band decided this bawling mob was never going to be won over, and – Peter and Michael at least – thought it would be a great idea to try to antagonise the crowd even more. 'Michael and I were rolling around on the floor, doing the Bump on stage and kissing one another,' laughed Peter Buck.

'It was like throwing meat to the lions.' Mike Mills and Bill Berry, however, were less than impressed. Berry walked off stage; the band followed him and a heated debate ensued. The crowd were booing so loudly that they just had to go back and play another song.

Other 1983 shows passed without such incident, and the band just enjoyed having the time of their lives. Speaking to David Stubbs in *Uncut* magazine, Michael Stipe recalled the era. 'I'm uncomfortable dredging up moments and emotions from that far back,' he said. 'Suffice to say I was getting laid and doing a lot of drugs, travelling around sleeping on floors – it was great fun.'

During a brief break for the band, back home in Athens, *Musician* magazine sent J. D. Considine to interview Michael Stipe. He found the singer late one night, standing outside the 40 Watt Club with an accordion and two friends. One had a xylophone and the other a snare drum. All three were making a racket, an open music case at their feet holding the $4 they'd earned. After an hour and some hassle from a passing drunk, they called it a night. Such anecdotes only served to enhance Stipe's growing reputation as a southern eccentric – quite a contrast to the cool rising star he could portray with R.E.M.

In 1983 Stipe met Natalie Merchant of 10,000 Maniacs, a folkish rock band from upstate New York. Stipe had heard good things about the band and checked them out when they came to play in Athens. At a party afterwards he was introduced to Merchant. At times he could still be incredibly shy. He handed her a paper bag and excused himself to go the bathroom. Too scared to go back to the party, he climbed out of the window and went home. Merchant was none too pleased to be left waiting. A second meeting, when R.E.M. played Buffalo, New York, went much better. 'I knew they were playing and I turned up at the sound check,' recalled Merchant. 'At that time I was into vintage clothing and I was quite a quirky little girl. I'd brought my juggling balls and I was wearing a pair of Victorian bloomers and a pyjama top.

Michael was wearing his pyjamas that day, so we made a pretty funny-looking couple when we went to this vegetarian restaurant. We talked about music and had a great time. He must have thought I was pretty cute, because we went on to become lovers.'

IRS was very happy with the first year of its association with R.E.M. and wanted to push the band to larger audiences, but not too quickly. They had already suggested a couple of opening slots with larger-profile bands, but R.E.M. had turned them down. Now the label came back with an offer for them to open for the Police during their summer stadium dates. It would be a big step for R.E.M. to be thrust in front of 70,000 fans who were really there only to see the headliners. It wasn't Michael Stipe's first choice of show but, having already turned down several offers, and having opened for the Police before – not to mention the IRS president being Stewart Copeland's brother – they felt they couldn't let the label down again and should play the shows to help push album sales. It was only seven shows. 'We turned down others because we didn't feel they were in the same frame of mind as us,' said Stipe. 'Opening for bands is a really difficult thing, and the more popular the band is, the more difficult it is. Which is kind of the reason we're doing the Police thing. Their fans are pretty frantic but I think it'll be interesting to see what 65,000 people think of us. You can't ignore that it's good exposure. I can't say that we hadn't thought of that, but we're certainly not imposing [sic] on our integrity to play Shea Stadium.'

Whereas the opening dates of the tour were played in large indoor arenas, the 18 August show was at the open-air New York Mets' Shea Stadium. Stipe was in mischievous mood as the band took to the massive stage. Mindful of the stadium's most famous rock concert, he greeted the crowd with 'Hello, we're the Beatles. We're gonna play five songs and get off.' R.E.M. played through pouring rain, which stopped as soon as they left the stage. Overall it was not a great experience for them: having gone into the dates with the attitude that it might win them some new fans, they ended the stint a little demoralised. They reckoned that perhaps they weren't ready for such a big stage, and second-guessed that no one had really cared a jot about them or their songs.

In September Stipe was visited in Athens by Laura Levine, a photographer for *New York Rocker*. They put together the idea of making a spoof film loosely based on the Bob Dylan film *Don't Look Back*. The Athens, Georgia, version was called *Just Like a Movie*, and its vague plot was that Michael Stipe and Linda Hopper each had a band and were competing to get people to go to their shows, which were taking place simultaneously. The film, 45 minutes long, has never been shown. Acting credits went to Michael Stipe (as Jiminy), Linda Hopper (as Simon), Lynda Stipe (as Cricket), Cyndy Stipe (as Lulu), Laura Levine (as Atmosphere), Bill Berry (as Folinda), Matthew Sweet (as Mary Ann) and Chris Slay (as Simple); Jerry Ayers also appeared. For Stipe this was the start of a long love affair with films. Around the same time he started experimenting on his own. 'I made a little Super 8 film with a friend,' he said. 'I filmed her taking a bath, and she filmed me, and that was that. Jim Herbert had a huge influence on me, both as an individual and as an artist. I remember seeing his films when I was 19 or 20 and being really stunned. They have a lot of flesh and peculiar movement in them. I think I was kind of a late bloomer in terms of having influences I could spot and name.'

To go with the film, R.E.M. members of the *Just Like a Movie* cast played a show at the Stitchcraft in Athens and performed songs that appeared in the film: 'I Got You Babe', 'Tainted Obligations' and 'Six Stock Answers'. R.E.M. then pulled out of town on a gruelling autumn tour, during which they made their network television début – on the *Late Night with David Letterman* show in New York. Stipe gave a great vocal performance of 'Radio Free Europe', even though between every line of the song he looked away from the cameras and down at the floor. He also held both hands high on the microphone stand and leaned in so that his head and face were mostly hidden from view – especially with his long hair falling down over his eyes. After the song, Letterman came over to shake hands with the band before the show went to commercials. The break over, Letterman asked Peter Buck a couple of questions while Michael Stipe slunk away to hide at the back of the stage, sitting out of camera shot. He returned to sing the second song of the show, 'South Central Rain', which was so new that it hadn't yet been named.

R.E.M.'s autumn shows were the band's best for some time. Playing to ever increasing numbers, they were the consummate live band with an engaging front man. Stipe would sometimes act the fool, though. At one show he tried a stage dive – pretty rare back in 1983 – and the crowd just moved out of the way, leaving him bruised and embarrassed on the dance floor.

In November IRS issued the *Talk About the Passion* EP in the UK, and R.E.M. made their first transatlantic trip to tie in with the release. On 18 November they made their European TV début on Channel 4's *The Tube*, alongside the sublime and the ridiculous (ZZ Top and Buck's Fizz!). In sharp contrast to early shows, Stipe stood still at the microphone stand, holding it in both hands and leaning in – as Liam Gallagher would do a decade later. Stipe's shoulder-length curly hair brushed his blue hooded top; wearing a standard pair of jeans, he looked like anyone you might see walking down the street. 'We're not from Atlanta, we're from Athens,' he announced, between 'Radio Free Europe' and 'South Central Rain'.

Two concerts were then played down in London (*The Tube* was filmed in Newcastle). The second of these, at the Marquee, came in a week when that venue also hosted the Mercenaries and Bernie Marsden's Alaska. The UK press heaped on the praise – but the band were already off for a couple of French shows and another in Holland. In their end-of-year poll, *Rolling Stone* listed *Murmur* as 'Album of the Year', ahead of Michael Jackson's *Thriller*. Michael Stipe would have to learn to cope with all the attention that was going to be coming his way, and fast. He might have felt he was carrying the weight of the world, but in reality he was just the singer in a rock and roll band.

Chapter Six

I Don't Believe You

1984 to 1985

'Kensey had a friend who worked at the funeral hall. Every once in a while they'd get a casket and put it on the back of his truck and drive to the parking lot at the mall. Kensey would climb inside of the coffin, cross his arms over his chest and close his eyes. His friend would close the lid of the casket and wait for women to come walking by.

'Kensey's friend would be sitting there with his arm hanging out of the window and he'd say, "Come here and look at this – Kensey upped and died." And she'd say, "I don't believe you." So he'd climb out of the truck and lift the lid of the coffin real slow and then the woman would put down her groceries and peer over the edge of the coffin. Kensey would open his eyes and go "Boo!" – it scared the shit out of them every time. Kensey disappeared about a year and a half ago and hasn't been seen since.'

— MICHAEL STIPE

R.E.M. WASTED NO TIME at all in 1984 before going back into the studio on 9 January to begin their second album. Though the line-up of band and producers, Mitch Easter and Don Dixon, was the same as it had been for *Murmur*, and the same Reflection Sound Studios were used, the approach taken by all was completely different.

Rather than spending time overdubbing lots of guitars and special effects, the band wanted a quick turnaround, and set about virtually recording the whole album live in the studio.

In fact they took just nine days to finish 17 tracks, displaying the same rip-roaring urgency that they provided during their shows on the road. One thing that didn't change during the sessions was Michael Stipe's unique lyrical approach. He was in the habit of carrying notebooks on tour and making notes as inspiration struck. So when the rest of the band came up with vague ideas for songs – or sometimes near-complete ones – he would consult his fragmented notes and use them as a basis for the lyrics.

Stipe's vocals on the second album were slightly clearer than on *Murmur*, but what he was actually singing about was often just as confusing – even to his band mates. The point was that even if you couldn't decipher the words, the style and mood of the song could be conveyed by the sounds Stipe was making. Sometimes he would miss out part of – or a whole – word, and he was equally likely to toss in a little bit of complete nonsense just because it went well with the feel of the song. 'Michael sings kind of funny,' said Peter Buck. 'The vocals are mixed into the band, rather than having them out front. But we wanted it like that. It creates a real band identity. We might not ever be as monolithically huge as say, Journey, but I don't want Michael to have to sing like a duck just so we can be famous.'

Stipe had finished most of the lyrics well before entering the studio. 'Seven Chinese Brothers' had been written way back in October 1982, 'Talk About the Passion' and 'Harborcoat' were almost a year old, and a major section of the album had been written during a spell of concerted effort late the previous summer. After such a hectic two years of touring it wasn't surprising that many of the songs written during 1983 concerned issues of travel and being away from home: 'Little America', 'Letter Never Sent' and 'South Central Rain', which addressed the pain of being away from home and finding out about the loss of Carol Levy. On 'Camera', which was directly about Levy, the band wanted to create a ghostly atmosphere, so they recorded Bill Berry rubbing a glass, Peter Buck playing bells and, most bizarrely, Michael Stipe holding a wok full of water and hitting it with a stick! 'Second Guessing' was Stipe's retort to the critics who had been trying to work him out, and Mike Mills's old song '(Don't Go Back To) Rockville' had the chance to take centre stage as the band played a country version, with Stipe putting on his best southern accent.

There were starting to be signs that Stipe was standing out slightly from the rest of the band. He had given up eating meat in 1980 after quitting his job at a steak restaurant, Le Château, in Athens. As a vegetarian he'd often had different dietary require- ments from the others but now, after a solid few years on the road, he seemed to be getting more picky about what he ate. He was more conscious of trying to eat well while on tour, to keep his strength up for what was an increasingly hard schedule, with more overseas trips and long stands away from home. For now Stipe was having a spell of wanting to purify his blood by eating copious amounts of garlic. Some of this came in numerous foul- smelling Tupperware packages of beans and pulses, some of it he just ate raw. As well as assaulting the senses of everyone else in the studio, his garlic overdose was stinking out every microphone he used. After each session the mics were taken out to be de- garlicked. When he wasn't flavouring the microphones Stipe was giving them nicknames: he called one of them 'Angela Davis' after the radical black activist. 'It was the funniest thing in the world because it looked like her,' said Mitch Easter. 'It had this big round windscreen on it that was this big, black fluffy thing. It was just brilliant for him to mention that.'

Again Easter and Dixon were happy to accommodate any studio eccentricities that Stipe displayed. When for this second album he wanted to sing alone in a stairwell off the main recording rooms, Easter and Dixon went along with it, even if it did seem more than a little strange. Easter recalls that Stipe would take scraps of paper, matchbooks and even toilet paper with lyrics scribbled on them into the stairwell. At the end of one take of 'South Central Rain' Stipe was putting so much passion into the vocal that he lost his footing and fell down some of the stairs, breaking a microphone stand in the process – which is why the vocal seems to end abruptly on the finished song.

The 'Seven Chinese Brothers' lyric came from a story both Stipe and Buck had heard as children. 'Michael and I were talking about it and that was like the most horrifying story I ever read as a kid,' recalled Buck. 'I remember the book which had drawings of a kid with the ocean in his mouth, spitting fish out, and I thought it was the most horrifying thing I'd ever seen. I had bad dreams about it until I was an adult. Turns out, after we talked about it and wrote the song, there were only five brothers. But once you've got the rhythm fixed, you can't change it.'

As the sessions sped along, the guys had time to take up darts and play marathon tournaments while still staying ahead of schedule. When the album was done, IRS had the surprise – but welcome – news that it was both early and under budget. It was named *Reckoning*, chosen in preference to such monikers as *Rate of Decay* and *Second Guess*. The reason for the choice was that the band saw themselves as under the microscope: had the success of *Murmur* been just a blip or could they carry it off again? It was their day of reckoning.

Michael Stipe's favoured choice for the cover was a painting of a two-headed serpent, and his first choice of artist to paint it was the Reverend Howard Finster. Stipe sketched out a two-headed snake and took the sketch to Finster to paint in his own inimitable style. Stipe called the 68-year-old Finster 'a man of vision and feeling'. He was certainly inspirational to Stipe and many other UGA students who would flock to his Paradise Gardens retreat as if on pilgrimage.

Finster had done numerous jobs through his life – carpenter, bicycle repairman, grocer, plumber, travelling preacher – until just after his 60th birthday in 1976. One day he was working on a bike, cleaning it up and using his finger to retouch some small scratches on the frame. During the task he fell into a trance, and had a vision. A small face from the paint on the end of his finger called out to him and told him to go and paint holy art. Finster, who had never previously painted, started using his fingers to paint an unusual brand of folk art, taking in such subjects as George Washington and Elvis Presley. He also built up Paradise Gardens into a maze of weird and wonderful objects: a full-size chapel, Coca-Cola bottles mounted into walls, and all kinds of structures and sculptures incorporating anything from rusted bicycle frames to old bathtubs.

On the last day of recording the album the band called in Howard Libov to film a video for 'South Central Rain'. Michael Stipe was dead against lip-synching, insisting that he sing live in the studio, but the rest of the band would be miming to a backing track. Libov set the three musicians up behind large screens and lit them from behind to throw large shadows, while Stipe was placed out front to sing with a pair of headphones clasped close to his ears. This video becomes a thumbnail of R.E.M.'s career: the band sheltered behind screens while Stipe the singer is thrust alone into the spotlight.

By the time *Reckoning* was issued in the UK on 9 April, the band was already in Europe for its first overseas tour, playing 15 shows before the end of the month and helping *Reckoning* reach the UK Top 100 for the first time – even if it did reach only number 91. The *NME* gave higher praise than the chart position reflected: 'R.E.M. somehow transcend period fetishism to make music similarly in tune with the times. In short, another classic.'

Back in the States, R.E.M. set about making a longer video project. Michael Stipe invited James Herbert to make a 20-minute film that would encompass all the music from *Reckoning*'s first side. The location for the film was Bill Miller's Whirligig Farm, near Gainesville, Georgia. On the site were hundreds of hand-made whirligigs, which the band wandered around and played with while Herbert filmed them. The unique thing about the final film was the way it was edited: Herbert used the frames speeding up, slowing down, stuttering like stop-motion animation, as well as zooming in and out, and the grainy, sometimes blurry images weave a hypnotic spell. While the film is an interesting experiment, it's hard to watch all the way through without getting a headache.

★ ★ ★

Something that Michael Stipe still hadn't come to terms with was the incessant probing of newspaper and radio journalists. In fact it was getting harder, as more and more scribes wanted to dig deeper and deeper into his brain. 'It seems like I'm being chased by an ever growing contingent of over-30 rock writers who want to delve into my psyche and try to pull out all these philosophical breaking points for this century,' said Stipe at the time. 'To my mind, if there's anything to what I'm writing, if it does go beyond nonsense and piecemeal phrases, it's exactly what they felt when they were my age and maybe never wrote it down or had any way to vent, to get it out. I just have this medium, a band, and I'm able to get it out.'

With Stipe's sometimes elusive interview technique and well-known left-field nature, rumours spread about his living behind big bamboo screens to protect his privacy, his not owning a TV, and his having no electricity or telephone – to name just a few. Some of these things might have been true, but most were exaggerated. Athens friend Lance Smith told writer Denise Sullivan that Stipe's home was indeed shielded by vegetation but only because he didn't have a gardener. 'Michael's house was 15 feet of weeds and grass, and when you looked out the window it was like looking into a jungle it was so green,' said Smith. 'I remember the first time I heard "Camera" the line "green light room" jumped out at me because I knew exactly what room he was talking about. That's all that room was – just weeds in front of you and the afternoon sun coming through and this blinding green glare.'

With their growing profile, several TV channels showed an interest in getting the band to play for them. Two of the more interesting appearances were on MTV for a new series called *Rock Influences* and the influential *Cutting Edge*. The *Rock Influences* show turned into a one-hour special which featured a number of bands performing before R.E.M. headlined the night and were joined on stage by some of the supposed folk-rock heroes. *Cutting Edge* filmed the band sitting around on cushions playing fully acoustic versions of '(Don't Go Back To) Rockville', the unrecorded 'Driver 8', 'Wendell Gee' and a horrific take of 'Smokin' In The Boys Room'. Stipe hid behind a large pair of sunglasses and sang through the songs in an exaggerated southern accent to add a twist of colour to them.

The band were travelling around the US in their newly acquired tour bus, having finally ditched the days of taking turns to drive a van. The new opulence made touring a wholly different experience, allowing them to do it for much of the next four years without a complaint. Starting in northern California and moving south, the first few shows went well. On 20 June Stipe spent the day at the beach in San Diego where they'd be playing that night. Somehow he stumbled and picked up a nasty cut to the bottom of his foot, which required medical attention on the spot. He then had to spend the next week or so on crutches – not the easiest way to run a rock show. Audiences were treated to the unlikely sight of Stipe perched on a stool with his leg bandaged. 'I challenged the ocean, and it bit me,' Stipe said that night.

The band then jetted off towards more new horizons. A trip to Japan was punctuated with a stop in Hawaii. In the Far East the band played to a mixture of curious locals and US citizens abroad, both civilian and military. At one show Stipe wore a black armband and told the crowd he was in mourning because Ronald Reagan had just won a second term as US President; this was one of the earliest signs of Stipe's making political or social statements from the stage – something that would accelerate over the coming years.

★   ★   ★

By 1985 R.E.M. were a well-established band, with well-defined roles within the dynamic of the organisation and well-defined ways of going about things. But they constantly wanted to change things around to keep things fresh. This is one of the major reasons that they have lasted at, or near to, the top of their profession for about a quarter of a century. The first signs that they really wanted to shake things up came when they were discussing what to do for their third album in three years – but what they decided on almost ripped the band apart.

First they opted to work with a different producer – not that they thought any less of the Easter/Dixon combo, but more because they wanted a change for change's sake. Peter Buck was adamant that he wanted to work only with someone who had produced albums of which he was a fan. A few names were tossed around, but then out of the blue came Joe Boyd. Boyd had been scheduled to work elsewhere but when that commitment fell through, the ex-Nick Drake, Richard Thompson and Fairport Convention producer was available almost right away. Stipe, in typical oblique manner, said he liked Boyd because 'his name was short and concise'.

Boyd said he was comfortable working only in England, so if it was going to happen they would have to record in London. The producer flew to meet the band in Athens, where they showed him the songs they had ready. He then watched them play a charity show in Atlanta at which they played ten of the new songs before a live audience. Both parties agreed that their going to London would be a good idea, and R.E.M. set off without a second thought. 'I literally jumped on the plane wearing what I had on, and [with] a toothbrush,' said Stipe. 'I got over there and after about four days

I started to stink a little and had to go out and buy a pair of tennis shoes, two pairs of socks, two pairs of pants and a shirt.'

London in March 1985 wasn't one of the most glamorous places to be: it was cold and damp – but for visiting Americans it was cheap to visit. The US dollar was at its strongest ever against the pound: the exchange rate was virtually one to one.

IRS had given the band a modest expense budget for their stay in London, but for some reason they seemed to blow it all on expensive accommodation in Mayfair – and then spent the rest of the time complaining about how poor they were. The studio that Boyd had chosen, Livingston Studios, Wood Green, made for quite a journey there and back every day from Mayfair. It didn't take long in a wet and miserable foreign city for the band to realise they'd made a mistake. Nerves were frayed, tension was high and on more than one occasion the band talked about giving it all up.

'It was another disaster unfolding,' said Stipe years later. 'We were so poor and so cold. And so out of place making that record. I drank coffee until I peed coffee, ate bad fruit juice-sweetened hippy cookies and wrote the whole record in three weeks.' (Which is a little confusing as the songs had mostly been ready before they even left Athens.) Stipe would be the only member of the band willing to get out and explore London, specifically its galleries and museums. The others sat bored in hotel rooms, trying to find something worth watching on one of only three TV channels.

'There were squabbles,' said Mike Mills. 'We were still growing up as people, figuring out who we were. It was a make-or-break time for the band.' Many of the squabbles seemed to be between Mills and Stipe. Speaking to David Buckley, Mills later added that 'Michael was trying to deal with being a really shy person thrust to the front of the band. And I was trying to deal with how somebody had an attitude when it was unnecessary.' Stipe was really at his wits' end and was pushed close to the edge during the London sessions. 'I didn't know if I really wanted to be in a band at all,' he recalled. 'I wasn't really secure with myself in terms of the position that we were in – how I perceived it – which was a very powerful place, and I was just real tired. We were travelling constantly, we were exhausted all the time, living on $5 a day each and sleeping in one hotel room. I had a breakdown. We were in England and it rained every day. It was a very dark period.'

Problems also showed up in the studio. Joe Boyd's working practices didn't always mesh very well with the band's. Boyd usually liked to work late into the night, making sure everything was just right before heading home, but 11- and 12-hour days in the studio just wore the band down, especially when they were travelling for the best part of an hour each way before and after every session. Boyd also found communication with Michael Stipe difficult at times. Stipe would tell Boyd how he wanted the songs to 'look', and that he wanted his vocals turning down, not up.

To top all of the problems was the album's subject matter. A cold and wet late winter in London was probably not the best time and place to catch the vibe of a set of gothic southern American songs filled with mysterious characters and ancient tales. While R.E.M. weren't a typical southern band, they did have strong connections with the area – Stipe in particular, having been born there and having family in Georgia. He'd also started taking a strong interest in southern folklore and traditions, which influenced his writing for these new songs. 'I was listening to cassettes recorded in Tennessee in the mountains,' he said. 'Appalachian folk songs, field recordings, literally someone with their tape recorder, recording an old man with a fiddle, with a woman in the background with her hand on the stove. That sort of image, I think, really infected the way I wanted it to sound. I also had this idea of the old men sitting around the fire, passing on these legends and fables to the grandchildren.' This was about as far from a wet tube station in north London as you could get.

Mixed in with fables, nursery rhymes, Uncle Remus stories and legends of the past that had been handed down through generations was imagery drawn from in and around Athens itself. Some strange characters crawled out across the album, intertwining themselves with the near constant themes of movement and time.

'When I was writing for this record I was thinking about *Brer Rabbit*, *The Wind in the Willows* and Aesop's fables, that kind of thing,' said Stipe. 'Some of the stories are so incredibly weird that you have this recollection of them from childhood. There's a very wonderful tradition of storytelling, I think it comes with every culture, but in the South it's been built up to a very wonderful thing. In a way I think I am carrying on the tradition although I'm not really telling stories, I've never been very fond of songs that have a storyline. It's the whole idea of storytelling, and that kind of ties in with lost heritage, the tradition of a story being passed on from generation to generation.' Trains also played a part in the writing on the album – most obviously the song 'Driver 8'. Athens was surrounded by railway lines and to get anywhere you constantly had to drive over train tracks, you'd hear the freight traffic passing in the night and the horns became part of the Athens soundtrack of life.

After the album, *Fables of the Reconstruction*, was completed and the band had flown home, they said they were unhappy with the finished product, a line they kept to for years afterwards. More recently they have relented and said actually it's pretty good, and even in the 21st century they've gone back to play some of these songs live in concert. At the time of its release it was well received in the music press. The title refers to the period after the Civil War when the southern states were rebuilt or 'reconstructed'.

The album opener, 'Feeling Gravity's Pull', immediately warned listeners that this was quite a departure from the previous R.E.M. albums. A staccato Television-esque guitar takes the song into Michael Stipe's ethereal vocal before the bass and drums kick in. The whole album's tone is set in the opening moments of this song: something isn't quite right, the mood is dark and brooding, string sections rise and fall. Stipe had wanted something different for the opening song, so arranged for the string players to come in and then conducted them himself. It wasn't an easy process, as Stipe had no classical training. 'They were utterly confused, very nice people, and very English,' he recalled. 'We were asking them to do things and they were listening back to the song and looking at their feet a lot.'

The 'legends' that Stipe was singing about were augmented by the 'maps' that he was interested in: 'I'm kind of fascinated by old maps,' he said. 'We have this book that we're going to sell on tour; it has some pictures in it but the whole background to the book is old maps culled from the library, from the 1700s.' This combination even gave rise to a song on the album. There must have been something in the southern water that year, a year in which Tom Petty also put out a 'southern styled' album, called *Southern Accents*. The rest of R.E.M.'s album is populated by an array of cryptic and eccentric southern characters, from the split personality of Brivs Mekis in 'Life And How To Live It' to the eponymous heroes of 'Old Man Kensey' and 'Wendell Gee'.

The last six months of 1985 took R.E.M. on the road for the *Reconstruction* tour, playing over 100 shows across Europe and the US and testing the water at some large outdoor summer festivals for the first time.

Stipe wanted to play out the theme of oddball southernness in the concert setting. Moody light shows accompanied the music, and Stipe would pause mid-show to regale the crowd with some-times lengthy stories, living up to the fables that he alluded to. Shows opened with a recording of a large train getting louder and then passing in the night. Everything came together as a whole package.

Stipe was certainly giving R.E.M. something that most other bands didn't have in a front man. The musicians were talented musical songwriters, but Stipe's air of lyrical brilliance put them ahead of the game. During the year he was constantly playing with his visual image. He grew an Abraham Lincoln-style beard, shaved off the top of his hair like a monk, dyed his hair yellow, cut it short, wore a long brown overcoat and hat, put on quite a bit of weight, lost it again and etched the word 'dog' across his forehead.

The band's videos from 1985 are hit-and-miss affairs. 'Can't Get There From Here' (which Stipe co-directed with Rick Aguar) was a joyful romp in which Stipe was keen to get involved as much as possible. He's seen leaping over haystacks, pretending to be at a drive-in cinema with the band, stripping off and covering himself in thick brown mud. He even allowed some of the song's words to be displayed across the screen. 'Driver 8' was a much more sombre affair. It uses local footage of rail depots and railway lines, which the band – who are seen only briefly, sitting in a darkened room – are portrayed watching on a large screen. It could be kindly described as a failed experiment. Both 'Life And How To Live It' and 'Feeling Gravity's Pull' used the stop-motion film techniques of a live concert. In 1986 Stipe would take a more hands-on approach to R.E.M.'s videos, and they'd start using the medium as an effective way of promoting their singles without selling out to the typical MTV devices.

Chapter Seven

Don't Worship False Idols

1986 to 1987

'Remember civil disobedience belongs in the town square and the home, not the concert hall, so please file out accordingly. Think about your neighbours, don't get your elbows stuck in their eyes and likewise. Above all don't worship false idols and don't forget to vote. And if you want some friendly advice, it's gonna be a hell of a winter, so I suggest you move south. But don't come anywhere near Clarke County, because we don't want you.'

— MICHAEL STIPE

I N EARLY 1986, Athens, Georgia, had a film unit lurking around town: film producer Bill Cody, director Tony Gayton and his film crew working on their documentary feature *Athens, GA: Inside Out*. R.E.M. agreed to be interviewed for the project and also contributed two acoustic tracks: the then as yet unreleased 'Swan Swan H' and a cover of 'All I Have To Do Is Dream'. Both were recorded at the disused Lucy Cobb Chapel. With Bill Berry perched on the back of a chair playing a single snare drum, Mike Mills and Peter Buck both played acoustic guitar while Michael Stipe stood swaying on the spot. A beret pushed back on his head, Stipe stood on the empty stage with eyes closed, holding a long piece of wood and shaking his head back and forth like a blind preacher.

'I got the impression [Stipe] was excited about some of the concepts we wanted to use,' said Cody. 'It was based on an art concept that if you throw a lot of ideas in, almost like a collage, you will get a better perception of the whole.' During one interview segment, Michael Stipe tells the camera how Mike Mills can smell ants. He's totally serious and explains that he knows only two people who can do that. Later he's filmed alone on stage with a clapperboard, as he demonstrates how 'Popeye exercises' before doing a little jig for the cameras. The film didn't go down well in Athens, as locals thought it missed too much of the important local flavour, but was well received elsewhere as viewers were fascinated by the insights into the apparently strange southern characters.

After the stresses of London and the 1985 tour, the band were staying home for a while; Peter Buck didn't change out of his pyjamas for weeks at a time. Michael Stipe, though, was hyperactive as ever. Though he needed a break from R.E.M. he was still keen to work. He accepted an invitation to sing with the revolving-door cast of the Golden Palominos. First he added vocals to the songs 'Boy (Go)', 'Clustering Train' and 'Omaha' and then appeared at three west-coast shows. He would rejoin the band in March for more shows and then again in July for shows in Switzerland, Italy and France.

After spending so much time on the road, R.E.M. had few new songs ready for their next album. In earlier years they'd been eager to work on new material at sound checks during a tour, so they'd have a batch of new songs ready for the next album. This time they had only a couple of lyrics plus a couple of instrumental tracks. They agreed to work with a surprising choice of producer in Don Gehman. Gehman was best known for his work with John Cougar Mellencamp and at first glance didn't seem an obvious fit with R.E.M., as he often produced albums with crystal-clear vocals and a big booming drum sound that was popular in the mid-1980s. He also hadn't been very impressed with the band when he'd seen them live in 1985. 'I felt a lot of their power was lost,' explained Gehman. 'They weren't able to get things across in a real direct manner. That was the essence of the experience for both of us, this conflict of my idea about the fact that things weren't really supposed to be that way.'

Studio time was booked with Gehman in Indiana for April and May, so in March the band called in at John Keane's Athens studio to work up some new tracks. In the main they actually went back to some older, previously discarded material and tried to rework it. These older songs included 'Hyena' from 1984, and 'Just A Touch' and 'Get On Their Way' (rewritten as 'What If We Give It Away?') from 1980. At another session the band met up at Michael Stipe's house to try to write some songs on acoustic guitar; 'Begin The Begin' was created there. To make up the numbers the band also decided to use a cover for the first time as Mike Mills sang the Clique's quirky 1960s tune 'Superman'.

Having confronted the nature of the South and its traditions on *Fables*, Michael Stipe turned his attention in a more political direction for the new album, as he had several ideas about the region's links to the country's history as a whole. Political writing was something that had so far escaped his remit, but Natalie Merchant talked him into trying it. 'Natalie was really the reason my work became politicised in the late Eighties,' Stipe explained. 'The work she was doing was real and important, all about the human condition. It was a very accurate reflection of the power and greed of the time, and I was impressed by her understanding. Through our conversations, I got to thinking that the plight of the Native American Indians was a very important issue.' Inspired by these conversations he penned 'Green Grow The Rushes' and 'Cuyahoga' for the next R.E.M. album. This was quite a change from a few years earlier when he'd been dead set against mixing music and politics. In 1983 he'd told *Record*, 'If you want to talk about politics or your love life or social problems or what it's like to live in 1983, then you should do it somewhere other than on stage.' His new direction showed how much he'd come to terms with his position, a seriousness in the way he perceived his role that made him change his mind to try to do something for the greater good.

The sessions were looser than those in London in 1985 had been, as the band had removed aspects of the process that they didn't like. The studios were set in nice grounds, with a lake. The apartments where the band stayed were by a golf course; it wasn't very rock-and-roll but made for a relaxing atmosphere. Michael Stipe was still working on his lyrics as the sessions progressed and would take long walks through the grounds.

Don Gehman had an input into each of the members' individual contributions to the album. He pushed Peter Buck to be even more dynamic with his guitar playing, Bill Berry's drums were amplified and given an extra punch high up in the mix, Mike Mills was steered towards using extra instruments such as the pump organ and piano, while Michael Stipe was questioned at every turn about his writing and what he wanted to say. 'I really hated Don at the time,' said Stipe. 'He's a great guy and a fine producer, but he was sparring with me in a way that no one had up to that point. What he did was good for me as a singer and lyricist, but he pushed me way too far and it took me several records to come back from that and recapture who I am and what I was trying to do. It was like throwing a baby into ice-cold water and just leaving it there.'

The album was called *Lifes Rich Pageant*, with no apostrophe (Stipe claimed there had never in the history of rock been a good album that had an apostrophe in the title), and Stipe decided he didn't want to face the press who would doubtless be quizzing him constantly about the direction his lyrics had taken. Instead he headed off to Europe, leaving the others to carry out the interview rounds. In Europe he hooked up with the Golden Palominos. In some live recordings of the shows he did with them it's apparent that he was still writing, because on various tracks snippets can be heard from 'Finest Worksong' and 'King Of Birds', which would be on the next R.E.M. album.

Yet again the album was issued to great reviews. Yet again the *NME* got a little carried away when it said, 'One of 1986's benchmark albums, it aspires to being nothing less than *The American Book of the Dead*, and it comes damn close, at that.' The artwork for the album featured some of Stipe's most cryptic work to date. What did the cover showing half of Bill Berry's face and a couple of buffalo mean? Paintings by Juanita Rogers give a folk-art feel, while a Sandi Phipps photo from the *Athens, GA: Inside Out* movie portrays the band.

As would become a feature of subsequent R.E.M. albums, *Lifes Rich Pageant* opened with a strong pair of uplifting songs. 'Begin The Begin' and 'These Days' clearly showed that Stipe had something to say and that he wanted people to hear it clearly and understand. 'Fall On Me' achieved wide international exposure, while 'Cuyahoga' bemoaned pollution and the fate of Native Americans. Stipe had spent time during the sessions wandering out by the lake and making notes for lyrics, and mentions of rivers and plants found their way into his writing.

With 'Fall On Me' chosen as the lead-off single from the album, IRS naturally wanted a video to promote it. Michael Stipe stepped in, saying that he wanted to make the clip and already had some footage he'd like to use. The result was one of the most un-MTV-friendly clips ever committed to tape – but that didn't stop it getting shown all over the world, and the single almost became the band's first hit single. The footage Stipe used was in black and white, the camera slowly moving over rocks and industrial buildings in a quarry. Overlaid on this was a selection of words and phrases from the song, flashed up in coloured lettering. It was pure Michael Stipe – as was the press release sent out with it: '. . . based on scenes outlined by German pre-constructivist and socialist Andheim Deirtinger in his essays concerning post-apocalyptic societies'.

With the 'Pageantry' tour slated to begin in September, the band had some time to prepare in Athens. Stipe brought in photographer Stephanie Chernikowski to take band portraits for the tour programme. 'I wanted to put mascara on Michael,' she recalled. 'He said, "Stephanie, look at my eyelashes." He's got the richest, thickest, longest eyelashes I've ever seen on any human.'

IRS art director Geoff Gans spent some time in Athens during the summer and got to know Stipe pretty well. He recalled that the week he arrived in Athens, Stipe's car had been vandalised; the singer was still a target to a small minority of the local populace and there was some nastiness around. 'The inside of Michael's house was kind of stark,' said Gans. 'One of the rooms was his bedroom, with a mattress on the floor and stuff around, paintings and sculptures. Mostly weird shit, like two or three of his paintings that I thought were unfinished but he told me they were finished. One room was just a bunch of cassettes piled on the floor. He knew I was into tapes and I told him I would organise his tapes for him. He thought that was really funny and called me the "Tape Queen". Another room where I stayed was totally empty. The happening areas were the patio and the kitchen.' The house was the hub of many social gatherings; Stipe loved to be around people much of the time. One night he invited a group of people over and had a fan-mail reading party, where each guest in turn would open a letter and read it out to the group.

This time the R.E.M. tour didn't leave the shores of North America. The band was not quite ready to jump from the large halls and auditoriums into the indoor sports arenas that held 12,000–20,000. Stipe also began the habit of giving some of the songs sarcastic or deadpan introductions. 'This song has absolutely no meaning,' he stated before 'Begin The Begin'. He was very aware of the responsibilities that came with playing larger venues; during a show in New York he halted the encore when a crush developed while a young girl was having an asthma attack.

Natalie Merchant and 10,000 Maniacs played just one support

slot in Buffalo, but the following night Merchant travelled with the band to Toronto, where she guested on four songs during the encore. Later on the tour, the band had Georgina Falzarano travelling with them as a guest. She worked as a teacher, and Stipe would question her about working at school and how she could influence people's thinking. 'He talked about the power of being in front of a group of people,' she said. 'Being able to manipulate them that way and how to control those impulses and use them.' This would be something that Stipe would make more use of as the tour went on, and come to master over the next few years.

The tour was quite compact, with a show almost every night for three months, and Stipe grew weary not just of the concerts and the travelling but of everyone who wanted a piece of him, both before and after the show. Wearing thin, he asked Falzarano to rent a car: the pair would drive to the next city without any of the circus that the tour bus attracted. Their trip from Salt Lake City to Boulder, Colorado, would become the basis of the song 'You Are The Everything'. The tour ended in Atlanta, after three nights at the Fox Theater, and Michael Stipe retreated for a well-earned rest.

★   ★   ★

In 1987 Michael Stipe tried a couple of new artistic avenues: a muted solo album and an acting role. The solo album, which had a working title of *Field Recordings*, has never leaked out, and possibly was never even finished. The only official comment about it on record came from Peter Buck, who said, 'Let's just say the world may not be ready for it yet.'

The acting role was in video director Robert Longo's *Arena Brains*. Alongside Stipe the cast was one that would gain fame in future years, including as it did Ray Liotta, Steve Buscemi and Sean Young. The story is based in New York, with Stipe playing the 'watcher'. In the opening scene Stipe is seen slumped in a chair; as he wakes up he seems to have a flashback and the movie unfolds. Not surprisingly for a film made in 1987 and set in New York, one of its themes is money and greed, but with the short movie being written by five different writers penning five interlocking stories, it's patchy and hard to follow. Stipe's character does little but watch from the shadows. His only real dialogue comes when he orders a sandwich in a deli; he goes home to eat it and the film ends. Unfortunately the film's only redeeming feature is its soundtrack, which included the Cure, Hüsker Dü and PiL.

★ ★ ★

John Keane's Athens studio, located just around the corner from Peter Buck's house, was becoming a vital tool for the R.E.M. musicians. Now whenever the trio had some new inspiration, they could put their heads together and work on it briefly at the West Clayton Street practice space, and then pop over to Keane's to get 16-track demos of the tracks at relatively low cost. R.E.M. again wanted to do things differently from on the last album, and didn't want to go into their sessions with so few fully-formed ideas.

The three musicians had started to employ a new method for working out new tunes. Peter Buck explained it was called the 'chaos method' as they would thrash away together until something came out of the jam. The idea was to keep things loud and 'angular'; they wanted to keep away from any too comfortably R.E.M.-like songs.

Berry, Buck and Mills also set themselves a strict schedule for working with these new methods. They would meet six days a week and jam for an hour or so. If things were going well they'd carry on until they were bored; if not they'd pack up and leave it for 24 hours and then try again. Practice makes perfect, and in this way they soon amassed over a dozen basic tunes to try out at John Keane's. Some of the tunes had been played in embryonic version on the 'Pageantry' tour, and Stipe had some lyrics ready for them, but others were bare-bones affairs which the singer would take away and work with on a C90 tape. A favourite method for him was to have these instrumentals playing in his car while he was driving; he would add words almost subconsciously as he travelled around.

As with the previous four albums, the band were ready to go fairly early in the year, and in late March they drove up to Nashville where they had five weeks booked at the Sound Emporium. R.E.M.'s last task in 1986 had been to record a song for the soundtrack to the film *Made in Heaven*; they'd had a song called 'Romance' sitting unused since 1981, which they decided to re-record and submit. First-choice producer Don Gehman was busy elsewhere, so he recommended Scott Litt for the job. The session went so well that when the time came to start a new album the band called Scott Litt again.

Stipe was happy to continue working on his lyrics right up to the last moment, and had an old typewriter set up in the studio's control room. When the noise made by his ancient clanking keyboard increased, the rest of the crew knew that Stipe had hit patch of inspiration and left him alone. The noise of the typing became such a feature of the sessions that the band decided to record it and use it on the album – hence the opening to 'Exhuming McCarthy'. The song concerned Joseph McCarthy, who been responsible for the anti-communist witch-hunts in the 1950s. Stipe saw the country as being in danger of returning to those wild days, and penned a stinging lyric which gave a damning view of 1980s capitalist excesses in the USA. The effect was completed by the addition of a recording of Joseph Welch, who had testified at the hearings back in 1954.

This was just the first example of Stipe really stepping forward with his political writing; on the first side of the album four songs could be taken as overtly political, and one as a tongue-in-cheek summation of the world situation as a whole. Like *Lifes Rich Pageant*, which opened with 'Begin The Begin', the new album, *Document*, had an equally if not more bombastic opening with 'Finest Worksong' – a real call-to-arms if ever there was one. 'Welcome To The Occupation' followed, as Stipe wrote about US interference in Central America. The lyric to this song was the only documented time when one of the band's objecting to something Stipe had written meant it was changed. Stipe had penned a line that said 'Hang your freedom fighter', but Bill Berry thought that went too far so it was amended to 'Hang your freedom higher'.

'There are more messages on this record than the last one,' said Mike Mills. 'Michael's just becoming comfortable with what he's doing so it's easier for him to say the things he feels. Plus, things are deteriorating to the point where he feels he should say something about it.' The band felt they were putting forward a statement on the current state of America, which was why the album was called *Document*.

It wasn't all serious topics, though. The euphoric spit-in-the-eye-of-fate nature of 'It's The End Of The World As We Know It' ended side one. 'I wrote the words to "It's The End Of The World" as I sang it,' said Stipe. 'When they showed me the song in the studio I just said, "It's the end of the world as we know it and I feel fine." I wanted it to be the most bombastic vocal that I could possibly muster. Something that would completely overwhelm you. The whole album is about chaos. I've become very interested in chaos and the hypothesis that there is order within chaos, so I guess that kind of carried over into the recording.'

Side two opened with 'Strange', a cover of an old Wire song, and then returned to some of the weird and wonderful characters first visited on *Fables of the Reconstruction*. 'Oddfellows Local' was Stipe's take on the old winos who used to live in cars as part of the Barber Street Motor Club. 'I think there was a guy called Pee Wee as well,' said Peter Buck. 'Michael knew them because he used to live right next door to them. Every once in a while you'd give them five bucks or drop off a bottle of wine.'

After earlier songs had edged around the periphery of the singles chart, *Document* finally provided the band with its breakthrough single in the shape of 'The One I Love'. With a catchy guitar riff, clear vocals and a double-crossing lyric, it reached number 9 in the USA. 'It was a feeling of complete anger and frustration coming out,' said Stipe. 'Originally I wasn't saying any word at all [during the chorus], I was just screaming. The whole chorus was me screaming, and then that developed into the word "fire" when it became time to put it down on tape.' Fire crops úp in several of the album's songs, and was included in the video to emphasise the point. '[Just as] chaos enters into every song, thematically speaking, [so] does fire,' Stipe explained. 'About everything you think about fire as being cleansing, something that destroys everything in its path. It's an element that's everywhere; the metaphorical and allegorical interpretations of fire are endless.'

'The One I Love' arguably changed Michael Stipe's life for ever. It thrust R.E.M. squarely into the spotlight and, as he was by far the most visible member of the band, he would be recognised in the street more than ever. It was his finest hour.

Document was finalised in Los Angeles. At the end of the mixing, Stipe, Buck and Mills stayed on to play an acoustic benefit show at McCabe's Guitar Shop in Santa Monica. The band had toyed with acoustic ideas before, but this show whetted their appetite for drastic changes that in the future would engulf them. It was ironic that this show came at the end of work on their noisiest album to date.

The R.E.M. trio were joined by Jenny Holmer, Kendra Smith, Steve Wynn, Natalie Merchant, Peter Case and David Roback, who each played two sets. Even IRS art director Geoff Gans got on stage to play some acoustic guitar. Tapes of the show were soon circulating in traders' circles, something that Peter Buck was pleased about. 'I was thinking I'd like to get it to a bootlegger and have him put it out,' said Buck after the show. 'If it came out as a real record it would build expectations into something that it wasn't. But it could be a fan-club cassette or a bootleg – there's some pretty neat stuff on there.' Stipe enjoyed the off-the-cuff nature of the performance, and R.E.M. would continue with these informal acoustic shows for the next few years.

Just before *Document* was released, IRS took the strange marketing decision to release a collection of B-sides and rarities on the compilation album *Dead Letter Office*. The collection did little but show how eclectic the band's influences were (Velvet Underground, Roger Miller and Aerosmith!) and that they had a humorous side, as they showcased spoof advertisements ('Walter's Theme') and hilarious outtakes ('Voice of Harold'). Most fans already had the majority of these songs as B-sides.

Once *Document* had been delivered to IRS, Michael Stipe took over the reins of producing a number of video clips and working with different directors. IRS helped to produce 'The One I Love' (directed by Robert Longo), 'Finest Worksong' (directed by Michael Stipe) and 'It's The End Of The World As We Know It' (directed by James Herbert).

The Stipe-directed 'Finest Worksong' caught the feel of the Russian motivational work posters that were used in the album's artwork. 'Technically, I was clueless,' admitted Stipe to Katherine Dieckmann, herself a video director, in *Musician* magazine. 'I did know what I wanted to see, and mostly that video followed what I had in mind – though it became much more frantic through the editing. There's some name for that very fast and aggressive editing, like "throttle" editing or something. I wanted the image to include the sweat that went into it. We were working really hard making that video, it was boiling hot, and we were all drenched. The footage almost dictated the way it was cut. Plus when we recorded that song, we added a 16 beat to it, a very fast little beat that creates a subtle motion in the music. I had to arm wrestle to get it in, because everyone else in the band felt it was manipulative and kind of crass. It's a subliminal seduction, you don't know what you feel so motivated by in that song, but it's the 16 beat in the high register. I was very conscious of that beat when I was editing, and that probably affected the visual rhythms.' The outcome was that the clip, all fires, furnaces and topless men sweatily stoking fires and shovelling coal, was described as homoerotic, which Stipe countered with 'It wasn't homoerotic, just erotic. It was fun to shoot.'

'The One I Love' was the first R.E.M. video that looked as if it was made to be played on MTV. While it wasn't just an example of the usual corporate rubbish that the channel loved to soak up, it was in colour, showed people dancing and had at least a vague connection to the actual song. Heck, the band even appeared at the end, even if only for a second or two. The girl shown several times in the clip with long black curly hair and a fine pair of eyebrows was Stipe's friend Caroline. She featured in many of his onstage stories during the 1987 tour.

James Herbert's film for 'It's The End Of The World As We Know It' was most like previous R.E.M. videos. The band are nowhere to be seen, and the action takes place inside a derelict house where a 15-year-old boy is sifting through piles of detritus on the floor. With Buck, Berry and Mills all absent from the three films, except for small cameos in 'The One I Love', the visual side of R.E.M. was becoming more Stipe-centric than ever. 'If it were up to me we wouldn't have any videos,' said Mike Mills. 'We leave it up to Michael; he represents us pretty well.'

R.E.M., almost always darlings of the critics, had their best ever set of reviews for *Document.* 'It's like being hit by an avalanche. It's bruisingly direct, explicit, stripped of ornamental diversions; they sound like young gods to me,' said the *Melody Maker. Sounds* added, 'R.E.M. are stage hypnotists in control; they will dictate the illusions you have whilst under their influence and they can be very intoxicating ones.' With the British press salivating for their return, and the public desperate for the band that had skipped the UK on the 'Pageantry' tour, there was great disappointment when it was announced they would play only one UK show – and only four in the whole of Europe.

The Hammersmith Odeon was at fever pitch when R.E.M. arrived for the show of 12 September, and the band lived up to the hype as they delivered a scintillating set. Playing mainly songs from *Lifes Rich Pageant* and *Document*, this new politicised band was a revelation, and Michael Stipe held the audience in the palm of his hand. Every nuance, lyric, word, syllable and grunt was gasped at and dissected. The crowd were blown away by R.E.M. but, just like a hurricane, they had gone almost as soon as they arrived. After the show the *NME* called R.E.M. 'perhaps the most crucial pop group in the world today'. For once they weren't far wrong.

The show in Utrecht, Holland, was equally good and was recorded for a possible live album. That never materialised, but various tracks from this show have been released as B-sides including the magically understated medley of 'Time After Time', Peter Gabriel's 'Red Rain' and 'South Central Rain'.

The major part of the tour took in North America. With 10,000 Maniacs supporting for six weeks, Michael Stipe and Natalie Merchant seemed to be inseparable. For the first time the band were travelling on two separate buses. The 'party' bus had all the drinkers and rowdier elements and was usually populated by Bill Berry, Peter Buck and Mike Mills. The quieter bus carried Stipe and Merchant. Usually she would join the band on stage for one or two songs. During an October show Stipe paused the 10,000 Maniacs set to bring out a birthday cake for Merchant and led the crowd in singing 'Happy Birthday'.

With the usual tour-ending party at the Fox Theater in Atlanta, the band were aware that in 1988 things were going to change. The five-album deal with IRS was now complete and there would be big decisions to make. Michael Stipe was now a bona fide rock star, plus people wanted to know what he had to say on a variety of political topics. He had mastered the art of being a rock front man in venues from small clubs right up to large indoor arenas, and was now starting to portray the band to larger numbers through videos.

R.E.M. were hurtling towards the mainstream, but they had already shifted perceptions of what the mainstream was, and the mainstream was also moving closer to them. The 3 December 1987 issue of *Rolling Stone* carried a group shot of R.E.M. on the cover, with the headline 'America's Best Rock and Roll Band'. The *Athens Observer* saw the significance of the article and put it on their front page too. Their headline was more to the point: 'It's Official: R.E.M. Hit Big Time'.

Chapter Eight

Running on a Parallel Axis

1988 to 1989

'In between New York and Los Angeles there is a place called the United States of America. This may seem boring to some of you but please bear with me. Running on a parallel axis to the continent are these things that are called rivers and every now and again there is a river that's named after, this is very popular in New Jersey I think, they take Indian names and apply them to little things. This particular name was a word that meant dying river.'
— MICHAEL STIPE

IF ANY PROOF WAS REQUIRED of R.E.M.'s growing status, it arrived in January 1988 with the news that *Document* had been certified 'platinum' – the first time one of the band's albums had achieved such sales (over 1 million copies). The news certainly helped pad their argument when they were looking to sign a new record deal. After five albums for IRS they were free to sign with the highest bidder, and labels were certainly queuing up to talk to them. Bertis Downs and Jefferson Holt put in many hours listening to everyone who wanted to make an offer, and said early on that they wouldn't be prejudiced against anyone in advance. After a couple of rounds of talking it was clear that Warner Brothers were in poll position. IRS, however, still held a sentimental place in the band's hearts and were still in the talks as well. IRS's top brass knew they wouldn't be able to compete financially with a multinational like Warner, and accepted that they'd helped take

R.E.M. as far as they probably could. The band's next step would be firmly into the mainstream around the world, and IRS just wasn't big enough to help push them there. IRS did want to help them to get a good deal, though, and wanted to keep on good terms with them – after all, they did control virtually all of the back catalogue.

The more cynical among R.E.M.'s fans were ready to brand it a sell-out if they signed for Warner, or any large label for that matter. What the fans weren't privy to was the fact that for any contract they were willing to sign the band were demanding complete artistic control. Most labels they spoke to respected the way the band had handled itself in achieving the unofficial status of the world's biggest cult band, and were happy to give them that freedom. The band also saw that previous independent spirits such as Hüsker Dü and the Replacements had signed with Warner – so they couldn't be that bad, could they?

One red herring the band gave out for not staying with IRS was the lack of success in Europe. Since the *Reconstruction* tour in 1985 the band had played only four European shows in two years, just as they were breaking through in America. The band complained that fans couldn't buy their albums in Europe. This wasn't strictly true – and the irony is they are now bigger in Europe than in their home country. On 20 April the talking was done, and R.E.M. signed a five-album deal with Warner Brothers Records. At the age of 28, Michael Stipe was now a millionaire.

For Stipe, more than the other members of the band, this was a watershed moment. Now he would be analysed and second-guessed for pearls of wisdom as never before, which is saying something. Would his shoulders be broad enough to cope with the pressure and interrogation? Initial signs were that he'd be the same old Michael Stipe and that the mainstream would have to get used to him rather than vice versa. Just after the signing to Warner, he was asked about how it would affect him. 'With significant energy and unprecedented outcome we have pummelled and joined critical mass,' he told bemused reporters. 'The present is at hand. We are now a fossil fuel.' In a quieter moment, though, he was more forthcoming about what he thought he might have to endure. 'It's terrifying, people come to Athens to find me, follow me around with video cameras, take things from outside my house,' he said. 'They want something I can't give them. A million people in America bought our last album [*Document*] and if just a quarter of one per cent of them decide they want to come and find me, that's a lot of people.'

Away from the negotiations, the musical side of R.E.M. was supposed to be taking a well-earned rest. For the first time since 1980 the band wouldn't be spending almost the whole year on the road. That didn't stop Michael Stipe being busy. In January he'd booked into the Cheshire Sound Studios in Atlanta for a week's work with Scott Litt. This was the first time he'd worked alone on R.E.M. material, without the rest of the band. He and Litt recorded a brass section courtesy of the Uptown Horns for use on a 'Finest Worksong' remix due to be released by IRS. Stipe also recorded his vocal part for a duet with Natalie Merchant on 'Little April Showers' from the film *Bambi*, for an upcoming Walt Disney compilation *Stay Awake*.

The other members of R.E.M. were also keeping busy. During the early part of 1988 they convened at the West Clayton Street practice space to work on instrumental versions of several new songs. What would become 'Pop Song 89', 'Orange Crush', 'Title' and 'Great Big' had been played on and off during the 1987 tour, and new tracks that were later titled 'Hairshirt', 'Get Up', 'Eleventh, Untitled Song', 'You Are The Everything' and 'Stand' were also fleshed out. In February they booked some time at John Keane's studio, where Michael Stipe joined them to lay down some guide vocal tracks which he'd work into complete lyrics at a later date.

Stipe had urged the other three to try to produce some 'non-R.E.M.-like' songs and so they experimented with different instruments. Peter Buck played around on a mandolin until he had the basis of 'You Are The Everything'. Mike Mills then added some accordion, and Bill Berry abandoned his drums to play bass. In fact many of the new songs were acoustic, and thoughts turned to making the next album full of such music. It was hard to disregard their electric instruments completely, though. Peter Buck came up with what he described as a stupid song, very upbeat and with a great riff. 'Michael fell over when he heard it and came up with some cool lyrics,' said Buck. That song would become 'Stand'.

After a week or so at John Keane's they had a dozen songs at varying degrees of completeness. Stipe went away to think about which direction he wanted his lyrics to go. He worked on some ideas while the negotiations with Warner were concluded. Once that was out of the way, the band split up for a few weeks' break. Peter Buck headed down to Mexico, where he married his girlfriend Barrie Greene, the owner of the 40 Watt Club. Stipe made a couple of trips, including one to New York where he joined Natalie Merchant on stage at the Pier, fuelling more rumours of romance between the two. They had been romantically involved on and off for a while, but had kept it a secret.

In late May they were all refreshed and ready to go into the studio. Memphis's Ardent Studios had been chosen for their first major-label album; Stipe said that the city had a weird kinetic energy and that he was looking forward to working there. Ardent had a reputation for being one of the most professional, but easiest to work at, studios in the South, if not the whole country. It was meticulously run by John Fry, who had opened it in 1971. Big Star had famously recorded their three albums at Ardent in the first half of the 1970s, and by the late 1980s many bands chose the studio for the Big Star link and Memphis's special atmosphere and deep musical heritage.

R.E.M. had booked Ardent for the best part of May, June and July, much longer than their normal recording schedules had previously been. This was partly because they had few completely finished songs to take to Memphis and partly because they wanted to experiment in the studio and try different approaches to their craft. Scott Litt, who was producing once again, was surprised by their new directions, but also aware of how seriously they were approaching this first Warner album.

Michael Stipe hadn't fully formulated the overall theme for the album, but certain songs were taking him into ever stranger territories and were sung from the point of view of some interesting characters. He took a repetitive mandolin line and turned it into a song sung from the perspective of a dog, 'Hairshirt'. 'Mozart', which was later renamed 'The Wrong Child', was another acoustic tune. Stipe had read the emotional story of a young child who had suffered horrific burns in a fire, and he turned it into a song from the child's perspective about not being able to go outside. 'Pop Song 89' was given an acoustic treatment that later turned up as a B-side.

Usually working from noon until eight, the band made good progress and left themselves time to enjoy the city as well. Because it was such a long stretch away from home, Mike Mills's girlfriend visited for part of the sessions, as did Michael Stipe's dog. 'I remember my dog was sick, and he was with us the whole time,' said Stipe. 'He had parvo, which is a horrible disease. Consequently I had to feed him a certain type of food and he just smelled horrible through it, and he wasn't house-trained. He was in the control room just farting his little doggy butt off for most of those sessions.'

A nearby Mexican restaurant garnered a lot of the band's custom and served up some mean margaritas by all accounts. Michael Stipe also took time off to see various bands who were playing around town. When Athens's own Love Tractor played a show he was spied at the front, dancing away late into the night.

After they left Memphis another trip was planned, this time to Bearsville Studios in Woodstock, upstate New York. Another six weeks were taken to record, re-record and mix the final album. Finalising the album saw its theme emerge. Stipe really wanted to push the green/environmental agenda, and the rest of the band were carried along with him. He had tested the water with some political songs on the last two albums; now he wanted the message to be at the forefront of the album's promotion. Giving the album the title of *Green* covered many bases. Most obvious was the environmental slant, which would become more pronounced through interviews and the 1989 world tour. Then there was the sly financial reference to 'greenbacks' alluding to the signing to Warner, and then the angle of being green and naïve which the band felt they were when it came to major-label music.

Luckily for Stipe, the rest of the band were as concerned about environmental issues as he was; if they hadn't been, it could have caused quite a rift. All of the band had other political, charity and social agendas, and helped out at a local level in Athens. Some causes weren't held as close to their hearts as others, though. Stipe was a vociferous supporter of the People for the Ethical Treatment of Animals (PETA) and recorded a song for their fundraising album, but Peter Buck was less convinced about that particular cause. He pointed out that he didn't have a problem wearing leather shoes, and that if some good could come from testing anti-AIDS drugs on animals he would support that, as he knew several people who were HIV-positive.

Once the music was sorted, the band had to begin on what would be a long road of promotion for the album. While still based in Woodstock they filmed a short promotional video for presentation to Warner Brothers' sales staff. Stipe, looking dishevelled with long greasy hair and a few days' beard growth, waved manically to the camera while Mike Mills spoke. When the album was about to be released the band took part in a live satellite linkup to a Warners staff conference, in which the whole of *Green* was played for them.

They also recorded interviews for a double promotional album, called *Should We Talk About the Weather*, which was to be sent to radio stations, and filmed videos for two songs that would be used as singles in 1989, 'Stand' and 'Orange Crush'. The latter video didn't feature any of the band at all, while for 'Stand' they were happy for director Katherine Dieckmann to have them leaping around Ithaca, New York.

On 25 September Michael Stipe made an increasingly rare live appearance in Athens, with local folk duo the Indigo Girls, as part of the Athens Music Festival. The acoustic trio put forward an eclectic set of covers ('First We Take Manhattan', 'Midnight Train To Georgia', 'All Along The Watchtower', 'Dark Globe' and 'Summertime'), Indigo Girls originals and sneak peeks at songs on the forthcoming R.E.M. album ('Hairshirt' and 'Eleventh, Untitled Song').

IRS wanted to maximise their financial return from R.E.M.'s back catalogue, and who could blame them? So they pre-empted *Green* by issuing a 'greatest hits' package, *Eponymous*, in mid-October, three weeks before *Green* was due to hit the shops. In keeping with the amicable nature of their split from IRS, at least for the time being, Michael Stipe worked with his ex-label on the artwork for the package – while Peter Buck penned some offhand liner notes about each track which seemed to indicate a complete indifference to their previous seven years' work. Michael Stipe also hit out at the choice of songs. 'I don't think I would ever listen to it,' he claimed. 'There are only two songs I like on it – the two I say in the liner notes ['Fall On Me' and 'Finest Worksong']. My greatest hits of the last five records would be very different from that and would probably be incredibly boring.' Evidently Stipe had little idea what 'greatest hits' was supposed to mean. His choice of songs would have had little to do with their chart placing.

Even though they'd had little success in the singles charts, most of the band's better singles were included in the *Eponymous* collection. For their part, IRS also managed to squeeze in some oddities to offer long-time fans some value for money. The original Hib-Tone version of 'Radio Free Europe' made its first appearance on CD, 'Gardening At Night' had the original vocal take, while 'Romance' and 'Finest Worksong (Mutual Drum Horn Mix)' were non-album tracks.

Stipe was probably happier with the packaging for *Eponymous*. He allowed the use of his high-school graduation picture with 'They airbrushed my face' written across it. 'It's something that everyone in America can connect to,' said Stipe. 'When you leave school they take your picture then they take it off to the labs and remove all your pimples and give you blue eyes. I didn't look anything like that, except for the Ian Hunter hair and the atrocious collar on my shirt.' Stipe wanted to use high-school photos of the other three, but they vetoed the suggestion. Instead he chose four recent photos of the band, with Berry and Buck playing bass and Mills playing accordion – all things they'd been doing for *Green* but not on any of their IRS recordings. Again a sign that they were looking forwards and not back.

Stipe's preferred choice of tracks would most likely not have gained the kind of praise that IRS's did. *Sounds* gushed, 'This reminds us that the decade's most consistently excellent rock band have kept us entranced by their dreams since 1981. Let's hope they don't wake up just yet.' Q magazine was equally enthusiastic, saying, 'An embarrassment of riches – just one of the drawbacks of being the best American band of their generation.' But then they gave the collection only 4/5.

Green was set to be released on 8 November, the day of the US presidential election between the Republicans' Reagan-replacement George Bush and the Democrats' challenger Michael Dukakis. Stipe talked about making sure people did two things on 8 November: they had to vote, and they had to buy the new R.E.M. album. He also went to great lengths to show his Democratic support. He was visibly upset that the Republicans might win a third term in office. 'Eighty per cent of males in Georgia said that they would vote for Bush. That terrifies me,' he said. Stipe and other members of the band donated money to the Democrats' campaign, but Stipe wanted to do more and even placed newspaper adverts to back his chosen candidate: 'STIPE SAYS DON'T GET BUSHWACKED. GET OUT AND VOTE. VOTE SMART. DUKAKIS.'

None of R.E.M.'s support managed to help the cause, and Bush won comfortably. The election result cast a shadow over the release of *Green*. Both Stipe and Buck gave interviews in which their frustration and anger boiled over. 'I think the whole country should rise up against him [Bush],' said Stipe. 'It's deeply insulting that we should have Bush as President.' Buck went much further: 'We're pigs! Americans are pigs!' he ranted. 'You can quote me on that. And d'you know what? I think I'm gonna be a pig that owns a gun! I'm so fucking furious, I feel like shooting people – George Bush first and then the people who vote for him.' Perhaps it was the need to be away from America that saw Michael Stipe fly to Europe later in November, to conduct press interviews on his own for the first time.

Once the anger had subsided, the band got on with the task of promoting the new album. To many listeners *Green* came as a shock. While Michael Stipe's vocals meant that you instantly knew this was an R.E.M. album, the songs themselves were very often far removed from the band's work of the last decade. The album swung between extremes, from the dour acoustic 'Hairshirt' and 'The Wrong Child' to the menacing and dark 'Turn You Inside-Out', and then to the uplifting pop of 'Stand' and 'Get Up'. In among this mix was what many saw as Stipe's most open lyric to date on 'World Leader Pretend'. This openness was further enhanced by the lyrics' being printed in the liner notes for the first time. It seemed that Stipe really wanted to make sure he got this particular point across. It was a million-mile advance from the shy mumbling on *Murmur*. 'I put down "World Leader Pretend",' said Stipe. '[It was] my attempt at a Leonard Cohen song, using military terms to describe something much more personal. That song was such a powerful step for me.' The song did seem to convey a strong look at personal politics presented in a unique way. '"Let my machine talk to me" is the turning point of the whole song,' Stipe said. 'It's very clear to me that the machine is the reptile brain or, in Jungian terms, the feminine side coming through and overwhelming the masculine, making the person in the song completely whole.' Stipe carefully explained that he was singing in character; but, the lines about raising walls to protect oneself and then deliberately breaking them down could easily be applied to his own withdrawing and then opening up to the extent that he was printing lyrics in the liner notes.

Another possibly 'real' lyric was used for 'Orange Crush', a song about the use of Agent Orange in Vietnam. Agent Orange was pumped out of helicopters over heavily forested areas to destroy any undergrowth that might be able to shield the Viet Cong. The press knew that Stipe's father had flown helicopters in Korea and Vietnam, so was this song about him? Peter Buck put the record straight – sort of: 'It's not about Michael's father's life, although his father sometimes thinks it is.'

Stipe did draw on personal experience for some songs, a couple of which were explained by his friend Georgina Falzarano. She recalled that 'You Are The Everything' referenced a trip the pair had made during the 'Pageantry' tour in 1986 from Seattle to Boulder, Colorado. She also said that the lyric to 'Stand' was based on a conversation she'd had with Stipe a couple of years earlier. 'It was written about a comment I made,' she explained. 'I have really bad direction; Michael asked me what I do. I told him I visualize I'm standing in front of my house because when I'm looking at my house I can tell that's north, then I can tell where east and west and south are in relation to where I am.'

Michael Stipe's philosophy of embracing mistakes and running with them showed up in the packaging for *Green*. Typing up some paperwork to submit to Warner, Stipe mistakenly caught the number '4' on his keyboard while he was typing the letter 'r' in *Green*. He liked the effect and it was eventually used on the album cover itself. If you hold the front cover at a slight angle you can see a number 4 under both the *r*s in *Green* and R.E.M. But what did it mean? Fans came up with all kinds of suggestions, but in reality it was just a simple mistake that Stipe liked the look of and decided to leave as it was. With the larger Warners budget, Stipe was also allowed to run with a special-edition package of the CD album and came up with a limited-edition cloth cover.

The album was a triumph. '*Green* is the world's smartest, most mysterious group in motion. Listen and absorb,' declared the *NME*. The conventional-leaning *Rolling Stone* magazine added that 'R.E.M. may be dangerously close to becoming a conventional rock & roll band, but *Green* proves it's a damn good one.'

Maybe to keep his mind off the disappointing election result, Michael Stipe kept busy to the year's end by returning to Atlanta and the Cheshire Sound Studios to produce Hetch Hetchy for a couple of days, before flying to New York City to film the bare-chested dancing scenes for R.E.M.'s 'Pop Song 89' video. He and his female friends all jiggled around topless as Stipe tried to make a sarcastic point about sexism in music videos. When censors asked for black bars to appear on screen to cover the women's nipples, Stipe made sure that his were blacked out too. After all, a nipple is a nipple.

★   ★   ★

By January *Green* had gone gold; a month later it was platinum. The move to Warner seemed to be paying off already as their superior distribution and marketing clout made its mark.

Michael Stipe was working on costumes, the light show, back-screen projections and images, plus dances, set-piece routines and speeches. He was going to make sure that people coming to see the tour got their money's worth and took home his environmental message.

The *Green* world tour, R.E.M.'s first truly world-encompassing jaunt, was split into four distinct portions, the first being Japan and Australasia starting at the end of January 1989. After almost a month of rehearsals in Atlanta with Peter Holsapple, who was joining the tour as a fifth member of the band, they flew west to Tokyo. Stipe sang only once at these rehearsals, having been busy working on all other aspects of the tour: programmes, caps, T-shirts and other merchandise were one side of it, light shows, back-screen projections and between-song banter the other.

The band took charities on the road with them – Greenpeace gained an estimated 50,000 new members at the shows. Other causes travelling with the tour set up information stalls at each venue. Stipe would urge people to stop at these stalls after the show, and his encouragement was clearly working. He also started to encourage the environmental debate during interviews. For example, on one occasion he was seen wearing a disposable razor as a pendant; when asked why, he explained, 'I was in an aircraft having a shave and it suddenly struck me. The razor to me is like junk culture. You take a single disposable razor and you throw it in the trashcan and you don't think about it. But if you think about how many disposable razors have been thrown away since 1971 and imagine them all in one place and how many mountains of disposable razors you might have, well it's kind of frightening.'

Japan, Australia and New Zealand comprised the first part of the tour; next was North America. On 2 March they played at Southern Illinois University, where Stipe had briefly studied over a decade earlier. The band's fan base had changed over the last few years; now they had people half their age attending. The venues were now larger than ever before and for the most part were sold out well in advance. R.E.M. had influenced a lot of new music over the past decade, and these large indoor arenas were

ipe's high school yearbook picture
om 1977 reveals the self-confessed
y, mixed-up teenager.

Stipe makes his way to art class on the UGA campus
around the time of R.E.M.'s first gig, Spring 1980.

e hides behind his fringe while visiting New York with his sister Lynda to support the Gang of
r in 1981.

Flyer for the Mad Hatter gig and a poster for the R.E.M. show at Hobo's in Knoxville, Tennessee, 1982.

Stipe takes a seat during an R.E.M. show at the Mad Hatter club in Athens, Georgia, March 1982.

Stipe and Peter Buck on stage at Merlyn's, Madison, Wisconsin, as R.E.M. spread their win from the Georgia-Carolina tour circuit.

Buck, Stipe, Mills and Berry (*right to left*) pose for the cameras during the Reconstruction tour in 1985.

Michael Stipe really wanted to get his point across in 1986, even to the extent of wearing his slogans on his T-shirts.

R.E.M. swept the board at the 1991 MTV Music Video Awards for 'Losing My Religion'. Here (*left to right*) Berry, Mills and Stipe celebrate with director Tarsem and a friend. Peter Buck never liked award shows so he stayed at home to watch it on TV.

Stipe models a self-penned T-shirt illustrating the band's tour itinerary during a host of charitable shows, October 2001.

After a worrying few weeks, R.E.M. relax during the Monster tour in 1995 after Bill Berry (*far left*) recovered from his aneurysm.

Stipe has long been a friend of the Phoenix family. Here he poses with Rain Phoenix at the New York premiere of *Stranger Inside*, 2001.

Stipe was genuinely pleased to get the chance to meet Nelson Mandela before the South Africa Freedom Concert in London's Trafalgar Square in April 2001.

A big sigh of relief greeted Peter Buck's 'not guilty' verdict in his 'air rage' trial in 2002.
Here Stipe poses outside Isleworth court with Peter Buck, Buck's wife Stephanie and Mike Mill

Since his rise to being an A-list media figure, Stipe has often been seen at premieres and charity
functions with his celebrity friends. Here Stipe is snapped with supermodels Helena Christensen
and Kate Moss, November 2003.

Stipe would often strip off during the 2003 tour. Here he is captured topless at the Starlight Theatre in Kansas City.

Stipe makes his political leanings clear for all to see during the Vote for Change tour in October 2004.

Stipe is a larger-than-life character as he works the crowd at London's Hyde Park during the momentous Live 8 concert in July 2005.

as big as they got before open-air stadiums. Right from their humble beginnings each member of the band had been unsure whether this would be a step too far, but Stipe controlled the situation perfectly. He really proved that he could handle the vast spaces and managed to make even the largest sports arena seem like an intimate setting. 'We've yet to play to an audience that I felt was too big,' said Stipe. 'Maybe it's the preacher's son in me, but my attitude is kind of, the more the merrier. I feel much more confident and comfortable with all of my chips on the table rather than balanced on my shoulder in some Dr Seuss fashion.'

Stipe had obviously put a lot of thought and effort into how he portrayed himself on this tour. He had a collection of set pieces and moves to go with each song and with the films being projected large above and behind him. Before 'Perfect Circle' Stipe started announcing how many times the band had ever played it in their 'long, illustrious career'; before 'Stand' he would announce 'This is the dumbest pop song ever written'; in Louisville, Kentucky, he came out to read the 'Group Participation Moment' as it was projected onto the screens:

'Hello [your city here] / Welcome to the show / We are the band R.E.M. / As you know / It's great to be in [your city here] / Please read along with us in this group participation moment / As we outline tonight's / Three / Simple / Rules / One / Please show respect and courtesy for those around you / Hello neighbor / Two / Do not throw things or hurl missiles / As someone may get hurt in the eyes or the head / Three / Please do not wait for the quietest moment / In the quietest song to yell / 'Radio Free Europe' / As Mike Mills doesn't like that / What a giant place this is / Let's see if we can hear a pin drop / Shhhhhhhhhh.'

The band did their best to keep this from being another by-the-numbers arena tour and accepted the chance to be involved in other projects as the tour progressed. When the oil tanker *Exxon Valdez* spilled millions of gallons of oil off Alaska the band – and Stipe in particular – were quick to speak out. Another song introduction was added as Stipe nightly dedicated 'Turn You Inside-Out' to the Exxon Corporation. As the song played, images of healthy-looking fish were projected onto the giant screen at the back of the stage, and Stipe sang through a megaphone to emphasise his point.

On 26 April Michael Stipe sat in on a press conference regarding the Savannah River Plant in Georgia. The plant had been set up in the 1950s to provide plutonium for use in the US government's nuclear-weapons programme. 'Everyone in Georgia knows how bad the Savannah River is,' said Stipe at the press conference. 'Anywhere below Augusta, the river is just teeming with horrible things. It's really polluted; it's really awful.' The band thought it was so important to publicise what was going on at the plant, and its effect on the environment, that they provided funds to Atlanta filmmakers Mark Mori and Susan Robinson. Their documentary film, *Building Bombs*, told a harrowing story of government cover-ups and intimidation.

The band did their best to keep things fresh and un-arena-like. For the 1 April show, at the Omni in Atlanta, the lights came up for the encore as a recorded version of 'Radio Free Europe' played over the speakers. On stage a set of five life-size cardboard cut-outs stood where the musicians should have been playing. What was going on? Then Mike Mills jumped from behind his cut-out to shout, 'April Fools!'

R.E.M. also had the luxury of taking along support bands of their own choosing. Several favourite bands were given widespread exposure this way, one such being the Indigo Girls. After working with Stipe in the studio and playing with him at the 1988 Athens Music Festival, the duo were invited to play on the *Green* tour. 'The problem with Michael is, he throws himself into one particular situation for a while and then just moves on to the next one,' recalled Amy Ray. 'Whereas for me it was a very special time in my life and then he just kind of moves on and you're kind of like, hey, wait a minute, I thought we had a bond! I guess you just have to appreciate it for the moment that it's there. Maybe it's something where he doesn't want to get too close to people.'

★   ★   ★

R.E.M. had played just one UK show in the last four years, so anticipation was reaching fever pitch as their arrival in May approached. They were due to play five shows in West Germany and the Pinkpop Festival in Holland before making 12 UK performances up and down the country. But after just one show in Düsseldorf Bill Berry was taken to hospital, seriously ill and with a nasty red rash spreading over his body. The German doctors were confused about what it could be. They decided to treat him for a viral infection – and luckily saved the drummer's life. The problem had been a case of Rocky Mountain spotted fever, well known in Georgia but unheard of in Europe.

'The first doctor that saw me before I got real sick thought it was some kind of viral thing and prescribed tetracyclin, which as it turns out is the correct antibody to use,' explained Berry. 'The doctors said I was lucky; I could have died if I'd gone untreated. I'd close my eyes and have visions and stuff, it was real scary. I'd see violent things, blood and stuff, and I had out-of-body experiences when my temperature was real high – that really scared me.' The other four German shows had to be cancelled, Berry not being well enough to resume drumming until a few days later. The UK portion of the tour opened without any medical emergencies, at the De Montfort Hall in Leicester. The initial batch of shows had been booked into halls that the band could have filled many times over, such was the fervour to see them.

Stipe was cutting quite a sight with his quirky between-song banter, props and theatrical drama. The song introductions were more like political sound bites and more to the point than the long rambling monologues with which he'd regaled audiences after *Fables*. As well as making the Exxon dedication for 'Turn You

Inside-Out', he told the audience that 'These Days' had three main points and said they'd be asked about them on the way out, so they had better pay close attention. Before 'I Remember California' he said that the closer he got to the Pacific coast the further away he felt, and before 'Begin The Begin' that it was a song of 'great political import' to paraphrase Janis Joplin.

Some observers tried to figure out what some of the props and designs were. Stipe's history of borrowing from people who'd influenced him meant that some of the moves on the *Green* tour were 'borrowed' from other sources. Back-screen projections had been used as far back as the mid-1960s by the likes of the Velvet Underground. Singing though a megaphone had been done by the Butthole Surfers in the 1980s, hitting a chair with a metal stick by the Gang of Four. Stipe's stage costume started off with him in sunglasses, baseball cap and oversized white/grey cotton suit, but as the show progressed he stripped back the layers until he was bare-chested and wearing just a pair of cycling shorts. This onstage strip had been done by Mimi Goese from Hugo Largo, and was the opposite of the act by Talking Heads' David Byrne, who had worn a suit that got bigger and bigger during the band's highly-regarded concert movie *Stop Making Sense*.

Quieter moments were creeping into the later stages of the set on a nightly basis. Tour manager David Russell would come on stage to sit in and play congas on a new song, 'Low', while 'King of Birds' was played as an extended take with Stipe sometimes introducing it as 'For the students in Beijing' – after the Tiananmen Square massacre inflicted by the Chinese government on its own people.

To document the experience, the band decided that the closing US stages of the tour would be filmed for future video release. Stipe also chose to mark the filming dates by having a weird haircut: fluffy on top, ponytail at the back and shaved down either side. 'My worst hair day lasted a year, 1989,' he said. 'It was a combination of every bad haircut from the '80s all rolled into one, kind of a fauxhawk and a rat-tail going down the back. It was beyond tragic. I'm just shocked that no one sat me down and said, "What the fuck are you thinking?"'

Tourfilm was filmed by several different filmmakers, each using a different format to record and each having a strongly defined identity within the finished cut. After the official tour was over there was a final benefit show in Atlanta, which was filmed too. As an end-of-tour celebration R.E.M. put on a unique show that included the whole of *Murmur* being played, in order, followed by the whole of *Green*, in order. 'For me, *Green* had so many connections to *Murmur*; it was very much in the back of my head the whole time we were working on it,' said Stipe. 'From the album cover to the topics of the songs and the way the songs were carried out, to me, there's a great connection there. Signing to another label was a new start for us. It did offer us an opportunity to sit back, scratch our temples and wonder, "Where are we and where do we want to go?"'

When it came out in 1990, *Tourfilm* was hailed as one of the best concert films ever. The juxtaposition of the different film formats, angles and colours married with the selection of songs, the theatre and drama of the shows and the band's being in peak form gave a show like never before. Certainly R.E.M. have rarely managed to reach such heights again.

So a wild decade of touring was over. In ten years the band had experienced the two extremes of the record industry and come out fairly unscathed. They had done it their way – but now they needed a rest. Michael Stipe said that it took him a whole year to get over the tour, and it was only much later that he could sit back and reflect on what they'd achieved as a band. 'I felt an obligation to the audience and the role I was supposed to be taking,' Stipe told *Rolling Stone*'s David Fricke. 'Talk about power, that's a fucking trip. Put your hand up and 20,000 people scream! After a year-long tour it's about a six-month period for me to really be able to sit down at a table with people and just be a regular guy. I remember coming off of a tour and sitting around with my family and some very close friends having dinner and they were all talking and doing what you do on a Saturday night. I was so far away from the conversation, it was just boring and . . . I had a little bit of an epiphany and I went, "These people are not boring and the situation is not boring, it's just real and there's nothing real about performing like that."' After *Green*, Stipe just wanted to be human again. As the 1990s dawned he felt like an empty shell, and he wasn't sure that he'd ever want to tour at that level again.

Chapter Nine

The Ground I Stand On

1990 to 1991

'I pledge allegiance and I'm gonna draw a flag. Caroline says I pledge allegiance to the ground I stand on.'

— MICHAEL STIPE

AFTER A DECADE of facing fans in person and playing hundreds of shows, in the 1990s the band took an abrupt turn. Suddenly R.E.M. didn't tour any more, they were seen only in videos and on TV – but the numbers of their fans just grew and grew. This also coincided with a musical change that had been hinted at on parts of *Green* as R.E.M. became more of an acoustic band. If a decade of touring in the 1980s was the first age of R.E.M., they had now entered the second age. And Michael Stipe was always seen wearing a hat.

Financially, R.E.M. didn't need to keep playing, no matter how much they loved it. Michael Stipe still wanted to push on, however, and even if R.E.M. weren't releasing an album or doing a tour he had things to say. He was acting on his own advice to think global but act local, by continuing to promote environmental issues large and small. As one of his smaller gestures he was photographed for teen magazine *Sassy* sifting through his rubbish bin and showing what could be recycled.

Stipe also started using film to make his political and social points. In association with Jim McKay and their joint C-Hundred Film Corp, Stipe acted as executive producer, editor, director and even cameraman on a series of informative public service announcements (PSAs). The subjects included everything from abortion rights and waste disposal to safe sex and homeless children. The series ran annually for three years and included contributions from R.E.M. video collaborators such as Jem Cohen, Tom Gilroy and James Herbert, *Sassy* magazine editor Jane Pratt, rapper KRS-1 and Natalie Merchant. C-00, to give it its correct title, was formed in 1988 when Stipe and McKay put out a promo clip for 'Talk About The Passion' based around black and white footage of city-dwelling homeless people. McKay said the philosophy behind C-00 meant that they put out films that might not otherwise be made. They wanted to present the viewers with non-mainstream thinking. 'We wanted to bring some alternative and independent-minded film and video work to the public,' said McKay. 'To expose the public to things we think they should see, and give exposure to other filmmakers. We're constantly thinking about how we can use the media. I think back on television and on my formative years and what was influential to me. Michael lives really low to the ground, meaning he wants to stay in touch with real life and stay grounded.'

The friendship that Stipe struck up with KRS-1 (real name Chris Parker) led to the pair's working on a hip-hop track called 'State Of The World'. Stipe even played keyboard for the track, saying, 'It's one of those K-Mart organs that you find in churches all over the South, with the chords on the left-hand side and the keyboard on the right. If you hit the black keys you pretty much can't go wrong!' Later in the year Stipe would ask Parker to appear on an R.E.M. track.

On 5 April, the tenth anniversary of R.E.M.'s début concert at the Oconee Street church, to commemorate the anniversary they played a short set at the 40 Watt Club. With no immediate band activities planned, Stipe then took off for a three-month spell of random appearances for various causes around the globe. The first of these took the singer to Maryland, where he joined Billy Bragg and 10,000 Maniacs for the Earth Day awareness show. He duetted with Natalie Merchant on 'A Campfire Song' (as he did on their *In My Tribe* album in 1987) and John Prine's 'Hello In There'. The following day the three acts again performed, this time in Washington, DC. For this show, also in aid of Earth Day, they were complemented by the Indigo Girls and actor Woody Harrelson! To publicise the cause further, Stipe wrote and recorded a PSA (to which Peter Buck added some musical accompaniment, with an acoustic guitar take on 'Fall On Me'):

Almost 20 years ago, more than 20 million Americans joined together on Earth Day to demonstrate concern for the environment, and their collective action resulted in the passage of sweeping new laws to protect our air, water and land. In the 19 years since the first Earth Day, however, the environmental health of the planet has become increasingly endangered, threatened by such problems as global warming, ozone pollution, toxic waste, exploitation of rain forest, insensitive industry and governmental policy, nuclear waste, all requiring action by all sectors of society. Earth Day is a national and international call to action for all citizens to join in a global effort to save the planet. Earth Day activities and events will educate all citizens on the importance of acting in an environmentally positive way by recycling, conserving energy and water, using efficient transportation, reducing their use of toxic chemicals and products and adopting more ecologically sound lifestyles by buying and using only those products least harmful to the environment and by doing business only with those companies that are environmentally sensitive and responsible. Earth Day activities and events will educate all citizens on the importance of supporting the adoption of legislative policies and other campus, local, state, federal and international policies that will help protect the environment.

We recognise now that we are all one family spread across the earth, supported by a planet on which each form of life is unique and necessary. We all have the same basic needs and the same hopes for freedom, spiritual health, justice and peace. We are all interconnected. All living beings depend on each other and on the earth; we care not only about our own survival, but also about the survival of all life as the future unfolds. We humans have the special ability to make conscious choices, to think creatively and to act responsibly. Because we have become aware of our relationship to the natural world and to the global human family we have the choice to change our thinking and our actions. To create a world that is peaceful and based upon co-operation with the earth, we pledge ourselves to these ideals: to respect and care for all forms of life; to share the earth's resources in a spirit of love, co-operation and responsibility for the earth and all beings that all may live; to cultivate the inner peace that leads to peaceful, universally responsible actions; to educate ourselves and our children to be responsible, caring, thoughtful citizens. Thank you for listening, for participating and for caring. Remember, the way-stream starts with you; you can make a difference. Let's make every day Earth Day.

Stipe, Bragg and Merchant reprised their act for three songs at the Big Day Festival in Glasgow. In what was billed as a short Billy Bragg set, the two Americans joined him for stark but emotional takes of 'Disturbance At The Heron House', 'Don't Talk' and 'Hello In There'. Stipe wore his greeny-yellow denim jacket and cap, a uniform that would accompany him for much of the summer. After the mini-show Bragg asked if the pair would like to travel with him to Eastern Europe, which was just breaking out from behind the iron curtain. 'I've known Billy Bragg for a number of years,' Stipe explained to the *Rockline* radio show. 'He and Natalie Merchant and I decided over a cup of tea that we should all go to Czechoslovakia together and tour. He was going over there and invited us to come. I have to say that it was one of the most educational and inspiring trips that I've ever taken, and I've been to a lot of places with a lot of different kinds of people. Billy is an incredible, incredible performer and he's a really intelligent and very politically wise person. I learned a great deal.'

As well as in Czechoslovakia – as it still was – the tour stopped off in the eastern part of the newly reunited Germany, in Finland and in the USSR. Stipe was excited about the trip, having wanted to visit Prague, especially, for quite some time. He'd written off the idea of getting a full R.E.M. show there because of the sheer logistics involved: they now needed about 20 people to do a show anywhere. 'It sounds like a postcard cliché, but I've never felt the spirit of revolution as I felt it in Czechoslovakia,' Stipe told *Musician*. 'We performed right around the time of the election, and most of the people we met were voting for the first time in their lives. You could hear jazz music in the streets. It was so electric. Billy did his regular set and was very well received. He'd been there before and has quite a following. It was pretty overwhelming for me to sing a song like "Disturbance At The Heron House" in front of people who are truly revolutionaries, who put their lives on the line last November and way before that. It was perhaps the most educational overseas trip I've ever taken. Regular touring leaves you with very little time and an ample amount of exhaustion. But 'most everywhere I've travelled, I've tried to avoid that cloistering thing that touring can bring on, and get out into the street every day and learn something about where I am – usually by not sleeping.'

While Stipe was globetrotting with Billy Bragg and Natalie Merchant, the three musicians in the band had been working on all manner of new tunes in Athens. When Stipe returned home, he joined them at John Keane's studio to add some guide vocals to the basic instrumental tracks. Then the quartet travelled north to the Bearsville Studios where they'd enjoyed working on *Green* two years earlier.

The music they'd produced was again very different from that on previous R.E.M. albums, but showing similarities to the likes of 'Hairshirt' from *Green* and 'Swan Swan H' from *Lifes Rich Pageant*. The reason was that the musicians had got fed up with playing their standard roles and instruments, so decided to ditch everything they knew and start again. Electric instruments were pretty much locked away for most of the trial sessions. Peter Buck would play banjo, mandolin and acoustic guitar; Bill Berry abandoned his drum kit to play bass and add various other percussion instruments; Mike Mills took a seat to play piano and keyboards. After they'd recorded in Woodstock and done the mixing at Prince's Paisley Park complex in November, the album was ready, except for a title. Warner called, pressurising the band for a final decision. They plumped for a title that described their current situation, *Out of Time*.

On 19 December Mills, Buck and Stipe made various guest contributions at the 40 Watt Club in Athens along with Kevn Kinney (with whom Buck had earlier recorded and toured) and Robyn Hitchcock (who had supported R.E.M. during the *Green* tour and had recently recorded with Buck in Athens). Michael Stipe sang just one song during the show, the début of a brand-new song with a curious title, 'Losing My Religion'.

As the world would soon find out, Stipe had set himself the challenge of writing an album's worth of love songs, something he'd never done before. In fact love songs had pretty much been off the R.E.M. agenda since the very earliest songs they'd written. 'Losing My Religion' soon became R.E.M.'s most easily recognisable song, the one that truly pushed them to worldwide superstardom. It was also the song that was most widely thought to have an autobiographical Stipe lyric. Even Peter Buck was quoted as saying he thought it was about Stipe. 'That's not about me,' Stipe responded. 'I rarely ever write about myself and when I do, I'm really honest about it. Not only with the band; if anyone else is involved with the song I tell them about it. None of the people has ever had to guess, "Is that horribly tragic figure me?" They would know before the record came out. I'm just not that fascinating a person to have had all those lives that I've written about.

'We toured *Green* for a year, which turned out to be the culmination of ten years of being constantly on the road. We were sick to death of touring. Peter was sick of being a pop star, the guitar god, and so he decided to teach himself other instruments. Among the instruments that he picked up was the mandolin, which gave us "Losing My Religion". It was really a reaction to what we had done for the better part of a decade that led to *Out of Time*.'

Just as they had done with previous records, R.E.M. released *Out of Time* when everyone else seemed to be moving in the opposite direction. No one else was really doing that kind of album; it was the noisier tones of grunge that were threatening to swamp the global rock scene.

Guest performers were all over *Out of Time* as on no R.E.M. album before: Stipe called up KRS-1 to provide a gentle rap for the album-opening 'Radio Song'; Peter Holsapple played; there were horn players and string players. Another guest appearance was made by the B-52's' very own Kate Pierson. She and Stipe had been friends for years but the chance to work together had just never materialised until *Out of Time*, on which she sang on three songs. The first of these is a song that R.E.M. have now all but disowned, the annoyingly jolly 'Shiny Happy People'. 'I had talked to Kate Pierson about singing together for years,' said Stipe.

'That song was about trying to match a vocal to this guitar line which wouldn't compromise the incredible happiness of the guitar. To me the guitar line was the greatest melody I'd ever heard. I told Peter for two months that I wasn't going to write a chorus because I didn't want to blow the guitar line by singing over it. But he insisted that I did and it worked.' Pierson also appeared on 'Me In Honey' and, as you can hear if you listen carefully, on 'Country Feedback'. This last song was meant as a Stipe experiment and not for release. He'd filled a page of his notebook with some fairly abstract lines, and then when he heard the music for the first time he just blurted out the whole song without thinking. When the band went back to the tape later they decided just to use it as it was, with Stipe's one-time vocal take as it stood.

This was the first time R.E.M. issued an album and didn't then embark on a promotional tour. They did travel to play for TV and radio shows across Europe and to a lesser extent in the US. Not to go on tour was a group decision, but it was Stipe who initially raised the issue. Still really burned out from the *Green* tour, he requested that the band not do that again for the foreseeable future, and the others were happy to agree.

Stipe was fielding questions about love songs and the band's change in musical direction left, right and centre. He repeatedly explained that he didn't want to be pigeonholed as a political writer, that being pretty much all he'd done for three albums in a row. Despite the lack of a tour and the subtle nature of the songs, the sales of *Out of Time* were phenomenal. By May it reached the top spot in the *Billboard* chart, a first for the band.

The music press were as delighted with *Out of Time* as the album-buying public were. 'This band does not carry a map,' said *Rolling Stone*. 'Not knowing what lies around the next curve is part of the fascination and fun of following R.E.M.' Ireland's *Hot Press* was just as excited: 'R.E.M. have stretched themselves further on this album than any of us had a right to expect and the end result is that *Out of Time* is as diverse, demanding and downright delightful a record as you'll hear this year. A classic.'

The band spent most of March promoting the album in Europe, but it was a lot less stressful than being on a 'real' tour. Radio sessions were recorded in Holland, Germany and Italy, and in London they made both TV and radio appearances: on BBC2's *The Late Show* and in a BBC Radio 1 special on the *Nicky Campbell Show*. Then on 14 and 15 March 'Bingo Hand Job' played a pair of shows at London's tiny Borderline club. Bingo Hand Job were in fact R.E.M. and friends, including Peter Holsapple, Robyn Hitchcock and Billy Bragg, all crammed onto a tiny stage. Michael Stipe was in his element, milking the crowd, telling bad puns, running through an eclectic set of songs, messing around on a little keyboard. For him it was a throwback to splinter events such as 1066 Gaggle O'Sound, but with his real band.

'We had to come up with something at this band meeting,' Stipe explained. 'I think Storage Box Hand Job was the original idea. When I came up with Bingo Hand Job, Bert Downs, our lawyer and sixth member, was depressed for three days. He wanted us to be called after a river in Virginia or something.' The new name was required as the shows were supposed to be kept a secret, but of course news leaked out that arguably the biggest band on the planet was planning a couple of shows in a club the size of a shoebox, and there were soon touts circling and people paying exorbitant amounts of money to get in. Each of the performers took a stage name, Michael Stipe being re-christened 'Stinky'. The shows followed a revolving-cast format, with Hitchcock, Holsapple and Bragg having their own mini-sets alternating with sections of R.E.M.'s trawl through their acoustic catalogue.

Back home in the USA, further shows were recorded for NBC and MTV. The former was an appearance on *Saturday Night Live* with special guest Kate Pierson for a rare live performance of 'Shiny Happy People', and the latter was a special recording of *MTV Unplugged*. R.E.M. recorded over one and a half hours' worth of music, which was edited down to a 50-minute programme for transmission.

Because they hadn't toured for *Out of Time*, the band went a little over the top with their music videos. Clips were shot for a total of eight songs from the album. The video for 'Losing My Religion' was the most memorable of these, and incorporated many genres and styles under director Tarsem Dhandwar Singh. Singh not only managed to coerce Michael Stipe to lip-synch, but he managed to get the rest of the band to look more comfortable in their video roles than ever before. Singh also used various elements of religious imagery in the video, which led to its being banned by Ireland's RTE television channel.

In September R.E.M. were back on MTV for the Video Music Awards show in Los Angeles and, despite having promoted an album of love songs for six months, Michael Stipe took the opportunity of standing before a massive TV audience to make a few political statements. The band had been nominated for a whole list of awards, of which they managed to win six, all for 'Losing My Religion': Video of The Year, Best Group Video, Best Alternative Video, Best Art Direction, Best Editing and Best Direction. Each time the band returned to the stage to collect another award, Stipe stripped off a T-shirt to reveal another one underneath. Each of the shirts had a simple but direct message: 'Rainforest', 'Wear a Condom', 'Love Knows No Colour', 'Choice', 'Handgun Control' and 'Free Pee Wee'.

While conquering the world with a love album, Stipe and the rest of the band were still getting involved with political matters at a local level. All four members of the band donated money to their chosen candidate (Gwen O'Looney) in the Athens mayoral election, and backed moves to help preserve Athens buildings of historical interest. Again their involvement was mainly financial, as the band paid for studies on how to incorporate old buildings in the warehouse district into modern redevelopments. They even sold a T-shirt depicting the warehouse section of Athens. Later

Michael Stipe would buy several buildings in and around Athens so as to protect them from future development; one of these buildings houses the Grit restaurant.

That wasn't the end of their politicising, though. In the US the practice of issuing CDs in a 'long box' was still being used, despite several artists' complaining about the waste of paper that went with it. R.E.M. decided to make use of the usually wasted resource to try to do some good. They included a cut out register card for people to fill in and return. The Rock the Vote campaign encouraged young people aged 18 to 24 to register to vote, something that many millions failed to do. In the 1988 election less than 20 per cent of that age group had bothered to vote, so there was a lot of work to be done. Part of the campaign was to pass a bill through Congress that would allow anyone with a driving licence automatically to be registered to vote. R.E.M. were fully behind the scheme. By the following spring 10,000 cards had been filled in and returned. Not bad for an album of love songs.

Chapter Ten

This Is Your Moment

1992 to 1993

'We're going to do a bunch of songs tonight, one after another, that's how this goes. This is our moment, this is your moment, this is the present, this is right now.'

— MICHAEL STIPE

OVER THE FIRST DECADE of R.E.M.'s existence, Michael Stipe had gradually come to accept the fame that he had attracted. It had grown slowly, and while he was used to being famous in certain circles he could still walk down almost any street in Los Angeles or New York pretty safely. That all changed when 'Losing My Religion' became a global hit: suddenly he was a media figure rather than a pop star. It took Stipe a while to come to terms with this change, which meant he could hardly go anywhere without being recognised by someone. Between 1991 and 1993 Stipe withdrew from the press, and R.E.M. didn't tour – but still the band grew bigger and he became more famous. It was like a predetermined course that Stipe could do nothing to arrest. During his time out of the direct spotlight, he came to the conclusion that he could either play along with his celebrity and embrace this new-found wider fame or be swallowed up and spat out by it. He decided he'd embrace it and have as much fun along the way as possible.

But Stipe's coming out to the media glare wouldn't be until

1994. For the next two years he would still be lying low, refusing all interview requests and letting the other band members carry that load, while he let the music do his talking and the videos allowed fans to watch him.

In 1992 Stipe was starting to get worried about his receding hairline. After wearing a hat during most public engagements in 1991, he was almost never seen without one during 1992–93. Baseball caps, cowboy hats and berets would all adorn the Stipe pate. This began right away, when R.E.M. played a small Athens show to benefit a local mental health charity: Stipe was afforded a hero's homecoming welcome as he took the stage, looking increasingly skinny, in a backwards-perched baseball cap.

When Michael Stipe was first called in during February to hear the music that the rest of the band had been working on, he was surprised that most of it was pretty mid-tempo or quiet. After talking about doing a loud rock album as a reaction to the subtle tones of *Out of Time*, the musicians just found that loud rock music wasn't flowing out of them. So with a batch of new instrumentals and a couple of leftovers from the *Out of Time* sessions (which would become 'Nightswimming' and 'Drive'), the band booked some studio time in New Orleans and then, before heading south, travelled up to New York for the Grammys.

At the music world's most prestigious event, R.E.M. were nominated for seven awards and won three of them: Best Music Video, Short Form for 'Losing My Religion', Best Pop Performance by a Duo or Group With Vocal for the same song and Best Alternative Music Album for *Out of Time*. Peter Buck for once upstaged Michael Stipe in the sartorial stakes, arriving in pyjamas, to make the point that awards shows made him sleepy. Stipe wasn't completely overshadowed, though, as he donned a black baseball cap with the words 'White House – Stop AIDS' on the front. He would wear this hat at several photo opportunities during the year and prompt various speculations in the press.

After partying into the night, the band regrouped for the trip to New Orleans and the Kingsway Studio of Daniel Lanois. Canadian-born Lanois was best known for his production work with U2 and Bob Dylan, but he was also a solo artist in his own right and had set up Kingsway himself. Like a stereotypical French-quarter residence on Esplanade Avenue – all wrought-iron railings, balconies and polished wood floors – it made for a very atmospheric recording environment, as did New Orleans itself. 'I've never been to another city quite like it,' said Stipe. 'If you look at the credits on each of our records, we've moved from city to city, record by record. We realised early on that working in a city can bring a certain flavour, a certain nuance, to work.' The band spent two weeks at Kingsway, though it was mainly instrumentals that came out of the sessions. One track that had been written before they arrived was 'Drive'; Stipe finished the lyric and added the vocals, singing in the telephone booth on the first floor of the house's large atrium. Overdubs were later added, but it was essentially this take that was used on the album.

Now, for a month, the familiar Bearsville Studios in Woodstock were used for the third album running. Scott Litt arrived, as the band now had 18 songs to work on, but a month later the majority of the songs were still lacking some vital elements. One song that was almost finished had been mainly written by Bill Berry. Michael Stipe had what he called some 'straightforward' words that fitted the music, and he sang through the first version of 'Everybody Hurts'. With such an emotive and heart-wrenching lyric there was always a danger that people would read it as being very autobiographical on Stipe's part – especially as in this first version he had a line referring to the 'singer of the song'. After some discussion in the band Stipe agreed that he should change the line to prevent people from jumping to too many wrong conclusions. After all, he had often had to explain that his lyrics *weren't* autobiographical; this would be like pouring petrol on the fire.

Next stop on the tour of studios was Criteria in Miami. The band felt that time wasn't an issue; they just wanted to play everything by ear, so to speak. With these pressure-free circumstances in mind, they rented a series of houses down on the beach facing the Atlantic. Despite travelling together and living next door to each other, the band were rarely functioning as one unit when it came to the studio. The lack of a deadline or any real time constraints meant that they were perhaps being a little too loose about their work ethic. Stipe had been experiencing writer's block, and the three musicians were tending to go to the studio alone or in pairs to work on little things here and there. In short, the whole process was getting fragmented. No one seemed to have a handle on where the album was going or what it would finally sound like. Many songs were still instrumental – and unfinished instrumentals at that. During the Miami session the band all decided they needed to take a break. Stipe set off to travel along the coast, driving with tapes of the instrumental sessions, wandering through countryside and taking walks along the beach. When the band met up again, the night before they were due to go back into the studio, Bill Berry heard Michael Stipe's typewriter tapping away into the early hours. At that point he knew that things would turn out OK: the writer's block had gone.

Finishing touches were still required, and several songs sounded as if they could be improved by the addition of some strings. Instead of the band's trying to tell classical players what they wanted – as they'd done in the past – Scott Litt got in touch with ex-Led Zeppelin bassist John Paul Jones, who agreed to write some specific sections to be used on the songs in question. He then flew over to conduct the players in Atlanta for four days. 'Drive', 'The Sidewinder Sleeps Tonite', 'Nightswimming' and 'Everybody Hurts' were all given the orchestral treatment; it was the latter that benefited the most.

Although all the basic recording was done, the band still had one more stop on this studio odyssey, with a trip to Bad Animals Studio in Seattle for mixing. One instrumental, given the working title 'C to D Slide' after the chord changes in the song, was a track the band had been pestering Stipe to find some words to, because everyone had great hopes for it. But while the rest of the album was being mixed, Stipe still hadn't managed to find anything that really worked. It was only when everything else for the album was done that he had a sudden flash of inspiration and penned what would be the lyric to 'Man On The Moon'. 'It was written and recorded on the day it was delivered to the record company,' said Stipe. 'Although it was a 40-hour day.'

It's fair to say that while most of the band members only tolerate having to make videos, Michael Stipe actually enjoys the experience. He's more than happy to come up with ideas, work on the early preparation stages and continue right through to post-production duties. As lead singer he's the one whose face is more often than not at the centre of these shoots – although over the years R.E.M. have been unconventional in that in several videos they don't even appear.

Peter Buck was quite open about his lack of interest in the visual side of the band when talking to Q magazine. 'That's his [Stipe's] job,' said the guitarist. 'The rest of us, I'm afraid to say, just don't give much of a shit. If it was up to me, the records would come out in white covers and they'd be titled '1', '2' and '3'.' Buck must have therefore been quite happy to have little to do in the seven weeks of work that went into producing the 'Man On The Moon' video. After the success of the 'Drive' video, which had been directed by Peter Care, Stipe wanted to work with him again, and the Englishman was glad to be involved. He usually liked to work using only his own ideas, but in this case most of the major ideas for the shoot were Stipe's.

The main thrust of the video was storyboarded with Stipe walking through the Californian desert until he hitches a lift on a truck (driven by Bill Berry) and goes to a truck stop. Stipe was filmed in jeans, white shirt and cowboy hat, reminiscent of James Dean in *Giant* or Montgomery Clift (about whom another song on the album was written) in *The Misfits*. Here the extras at the truck stop all sing lines of the song while members of the band play pool, serve drinks and generally hang out. Stipe worked closely with Peter Care and his team, starting with the initial location-scouting of desert sites and two different truck stops (one for internal and one for external shots). Stipe was also sure that he wanted images of Andy Kaufman and various other footage to be shown in the desert sky above him. The result was one of the 1990s' most iconic videos and further pushed the band – and especially Stipe who was clearly its centrepiece – to the epicentre of popular culture.

Not wanting to feel pressurised to find an album title, Stipe decided to put some plans in action as soon as everyone returned to Athens in August. After running his idea past his band mates, he took Bertis Downs to a local Athens eatery called Weaver D's Fine Foods, down the hill on Broad Street. Advertised as a soulfood restaurant, the small establishment served up some of the best in the area. But Stipe hadn't just taken Downs along for some good food: he wanted to speak to the owner, Dexter Weaver, about a business proposition, and needed Downs's legal nous. The three sat down, and Stipe explained that for the title of their album R.E.M. wanted to use Weaver's restaurant motto, 'Automatic for the People'. Unlike previous R.E.M. album titles it had little if anything to do with the album, but all four band members liked it anyway. Weaver was only too happy to comply, Downs sorted out the paperwork and Warner were told of the decision.

The single chosen to precede the album's release was 'Drive' – a surprise, given its stop-start, brooding nature. The single benefited from a memorable video, shot by Peter Care at the Sepulveda Dam in California. Volunteers turned up to allow Michael Stipe to be filmed crowd-surfing, rolling across the top of hundreds of hands – while the rest of the band were blasted with water. (Guess who drew the short straw there.)

With the album set for an early-October release, it was Peter Buck and Mike Mills who stepped forward to carry out the advance interview duties. The question they had to field most often was 'Where's Michael?' or maybe 'Is Michael ill?'. The answer to the first question was that he was removing himself from interviews for the foreseeable future, and the answer to the latter was no, he's perfectly well. It is fair to say that he was looking very thin and gaunt, was thinning on top and, an AIDS activist, had just written an album of songs about death. Rumours began that Stipe was ill with AIDS, and they refused to go away. 'To go public and deny I had AIDS would denigrate those who are suffering from HIV and AIDS,' he said later. 'I didn't want to dignify the rumour.' The band actually hired a private detective to track down the source of the rumours, a trail that led to a friend in Los Angeles.

To accompany the album the band prepared a short promotional film, which was sent to reviewers and various TV companies. Even on this preview, however, Stipe refused to speak, although he appeared to sing a bare-bones take of 'Find The River' live in the studio. 'I went through a period where I was really tired of seeing and reading about myself,' said Stipe. 'If I'm tired of me, I'm sure the public is as well. For years I would do press for one record, then not do press for the next record. I hopscotched like that for four or five records. I just felt like I'd run out of things to say – in a way I feel like that right now. I'm not sure that I have anything really new to say.'

Rarely has an album received such universal, 100 per cent approval. Almost every review bestowed top marks and unreserved praise. *Vox* and *NME* both gave 10/10, *Rolling Stone* and *Select* gave 5/5. *Melody Maker* didn't give scores but added, 'Listen to it, and let it stone you to your soul.' This time the reviewers got it absolutely right. The album was clearly a career peak. Stipe's voice came across with great authority and feeling, his emotions veering from despair to hope, from gloom to ecstasy and anger across the 11 songs. 'Digital recording makes me sound like what I've always wanted to sound like,' he said. 'I think people who were fans of the band early on might not like the progression my vocals have taken, but there's not a whole lot I can do about it. I'm ten years older, I know what I'm doing now.'

The writing on the album was also exemplary, with cultural references in abundance (President Bush, Andy Kaufman, Montgomery Clift and Elvis to name just a few). Almost every song could be considered a highlight – though 'Nightswimming' must be one of the band's understated masterpieces. The song harks back to a time before innocence was lost, Mike Mills's piano and John Paul Jones's string arrangements perfectly offsetting Stipe's slightly gravelly vocal. Stipe himself tells a clever story with the imagery of a photograph being lit up on the dashboard of the car while it's driven past street lights. It's the quintessential moment of Stipean lyricism. In a few simple lines he manages to convey the wistfulness of memory, zooming in on a detail of the picture and still managing to get his whole point across.

Stipe took part in photo shoots for several magazine covers during the autumn, doing among others a cheeky bare-chested shot for *Select* in the UK. Though refusing to give interviews, Stipe was not being so coy when it came to speaking out on non-musical issues close to his heart. With a US presidential election fast approaching, he attended a Democrats rally in Athens and took the stage to introduce vice-presidential candidate Al Gore. With a keen sense of where he was and who he was listening to, Gore said, 'George Bush is "out of time" and Bill Clinton and Al Gore are going to be "automatic for the people".' The Clinton–Gore team won 43 per cent of the popular vote – 5 per cent more than George Bush – as they swept into the White House.

After heartily celebrating the election victory, R.E.M. spent five days at John Keane's studio rehearsing for a Greenpeace show at the 40 Watt Club on 19 November. The event was to showcase

Greenpeace's new solar-powered mobile recording truck, which was touring around and recording different bands for a compilation album. R.E.M. wanted to donate a live take of 'Drive', and decided to play an hour-long show which featured the live débuts of four songs from *Automatic for the People*. 'Drive' was delivered with a harsh funk and was not at all like the album version, 'Monty Got A Raw Deal' was given a more moderate treatment, 'Everybody Hurts' brought the house down with its epic majesty and 'Man On The Moon' did likewise. The show was performed in front of family, friends, fan-club members and the press, and soon found its way onto bootleg CDs.

The last order of business before the traditional parting at the end of November was a final video shoot for the next single, 'Everybody Hurts'. Director Jake Scott flew the band to San Antonio, where he got permission to close part of a freeway while he filmed the clip. Like the 'Man On The Moon' video, this would become one of the band's most famous and increase their worldwide appeal, becoming another of the most iconic musical images of the 1990s. In the video, the band are stuck in a car on a gridlocked freeway and Stipe decides to get out and walk, giving one of his most mournful performances as he clambers over cars and leads everyone away. The band were dressed in black suits and white shirts (with Stipe wearing an obligatory hat), with Bill Berry and Mike Mills especially looking as if they'd just left the set of *Reservoir Dogs*.

Stipe was acutely aware of the power of the video by the 1990s. When he was in town on a Saturday night he'd invite a group of friends over for food and drinks while they watched the latest videos on MTV's *120 Minutes* and give their critiques of each in turn.

The band were now selling millions of copies of each new album and had reached a peak in the public's awareness. Michael Stipe, especially, was a cultural icon – and was also there to be, figuratively, shot at. The first person to fire a shot was the Manic

Street Preachers' Nicky Wire. During an 11 December show at London's Kilburn National, the guitarist felt it was a good idea to spout, 'In the season of goodwill, let's hope Michael Stipe goes the same way as Freddie Mercury.' The reference was clearly to the former Queen front man's death from AIDS. The British press had been speculating about Stipe's health for some time; whether he was ill or not, it was a comment in the poorest taste and extremely disrespectful to people with the illness – who might even have included Manics fans in the audience that night.

Wire was roundly condemned and took a bit of a pounding in the press. Stipe himself kept quiet, obviously seeing the comments for what they really were, a grasping attempt to try to get some cheap publicity. A January 1993 issue of *NME* poked fun at the incident when it announced R.E.M. as winners of their readers' poll with the front-page banner headline 'Stipe Lives!'. US comedian Denis Leary did it better when he worked a gag about R.E.M. being shiny happy people into his routine. When he later met Michael Stipe he explained that it was just for laughs and that he was actually a fan of R.E.M..

January 1993 had been a long time coming. The last Democratic inauguration had been for Jimmy Carter way back in January 1977. Mike Mills and Michael Stipe flew up to Washington, DC, for the week, to join the celebrations. Stipe appeared at the opening event where he read Woody Guthrie and (environmentalist) Lester Brown quotes. Many Clinton supporters converged on Washington; Stipe later said that the highlight of his week was meeting Sidney Poitier and Harry Belafonte with whom he talked about photography and activism.

There was a series of concerts across the capital, but Stipe and Mills weren't expecting to perform – not, that is, until they met Larry Mullen and Adam Clayton from U2, when someone suggested they could all play as one band. The concept spread from there; names like 'R2 U2' and 'Automatic Baby' were bandied around for the makeshift grouping, and the latter was chosen.

They performed just one song, a haunting version of the U2 track 'One', at the MTV Rock and Roll Inaugural Ball. Michael Stipe also paired up with 10,000 Maniacs to sing 'Candy Everybody Wants' and a rousing 'To Sir With Love' with Natalie Merchant.

Stipe spent the spring visiting friends and getting involved with his first love, photography. When Jem Cohen signed up to film a video clip for 'Nightswimming' in southern Georgia and Florida, Stipe tagged along as the video shoot's official photographer, snapping pics of naked boys and girls along the way. 'The goal is to get to the essence of a song,' said Cohen about the lengthy clip. 'I try not to overpower it with fast edits and fancy effects. We also wanted to make something sexy – for girls, boys and older people as well – that didn't depend on exploitation, on "perfect" models in bikinis, on things that have little to do with real life as most of us live it.'

In May it was back to the White House as guest of the President for the second time in four months. This time it was because the Motor Voter Bill had been passed and R.E.M.'s work to get more young people to sign up was being recognised, as Stipe, Mills and Berry met the President for a photo opportunity on the White House lawn.

With little going on over the summer, Stipe encouraged people to catch the 10,000 Maniacs' summer dates through the R.E.M. fan-club newsletter: 'Go directly to the nearest 10,000 Maniacs concert – absolutely do not miss this band on the greatest tour of the summer! THIS MEANS YOU!' he wrote.

On 24 August Stipe gave one his most surreal performances with local singer Vic Chesnutt at the 40 Watt Club. Dressed in a powder-blue suit, foppish white shirt and cowboy hat, Stipe strolled on stage to a backing tape of Glen Campbell singing 'Rhinestone Cowboy', to which he lip-synched, before being joined by Chesnutt to run through more Campbell numbers ('Wichita Lineman', 'Galveston', and 'By The Time I Get To Phoenix') and a few other covers for good measure.

R.E.M. made a surprise appearance at the MTV Music Video Awards in early September in Los Angeles. Though they weren't there to collect any awards this time, they played 'Everybody Hurts' and 'Drive' to a massive worldwide television audience. Michael Stipe had changed his look again, having last been seen by the general public in white T-shirt and sunglasses, for the press photos to promote *Automatic*. Now he wore a straw hat, had large black eyebrows painted on his face and sported a goatee beard. Also showing off a new image was Mike Mills, who had developed a full-blown rock-star persona and had long curly hair, while wearing a Gram Parson-like Nudie suit with large flame patterns on the jacket and trouser legs.

Stipe's last public engagement of the year before a planned linkup with rest of the band to go back into the studio was at the Telluride Film Festival in Colorado. Here he sat in on a panel discussion about music videos where 'Low', 'Belong' and 'Man On The Moon' were screened.

★　★　★

When the band regrouped to talk about a new album, Bill Berry had already sketched out the tune for 'I Took Your Name', and early versions of 'You' and a song Stipe initially called 'Yes, I Am Fucking With You'. They headed back to New Orleans and Kingsway Studios with these new ideas and a few more, which all sounded far removed from anything on either *Out of Time* or *Automatic for the People* and nothing like the R.E.M. of the IRS years either. In the back of their minds everyone knew they wanted to tour with the next album, and so worked on ideas that they hoped would reproduce well in what would be very large concert halls and stadium settings. After ten days' working on rough versions of 20 new tracks, the band took a break.

Shortly after going home to Athens, Stipe received some chilling news: River Phoenix had died in Los Angeles. Phoenix had risen to fame with the film *My Own Private Idaho*; like Stipe he was a vegetarian, cared about the environment and loved music. The two had become friends, and Stipe had shown an interest in Phoenix's band Aleka's Attic. Phoenix was in Los Angeles to work on a movie called *Dark Blood*, and had signed a deal to appear in *Interview with a Vampire*. On 30 October he stumbled out of Johnny Depp's club on Sunset Boulevard, the Viper Room, and collapsed in the street. He was rushed to the Cedars Sinai Medical Center but pronounced dead. His post-mortem examination showed high levels of cocaine, morphine, Valium, marijuana and ephedrine in his system. Unsurprisingly the official cause of death was 'acute multiple drug ingestion'. He was 23 years old.

'Upon River's death I had to re-evaluate all the people in my life that had passed away and what they had meant to me,' said Stipe. 'I realized how much more profound his loss was than any other that I had experienced. Possibly just because it was so tragic, so incredibly tragic, an awful, awful mistake. He was my brother, I loved him a great deal. I couldn't write for five months. We had started the record in September. I'd written two songs and then River died. And, having written *Automatic for the People*, I was not about to write another record about death and loss. So it took me five months to sit down and write again.'

Away from R.E.M. Stipe hosted guests in Athens. Courtney Love, Kurt Cobain and their young daughter Frances Bean stopped by while working in Atlanta. Though Stipe didn't know Cobain that well, he knew that Cobain respected R.E.M. to the point of being almost in awe of them. Stipe was happy to play Cobain his latest demos of 'You', 'I Took Your Name' and 'What's The Frequency, Kenneth?', but Cobain was more interested in going the opposite way to R.E.M.'s new louder direction. He wanted to explore more acoustic ground, and spoke to Stipe about R.E.M.'s previous two albums.

It was about this visit to Athens that Courtney Love later made some controversial claims, speaking to *Vanity Fair* in June 1995.

Apparently she had wanted Cobain to experiment with his sexuality with Michael Stipe. 'I left him with Michael Stipe one night and told him to go explore his cravings. "Big talker, go on!" I told him. All he'd ever done was kiss some guy in high school and some kid in a club. He came back the next day, and I started screaming, "What happened?" He said, "I dunno. It was just weird. Nothing happened, but sort of." I'll never know. Michael's never told me.'

'That was a little crazy, I'm not sure what that was about,' said Stipe when asked about Love's article. 'He slept somewhere else. Kurt and I had a kind of intimacy, sure, but intimacy can be acquired in all sorts of ways. It wasn't sexual on either side. That's ludicrous. The thing about Courtney, she just likes building myths.' Later he spoke to gay men's magazine *Out* about the whole episode. 'The baby and the nanny were with us the whole time,' said Stipe. 'What a night of sexual escapades that would have sounded like if that had been mentioned. If I slept with everyone I was supposed to have, I wouldn't have the energy to eat.'

Stipe sang with Annie Ross and the Low Note Quintet on 'Full Moon' for the soundtrack to Robert Altman's *Short Cuts* movie. Ross and producer Hal Willner took a 12-seater plane down to Athens for a midnight vocal session with Stipe at John Keane's studio. The next visitors were Kristin Hersh and a film crew to make a video for 'Your Ghost' for her début solo album *Hips and Makers*. Stipe had already duetted on 'Your Ghost', and the clip was directed by Katherine Dieckmann who had done 'Stand' and 'Shiny Happy People' for R.E.M. 'It's a great song and video,' said Stipe. 'Kristin's voice resonates with loss, humour, pathos and yearning. She can really wail. Her song writing is brilliant on the whole record and "Teeth" is as close a response to "Country Feedback" as I've heard. This is really good stuff.' Finally, to end a strange year, Stipe posed as a model for a 1994 calendar in aid of the Athens Area Rape Crisis Center.

Chapter Eleven

Over a Wall to Get to the Gig

1994 to 1996

'I had to jump over a wall to get to the gig, a 15-foot wall, with my friend Sue, and these two big guys had to help us down the other side. There was a highway that we dropped on to. So I performed that night with my clothes covered in white stuff from the wall.'

— MICHAEL STIPE

WITH MICHAEL STIPE STILL IN SHOCK over the death of River Phoenix, R.E.M. put off resuming work on the next album until March. While Stipe couldn't bring himself to write words, he did move forward with a film-related project as his Single Cell Films production company signed a deal with New Line Cinema. 'I'm really excited to have the opportunity to work on Hollywood-budget-sized films on one coast and underground films on the other,' he said. At the end of February the band were guests of honour in New York where they were presented with the first of the annual Rock the Vote Patrick Lippert Awards. At the ceremony a video message was shown from President Clinton, who managed to include another R.E.M. reference: 'R.E.M. prove that if you work at something long enough,' he said, 'and hard enough, you can get there from here.' Michael Stipe made an acceptance speech on behalf of the band and used a quote from *Slacker* director Richard Linklater: 'Withdrawal in disgust is not the same as apathy.' It was obviously a quote that had struck a chord with Stipe, as he was using it in the song 'What's The Frequency, Kenneth?'

By March 1994 Stipe was ready to get back to work, but it was a strange time for the band. Each member's life seemed to be moving in a different direction. Michael Stipe was becoming increasingly involved in film and politics; Peter Buck had moved to Seattle, and his girlfriend was expecting twins; Bill Berry had set up a hay farm outside Athens; and only Mike Mills seemed to want to be a rock star – and in fact he was embracing the idea more than ever before. To get everyone focused on the job in hand, and to concentrate their minds on what they were and what they were trying to do, they hired the Crossover Soundstage in Atlanta. Here they could set up their equipment as though they were playing a show and work out songs on a stage, instantly giving themselves a feel for what they would be able to do with the new tunes when they finally took them on tour.

After a slow start the band hit a purple patch and the songs really flowed. Everyone was having fun just playing as a band again – but then they were hit by the first in a long line of problems. Mike Mills was rushed to hospital with appendicitis. While he recovered from surgery the other three went back to work. Then Bill Berry caught a particularly aggressive viral flu and was bedridden. When eventually they were all fit and ready, they decided to head down to Miami and Criteria Studios for some sun.

Just as they were re-starting, Michael Stipe called for some time out so he could visit his sister Lynda who had just given birth. As Stipe returned, Peter Buck flew home to Seattle as he was about to become a father: his partner Stephanie had healthy twin girls, Zoe and Zelda.

Then some tragic news came out of Seattle. Kurt Cobain had been found dead at his home. Most of the world was in shock – but Michael Stipe was more depressed than shocked. He'd been keeping in touch with Courtney Love, and knew that Cobain had been in bad shape for a while. At one point he'd sent some plane tickets to try to entice the Nirvana singer to visit him in Georgia, but all attempts to reach out had failed. When Stipe heard that Cobain had been reported missing, a couple of days earlier, he had feared the worst. 'I had been talking to Kurt and when he disappeared, I knew it, we all knew it,' said Stipe. 'For seven days nobody knew where he was. I knew that a phone call was going to come, and I was just hoping that it was going to be a good one. Everything stopped cold. Everyone in the band knew he was missing and we knew that a call was gonna come. But it was bad, really bad. We all loved and respected and admired him a great deal. It was a deeply painful loss, not only because he was a brilliant songwriter and musician, but also personally, because I really had a great deal of respect for him and liked him a lot.'

As Stipe already knew, that respect had been mutual. Years later Cobain's biographer Charles Cross reported that the CD found in Cobain's stereo after his death had been *Automatic for the People*; it was possibly the last album Cobain ever listened to. 'He was under immense pressure,' said Stipe on Australian TV. 'He had a lot of physical problems and he was a drug addict. I kind of maintain, and this is my stupid theory, who knows, that as a performer, whether you are a Chinese acrobat or a sports figure, a basketball player, rugby player, or certainly if you are an actor, singer, musician, the amount of adrenalin coursing through your body is unbelievable. It's the most powerful drug that I have ever taken. I did a lot of experimenting when I was very young. I think that people that have that kind of adrenalin as a part of their life maybe are just looking for a balance, and that balance might be in drugs or alcohol. It's self-medicating. Sometimes it's a slippery slope.'

Stipe also spoke of the pressure that Cobain must have been under having tasted such massive success so quickly, and he felt lucky that R.E.M. had been able to build up slowly. 'If *Murmur* had sold millions I might not have survived,' he told *The Face*. 'I would have killed myself, probably with drugs. Accidentally. The kind of people who are drawn to this job have a similar chemical make-up, unbalanced. And those same people are attracted to or drawn to mind-altering substances.'

Stipe had to take more time out. He badly wanted to stay away from writing more songs about death, but now he'd been affected by two in a matter of months. He couldn't avoid it any longer, so he sat down and penned the words to 'Let Me In', a song about Kurt Cobain. It was a way of releasing some emotion and being able to move on with the recording sessions.

The band decided on yet another change of scenery, this time going to Ocean Way Studios in Los Angeles. Again, just as things were getting going, problems struck: this time Stipe had a medical problem with a tooth abscess, which halted things yet again.

As the album staggered to its conclusion, the band were bushwhacked. Arguments would spring up over mixing and track selection. The album was way, way overdue, something that had never happened before; Buck was away from two young babies; medical and emotional problems were rife among the band. Why wouldn't they be arguing? At the end Stipe was drained. He recalled, 'We reached the point where none of us could speak to each other. We were in a small room and we just said "Fuck off", and that was it. We were crazy making the record, our eyes were like kaleidoscope whirly things. All of us were nuts. At the end of the last phone call after the last mastering I fell on my knees and wept like a baby. I kissed the ground before me.'

The album, aptly named *Monster*, was released in late September and dedicated to River Phoenix. Stipe also had Kurt Cobain on his mind and was keeping in close contact with Courtney Love through difficult times. He would often call and e-mail her, which she took great solace from. 'He probably doesn't know how much he kept me alive,' she told *Rolling Stone*. 'He very telepathically called me at strategic moments.' She also asked him to take care of Frances Bean if anything were to happen to her – but he said no. He didn't want Love thinking that way, and declined in order to make sure she knew it was her responsibility to stay around and look after her daughter.

The publicity rounds for *Monster* took place in Los Angeles, and the band holed up at the Chateau Marmont hotel to receive journalists from around the world. Freed from the clutches of the album beast, Stipe was in playful mood. One photo shoot saw him drop his trousers (along with Berry and Mills) for the cover of *Select*, showing off his stripy boxer shorts. Another photo of Stipe dropping his trousers and boxers gave a rear-view picture of him trying to hitch a ride in the suburbs.

During the stay at the Chateau Marmont, Stipe went to a party held by Naomi Campbell. He left early and was spotted by a reporter hauling a huge bag of laundry up some stairs after finding that the local laundry was closed. The fact that he still did his own laundry was apparently now a newsworthy item.

From the first chords of the album-opening 'What's The Frequency, Kenneth?' R.E.M. fans knew they were in for a completely new ride. The mandolins had been well and truly banished and the amps were turned up to 11. The song's crunchy guitar and Stipe's rattlingly fast vocal gets the pulse racing. It was chosen as the first single from the album; the band wanted to re-announce themselves with the video. After his sterling work on the *Automatic* videos, Peter Care was called in for the job. Filmed in a warehouse, it features the band playing live, stylishly shot by Care. The opening moments show Michael Stipe from the shoulders down only, wearing what would become his trademark green T-shirt with a red star on the front. As strobe lights crackle and fizz about the set, the camera pulls back to reveal his newly shaven head. It's an image that still, many years later, is instantly recognisable as Stipe.

The second song on the album, 'Crush With Eyeliner', showcased

Stipe messing around with some vocal effects. He sang his lyric directly into a recording Walkman. '"Crush With Eyeliner" is completely a paean to the New York Dolls,' he said. '[The] reference to "Frankenstein", which is of course one of their songs, and a lot of this album is referring back to Iggy and the Stooges and Patti Smith and Television. I went back and listened to *Marquee Moon* while we were making this record.' The Dolls' glam influence is evident in Stipe's vocals, writing and later stage performance.

'I wanted to write a record about sex,' said Stipe. 'I thought that would be kind of fun, kind of cool. I could come at it from all these different angles. I was thinking about this the other day, because I know that with this record people are going to ask a lot of questions about sex. I've had this pat answer about my idea of sex, that sex is nothing more than friction and ego, and timing. These songs are meant to be in your face. I kind of wanted something that was brash, fucked up and sexy. Dysfunctional. Kind of a gender-fuck train wreck just thrown out there.' Stipe later commented that some of the *Monster* lyrics were 'gross and disgusting' but that he enjoyed playing that particular role. Several reviewers forgot Stipe's golden rule about not confusing the singer and the song. Few, if any, songs on the album were really about Stipe, despite what you might have read.

Much of the album revolved around the crunchy guitars, reverb and throbbing bass lines. Michael Stipe also managed to showcase several vocal styles across the album. 'King Of Comedy' was sung in an affected accent, 'Star 69' was a breathless rant, 'Strange Currencies' was a throwback to the fragile emotions of 'Everybody Hurts', while 'Tongue' displayed his best falsetto. *Vox* magazine commented that 'This monster comes out with fists flying, snarling like a Rottweiler, set to knock you into oblivion.'

Like R.E.M.'s other Warner albums, *Monster* was also released as a special-edition CD. This time it came in a hard-backed book which earned a Grammy nomination for Stipe, Chris Bilheimer and Tom Recchion who had worked on it.

R.E.M. had put themselves out on a limb with 11 months booked up for touring during 1995. Michael Stipe was looking forward it immensely. 'You're gonna be sick of me in about ten months' time. I'm gonna be everywhere,' he grinned. The band were still a little surprised that they had reached such large sales figure over the last four years and really expected their bubble to burst before too long, so they were going to do their best and make the most of it while they could because they probably wouldn't be this massive ever again.

Monster had been recorded with touring in mind, so it wasn't surprising that every song was played live – and Stipe played up the sexuality of the material while on stage. He'd dedicate 'Tongue' to all the ladies in the audience, swagger across the stage and give off an aura of having a real attitude. This was far removed from the Stipe who patrolled the stage during *Green*. Now he was more likely to stand on the monitors, hitch up the back of his shirt or jacket and bend forward to give the crowd a good view of him shimmying and shaking his butt.

Now in his mid-30s, he was happier than usual to talk about his private life and would talk about being sexually interested in both men and women. 'I'm an equal-opportunity lech and I'm pretty comfortable with it,' he said. 'I've dealt with it for over 20 years.' He had his long-term boyfriend with him for parts of the tour, and Stipe would be the band member most likely to be seen out partying into the night, wherever they were in the world. He was especially keen to enjoy the nightlife in Australia. Grant Lee Phillips of support band Grant Lee Buffalo was swept along for some nights out with Stipe and his entourage. Phillips recalled to Q magazine that he'd never drunk so many 'blue drinks' in his life. 'We were in a bar and Grant Lee and I started dancing on this table,' said Stipe. 'This bouncer came over and said, "You can't do that," so we got down. Then as soon as he went away we got back up and he came back and throttled me, literally lifted me off the table!' Another social event on the eve of the tour was Peter Buck's wedding. He and girlfriend Stephanie were married in Perth.

Unlike the *Green* tour, which had some strong political and environmental messages, the *Monster* tour was more about raw fun and entertainment. Again there were films and slides projected onto large screens, but this was mostly abstract footage, and Stipe had cut down on his between-song pronouncements and introductions to songs. He could be quite animated on stage, and instead of just standing in the middle he moved out to the extreme edges to make sure everyone the large arenas got a good view, but anyone looking for profound statements was disappointed. Often he wouldn't speak at all for the first few songs, and then it would probably be 'Hello, here's another song' or 'Hi, here we are and here you are, and here's another song'. He was using a music stand as a prop, but also for real: he needed the words to lots of the older songs.

The new songs from *Monster* were mixed with 'new' songs from *Out of Time* and *Automatic for the People*, neither of which had been played live on such a scale. So the band had 30-odd new songs to add to the IRS back catalogue. During the early part of the tour Stipe would play guitar for one song, even if it was just a single chord for 'I Don't Sleep, I Dream'. He was wearing more outlandish outfits too. Instead of the *Green* tour's sombre suits it was all fake fur, woolly hats and big goggles.

After dates in Japan, Australia, New Zealand and Taiwan, the tour hit Europe in the late winter. The weather was miserable and wet, and after the initial adrenalin rush of the early dates everyone was now settling in for the year-long slog. Many of the crew members had heavy colds as the tour reached Lausanne, Switzerland, on 1 March.

Part-way through the show Bill Berry was taken ill, with what was at first thought to be just a severe headache, and Joey Peters from Grant Lee Buffalo stepped in to play drums for the rest of a shortened set. Berry was taken to hospital, where some of best brain surgeons in the world ascertained that he had an aneurysm and needed emergency surgery. The operation was a success, but Berry would need a while to recover. The band never entertained a thought of replacing him, so they had no choice but to cancel all forthcoming shows – a total of 31 in Europe and a further eight in the USA.

★ ★ ★

Michael Stipe had not eaten meat since 1980, and had added fish to the list of no-nos in 1988, but during the 1995 tour he began eating fish occasionally. He claimed that his body knew when he needed some protein and he followed his instincts; if he felt like having a tuna steak, he'd have one. Given the physical rigours touring demanded of his body, allowing himself to eat fish was probably a good idea for his overall health. Stipe did a little travelling in Europe until Berry was well enough to go home; then it was a case of sitting and waiting to see how long it would be before he could play a show again. Amazingly Stipe had to wait only 75 days between Berry's being taken ill and his return to R.E.M. for a show in San Francisco.

When the tour got back to Europe, Mike Mills fell ill and was rushed to hospital in Germany for a laparotomy to release an adhesion on his small intestine. When he was back on stage just a few days later, everyone was hoping that was the end of the medical dramas for one tour.

For the outdoor summer shows R.E.M. had often hand-picked their choice of support bands. One of these was Radiohead, and their lead singer Thom Yorke was a big fan of Michael Stipe. 'At the first gig, Mr Stipe came in to say hello before the show,' recalled Yorke. 'He said, "Hi, I'm Michael. I'm really glad you could do this. I'm a very big fan." When someone you really admire gives you something like that, your shoulders get a little lighter. You feel a little stronger.'

The final date of the European portion of the tour was in Prague.

This show had already been cancelled twice – once when Bill Berry was ill and again when Mike Mills was ill. On the afternoon of the show, Michael Stipe went exploring through the city's historic old town, and came across some people handing out flyers for that night's R.E.M. show. To the bemusement of the locals, Stipe took a handful of flyers and began handing them out to passers-by himself. Most people had no idea who he was in his Sonic the Hedgehog T-shirt, sunglasses and beret. On returning to his hotel, Stipe complained of stomach problems; later that afternoon it was found he had a hernia and would need surgery right away. But Stipe was adamant that he wasn't cancelling the show for a third time, so he was given heavy strapping around his stomach and the band changed the set list so he wouldn't have to strain for any high notes. The show was a success and Stipe flew back to Georgia for surgery at Emory Hospital in Atlanta the next day.

By the autumnal home stretch the band had quite a few new songs in the set: 'Undertow', 'The Wake-Up Bomb', 'Binky The Doormat' and a song called 'Departure', which Stipe had written back in February on a flight to Spain, about a dream he'd had featuring River Phoenix. He awoke in the early hours to see most other passengers fast asleep. 'Just these lumps of polyester blankets. It was sweet, like a nursery or something,' said Stipe. He looked out of the cabin window and saw that the plane was passing over a thunderstorm below. 'There was this bright orange storm over the sea,' he continued. 'One of the most beautiful things I've ever seen in my life, and it was all mine.'

The tour wasn't all about fun and sex. There were deeply poignant moments too. 'Everybody Hurts' and 'Strange Currencies' always had a strong impact, as did 'Let Me In'. When they started the encores with this song it was usually just Stipe and Mills who would return to the stage, with Buck and Berry joining in as it progressed. An extra level of meaning came from the fact that Mills was playing the song using one of Cobain's own guitars, which Courtney Love had given to the band.

Stipe continued to play with his image as the tour wound down in North America. He wore upside-down hockey shirts, and pumpkin masks, and on one occasion painted his head blue. As on the *Green* tour, the final dates of the *Monster* trek were filmed, this time by Peter Care for the live *Roadmovie*. The tour ended in Atlanta as was usual, and a collective sigh of relief was breathed by all. 'We weren't unlucky,' said Michael Stipe. 'We were extremely lucky to all be here to tell the tale.'

The *Monster* tour would have lasting ramifications for the band, of which they were as yet unaware. Everyone expected R.E.M. to disappear for a year, but within a couple of months they were well into their next album. On 19 February 1996 Stipe sang two of the new songs, 'Low Desert' and 'Undertow', at a charity benefit for the Tibet House organisation in New York on 19 February 1996. In late April he also sang at the VH1 Honours Benefit with Natalie Merchant and Peter Gabriel. In between these fundraisers he attended the Sundance Film Festival, this time as an actor as well as a producer.

Stipe played the part of Skeeter in Christopher Munch's *Color of a Brisk and Leaping Day*, the story of one man's battle to save the Yosemite railroad just after the Second World War. Munch had earlier gained critical praise for *The Hours and Times*, a fictional portrayal of a weekend spent with John Lennon and Brian Epstein. *Color of a Brisk and Leaping Day* won the Best Cinematography award at Sundance for its excellent monochrome vistas, but Stipe's performance was described as 'stiff and strange'. In the future he would keep to producing films rather than appearing in them. After Single Cell Pictures' deal with New Line Cinema ran out, they signed another distribution arrangement with October Films, who saw the potential of forthcoming Single Cell projects such as *Being John Malkovich* and *Velvet Goldmine*.

★　★　★

Ambitious as ever, R.E.M. had considered recording a new album's worth of material live on the road during the *Monster* tour and releasing it in early 1996. But after the problems encountered during the year they didn't have enough material to carry this off. Instead they set to work on some new songs they'd messed around with alongside the half-dozen or so new songs that had been recorded on the road.

This next album would be the final one under the five-album deal they'd signed with Warner back in 1988. The deal had obviously been great for both sides and R.E.M. were now touted as being the biggest, and best, band in the world. It would be the perfect time for them to negotiate a new deal, either with Warner or elsewhere. Stipe really wanted to try to capture the essence of being on tour, the movement, the distance and even the religion. Over 100 hours of 1995 recordings were archived and the best takes were picked out for possible use. The band also dusted off some *Monster* outtakes and a couple of new songs written early in the new year. In just three months they had the new album completed.

'I really wanted this record to have heart,' said Stipe. 'I just wanted to document what happened to us over the last year or so. It turned out great. I can't believe I was doing it 12 months ago. It seems like four years ago.'

New Adventures in Hi-Fi covered a lot of ground and seemed to be following Stipe's arty idea of throwing everything together to see what comes out. For the first time Stipe was making lots of religious references in his songs. This might be apparent from the first song, 'How The West Was Won And Where It Got Us'; it's definitely the case in 'New Test Leper' (short for New Testament Leper) where Stipe quotes from the gospel of Matthew. The same gospel tells the story of Jesus curing a leper. In 'Undertow', which had been recorded on the *Monster* tour, Stipe sings that he doesn't need religion or heaven; then in 'Be Mine' religion is everywhere. Stipe sings of the modern-day commercialism of Christmas and

Easter, of having visions, and of washing someone with his hair, as Mary Magdalene did to Jesus's feet.

Other songs concern more typically Stipean subject matter – travel, distance, writing home and loss. These are covered on the likes of 'Departure', 'Leave' and 'E-Bow, The Letter' which finally saw him share vocal duties with Patti Smith on an R.E.M. song. As usual Stipe was at the centre of designing the artwork. He'd been taking lots of photos on the road while recording the songs, and he wanted the artwork to match the travelogue nature of the music; several of the pictures were shot from the tour bus as it drove along. Q magazine was ecstatic about the hotchpotch nature of the album: '[The album] hits its many different targets virtu-ally every time,' it declared, while awarding 5/5.

In between their finishing the album in May and its release in September, the band went through a harrowing time. In May manager Jefferson Holt ceased to be part of the R.E.M. camp, his duties being taken on by Bertis Downs. For the tight-knit R.E.M. 'family' to lose a member was more than a little surprising to outside observers. He'd been with the band for 15 years, appeared in videos and was generally considered to be a nice guy. So what had happened? The R.E.M. office put out a short statement saying it was an amicable split by mutual consent. More of a clue to something being not quite right came in the lines 'The reasons for this decision and terms of the termination are private and confidential, and no further discussion of these matters will be made by any of these parties.' Suddenly the split didn't seem very amicable after all.

Even more puzzling was the timing: the band were deep into negotiations with Warner for a massive new five-album deal. Michael Stipe has never openly commented on Holt's departure, but Peter Buck has: 'There are plenty of rumours going around and they're all pretty interesting,' he told Q magazine. 'But y'know, I may not be a gentleman or whatever, but I know how a gentleman would act, and I'm not going to say anything about it. It wasn't amicable on either of our parts, but y'know, big deal. Jefferson has said the only thing that's been quoted in public and he said that sometimes people change and go on to different things, and that's true and maybe that's what it's all about. Maybe not. Who knows. I know, but I'm not gonna tell you.'

Over the summer sketchy details of the new contract with Warner leaked out. The figure most quoted was a whopping $80 million. Large signing bonuses were paid directly to the band, their royalty percentage was hiked up and better deals for their back catalogue were included. R.E.M. were now financially set for life. Or even for several lives. Michael Stipe sidestepped all the controversy of the summer – over the departure of Holt, the new contract, the new album and even the new concert film, *Roadmovie*.

Peter Care did a decent job of capturing the band and used some of the techniques employed on *Tourfilm*, namely filming with different stock that gave images ranging from slightly grainy to crystal clear. The major difference, apart from the songs, was that it was all in colour and the band had the crowd surrounding them 360 degrees. This meant the films and projections lost some of their impact. *Roadmovie* was always going to be compared with *Tourfilm*, and it comes off a poor second best. The film was premièred in August 1996 at the Edinburgh Film Festival, where Michael Stipe was due to appear – but as fans arrived they were informed he'd had to cancel owing to 'rescheduling of commitments'.

R.E.M. for the first time ever had nothing at all planned for the foreseeable future. A rollercoaster three years had seen the loss of friends, the loss of a manager, two albums released, a massive world tour completed and a new movie issued. Some fans bitched that they weren't the same band any more, but how could they be? Everyone changes through life, and now being closer to 40 than 30 they had changed both as people and as a band. The financial security of the new Warner deal meant that what the band members wanted and needed was now very different from before and they were a multinational corporation in their own right, quite removed from their Athens roots. Friends had changed; circles they moved in had changed.

Stipe still had his basic political beliefs intact, though – as well as his mischievous sense of humour. As Bill Clinton campaigned to gain a second term in office as President, Stipe spoke at a Clinton rally in Atlanta. He also told of an earlier incident in Seattle. 'We landed at this private airport and there's just two planes on the tarmac,' he laughed. 'The other one's this huge plane. And suddenly there's all these cars driving around it and they've got flashing lights on and are circling the whole plane. And we're like, "What the fuck's going on?" Then the plane turns really slowly and it says down the side "Dole for President 1996". They were all Secret Service people driving in a circle around the plane. So I ran out on the tarmac and pulled my pants down . . . I had to . . . and mooned it.'

Chapter Twelve

The Further Away I Feel

1997 to 1998

'The Pacific coast. The closer I get, the further away I feel.'

— MICHAEL STIPE

THE FIRST AGE OF R.E.M. was the constant touring of 1980 to 1989, while the non-touring/breakthrough years of 1990 to 1996 constituted the second age. The supposed year off, 1997, would herald the start of R.E.M.'s third age, that of being a three-piece.

Michael Stipe started the year well away from R.E.M. as he worked on Single Cell's latest film project, *Velvet Goldmine,* in London. As executive producer he helped raise the finance required to get the screenplay through to the big screen. He also worked the city to rustle up musicians for the movie's soundtrack. As well as the bands he was expected to draft in (Radiohead, Grant Lee Buffalo, Brian Molko) he enlisted the participation of Jarvis Cocker, Sonic Youth, Bernard Butler and Mudhoney.

The movie tells the story of sexual and music exploration as glam rock took hold of the UK. The film captures the colour, the clothes, the make-up and, of course, the music from the era. The cast list was impressive: Ewan McGregor, in his follow-up to *Trainspotting,* as Curt Wild; Jonathan Rhys Meyers as Brian Slade, who fakes his own death to escape stardom and all its trappings; Christian Bale as Arthur Stuart, the journalist charged with tracking down Slade; Toni Collette as Mandy Slade; and long-time pal of Stipe's, Eddie Izzard as Jerry Devine.

After the exertions of the *Monster* tour, Peter Buck had bought himself a house in Hawaii to relax in. But being the workaholic that he is he also set up some recording equipment there, just in case he felt the need. The other three members of R.E.M. visited Buck to talk tentatively through a few new ideas and to mess around in his new studio. Everyone agreed that they wanted to try some radical new recording methods – at least radical for R.E.M. Buck had collected some old analogue drum machines and synthesisers, and the primary new writing was being based around these electronic instruments. Bill Berry didn't really throw himself into this, even though it was really just a bit of fun. He did help out programming some of the drum patterns, but he'd spend more and more time on his own, wandering along the beach or driving around. No one said anything; they knew he was in the midst of a divorce from his wife Mari after 11 years of marriage. Little did they know that he had more life-changing things playing on his mind as well.

With a few ideas sketched out, the quartet split up to go their separate ways. Mike Mills relaxed by playing golf and working on a film score for *A Cool, Dry Place*, Bill Berry went back to work on his farm and Peter Buck linked up with numerous collaborators on the Magnificent Seven vs. The United States tour. The last show of this tour took place on 31 May at the Variety Playhouse in Atlanta. Since Atlanta was just down the road from Athens, Mills, Stipe and Berry came to see the performance, and inevitably the idea of their all joining in at some point was raised. Mills and Stipe were up for the idea, but Berry made his excuses and left before the end of the show, driving home alone. He missed Stipe sing 'New Test Leper', Suicide's 'Ghost Rider', Chris Isaak's 'Wicked Game' and Iggy Pop's 'The Passenger'.

Stipe had spent the spring travelling, taking photos and helping out with a couple of charity causes, including one aimed at raising awareness about the plight of Tibet. In February he'd joined Patti Smith to sing 'E-Bow, The Letter' in New York on a night that included contributions from Billy Corgan, Allen Ginsberg and Ben Harper. He was also invited to sing at a large outdoor festival on Randall's Island, New York, in June. He wanted to try to get R.E.M. to perform a short set on the bill, which included Noel Gallagher, Björk, Radiohead and Foo Fighters and was organised by the Beastie Boys' Milarepa Fund.

The first Tibetan Freedom Concert had been played in San Francisco in 1996 with Beck, De La Soul and others giving their time. Now, in New York, the show was bigger and more publicised. The next year would see it expand even further and play in Washington, DC, on the President's doorstep. For now, though, Michael Stipe wanted to play this show but was having difficulty with the logistics of getting the band together. Peter Buck was working with Tuatara and Mark Eitzel before flying to Europe, and Bill Berry still didn't want to play. So Mike Mills and Michael Stipe decided they would play alone. There was some discussion as to whether they could be advertised as R.E.M., but in the end that was vetoed and they were listed as Stipe & Mills.

The R.E.M. duo played their short set on the second day of the festival, 8 June 1997. They started with a stripped down, acoustic arrangement of 'Undertow' – a massive departure from the overblown guitars of the album version – following it with the usual acoustic take of 'New Test Leper' before the drum machine was revved up for 'Electrolite'. Mike Mills sat at a piano to play a beautiful version of this song, with Stipe's vocals softened to blend perfectly with the accompaniment. 'Be Mine' was suitably stark, as had been the B-side version of the song in 1996, before the last three songs called in some help. Pearl Jam's Eddie Vedder and Mike McCready joined in on 'The Long Road', with the latter hanging around to add extra guitar on 'Ghost Rider', before they closed out with the Beastie Boys' Mike D drumming on 'The Passenger' to end an unusual but satisfying set.

With nothing planned for the rest of the summer, Stipe kicked back and relaxed, knowing he had until early October, when the band had arranged to meet in Athens for some demo sessions. Then he would listen to the music evolving from the electronic experiments and start to work on some lyrical ideas to match it. He was spotted by paparazzi with Courtney Love at various film premières, but generally he kept a low profile.

The night before the band was due to reconvene at the West Clayton Street practice space, Bill Berry called Bertis Downs and said he'd made a big decision. He was intending to call the others in the band to tell them, but Downs said it ought to be done in person. So the next day Berry came in with his shattering news: he was leaving R.E.M.

Like the rest of the band, Michael Stipe was stunned; he felt as if the carpet had been pulled from under his feet. He immediately set about trying to change the drummer's mind, but Berry hadn't just decided this on a whim; he'd been giving serious thought to leaving for a long time. Some thought the aneurysm was behind his decision, which it wasn't – at least not directly. What it had done was give him time to think about his life and reassess what he wanted to do. He'd decided that after playing drums since being a teenager, he wanted the rest of his life to take a different course. Despite Stipe's protestations, Berry was adamant. What Stipe did get Berry to agree to was a cooling-off period. The imminent sessions were cancelled and Berry went home to think about things for a few weeks, as did the rest of the band.

During this period Stipe took it upon himself to drive out to Berry's farm and have a heart-to-heart with the drummer. What they discussed was so private that Stipe said he'd never tell anyone what went on, not even Mike Mills and Peter Buck. What Stipe did later disclose, though, was that after this talk he was sure that Berry knew what he really wanted and that he was making the correct decision for himself. With this in mind, Stipe knew he had to let it go. Berry did offer to stay on if it meant keeping the band together. As he put it himself, he didn't want to be the one who broke up R.E.M.

On 30 October the band called a press conference at their Athens office and announced Berry's decision to the world. Photos were taken showing Berry smiling apologetically, Mills looking stunned, Buck frowning behind pair of sunglasses and a sad-looking Stipe who could have been on the edge of tears. Stipe had been the most vocal in the past about the band's ending if ever any one of them wanted to leave. Now he was having to back-track and explain that the rest of the band would be continuing as R.E.M. after all. 'I guess a three-legged dog is still a dog,' he said. 'It just has to learn how to run differently.' Just how different it was going to be for this dog wasn't apparent to anyone just yet.

Once the round of interviews and online chats was over, Berry was given his wish and allowed to slip into anonymity on his farm. The others were left with a big hole in the band and no idea how to fix it. They decided to go away and leave it until after Christmas; they all had a lot of thinking to do. Of the remaining trio Peter Buck seemed most upset and angry about it, but Michael Stipe realised it was only fair to let Berry go. He was sent into an emotional spin, though. 'It was like a knife through the heart for me for a long time,' said Stipe. 'It had a profound impact on an already difficult task.' What he meant by this was that Berry's exit stopped him dead as far as lyric-writing went and it would be a long time before he could get back on track.

★ ★ ★

Before Bill Berry walked away, each of the four members of R.E.M. had written a list of the cities in which he'd like the band to record the next album. Only one city had been on all four lists and that was San Francisco. Though Berry had gone, they saw no reason to change their plan, and settled in at Toast Studios – which studio manager Chris Lyon describes as having the ambience of 'a chic California living room'. Located on the legendary Mission Street (epicentre of many Beat writers' adventures), the studio seemed to have the laid-back atmosphere that R.E.M. needed to ease into a new way of working as a trio.

With Jefferson Holt out of the picture and Bill Berry gone, if as they say troubles come in threes that left one more to come: for the first time in 12 years the band wouldn't be working with Scott Litt as producer. Litt was busy trying to establish his own record label and wanted to move away from being a producer, so R.E.M. turned to Pat McCarthy as a co-producer. McCarthy had assisted Litt by engineering both *Monster* and *New Adventures in Hi-Fi* so he knew the band and their methods fairly well, but of course this would be a new beginning for them all. Through parts of February, March and April the band set themselves a strict itinerary of working consecutive six-day weeks.

This hard schedule served only to heighten tensions that were building within the band. Ever since Berry's announcement, Michael Stipe had been unable to write and was sometimes verging on the edge of panic about what they were going to do and how they were going to do it. When the San Francisco sessions started he was still reeling and had little lyrical input to offer. He'd always felt some pressure: he added the words to the songs last of all, so until he was happy with his contribution an album could never be finished. As time ticked away in San Francisco, he was still struggling to write, while Buck and Mills grew more frustrated. The tension growing, the trio became less willing to discuss things, which only enhanced the resentment and made working even more difficult. When they decided to break off recording until summer, all three went away feeling dissatisfied and worried about the future. 'I completely shut down during the making of that record,' Stipe told Q magazine. 'I had the mother of all writer's block, just because the band was falling apart. At one point, I had to get used to the idea that we had completely split up. I was working on what I thought would be our last will and testament. When you see relationships that are that important to you fold and collapse, and you can't find a solution to it. I'm really not overstating anything here. It was awful.'

'Michael was having writer's block,' added Peter Buck. 'We'd booked all this time, and then we had all this stuff to do. I was away from my family for three months, sitting around, and not one single bit of work would be done. It'd be, "I'm going home, this is ridiculous." "Well, we have interviews on Tuesday." "Fuck! Why are we doing interviews?" "Well, because we're playing the Tibetan benefit festival thing." I spent the hottest two months of the year sitting around. If you've got a family, it's tough.'

Stipe refocused his attention and got away from the problems by flying to New York to promote a book of his photographs, *Two Times Intro: On the Road with Patti Smith*. Stipe had tagged along with Patti Smith as she supported Bob Dylan on ten dates during December 1995, right after Stipe stepped off the gruelling *Monster* tour. Between Danbury, Connecticut, on 7 December and Philadelphia on 17 December Stipe blended in with the tour crew and snapped away with various cameras, using up 18 rolls of film.

In 1998 he spent late April and May promoting the book and a couple of upcoming gallery shows that showcased the photos from it. 'I never felt like my role was documenter; it was more like I was there as a friend and I was taking pictures,' said Stipe. 'I do that anyway, I mean I have about the same photographs of just about anyone and everyone I hang out with. But she's a pretty compelling subject.' It wasn't with the intention of publishing a book that Stipe travelled with Smith. As he says it was just something that he liked to do. 'When we got the contact sheets back, they were really beautiful, and at some point I mentioned that I wanted to do a book of photographs,' says Stipe. 'I just wanted it to be a documentary kind of book of that ten- or twelve-day tour. The air was just bristling with excitement the whole time, it was so exciting every night. And it was great for me to be in the audience and be such a fan. Nobody knew I was there, nobody expected to see me there, so I just pulled my cap down and went out and stood in the 12th or 13th row and rocked and cried and beat my chest and all the stuff that you do when you love music.'

Stipe's black and white images cover airport lounges, hotel rooms, candid backstage shots and sound checks. They don't just focus on Patti Smith either. The whole band is captured, along with tour personnel, friends who called in (such as Allen Ginsberg) and the odd self-portrait. The images do show a photographer with a keen eye, and Stipe manages to capture the emotions of the tour very well. His own mini-promo tour included a TV spot on the prestigious *Charlie Rose Show*. The photos from the book were exhibited at the Robert Miller Gallery in New York during May and at the Photographic Resource Center in Boston that September and October.

'I still feel like a geek, and even though a lot of those people are known to the world as pretty glamorous people, when it comes down to it, we're all geeks, each in our own way,' said Stipe. 'I've tried to demystify that celebrity thing a little bit. Maybe it's more like a work ethic; there's this group of people that just travel a great deal all the time and tend to bump into each other a lot. I'm a sap at heart, and it was really something to see her and Bob Dylan singing together, to recognise the influence he had on her, and then the influence she had on me. I'm just one of a whole lot of people who really owe a great deal to her for her body of work, but I have the added benefit of being a real good friend, and I'm very honoured by that.'

'Frankly, I was afraid of how I was going to officially enter the world of photography,' Stipe told *Smug* magazine. 'Photography is such a great passion of mine that I was worried that if I came out with a bunch of photographs, especially a book of photographs of famous people, that would be kind of dismissive. I wanted to be careful about how I presented myself and the photographs to the world because I don't want to be easily dismissed.'

Stipe had previously said that he sees things before he hears them in the studio, and he tried to explain to at least one producer how a song should look. Billy Bragg told *Mojo*, 'Americans as a song-writing nation write in a very cinematic way. Their culture is very visual. [Michael Stipe] notices the things you tend to over-look.' Stipe had referenced photography in R.E.M.'s music as far back as 1984, when he'd written 'Pretty Persuasion' about a dream he had about photographing the Rolling Stones for an album cover. Later songs including references to photography were 'Nightswimming', 'Photograph' (of course!), 'The Flowers Of Guatemala' and 'Cuyahoga'.

Next up for Michael Stipe was another non-music project. This time it was a poetry project: a book of haikus, to which Stipe contributed. The book, *The Haiku Year*, actually contained the so-called 'Western haikus' as conceptualised by Jack Kerouac in the 1950s. These little poems had strict rules in that they had to be three lines long and the lines had to contain five, seven and five syllables respectively. During 1996 a group of seven friends took up a challenge to write one haiku each every day. The result of what started out as a bit of fun between friends was later published as this book. Around 30 of Michael Stipe's compositions were included. Joining Stipe among the group were Tom Gilroy, Jim McKay, Grant Lee Phillips and Douglas A. Martin.

Martin later gained a measure of notoriety when he published a book of his own, *Outline of My Lover*, in 2000. This book was marketed as a novel, but few reviewers or readers wholly fell for that. The publisher's blurb from Soft Skull Press reads: 'In the sleepy college town of Athens, Georgia, a young man goes off to a college miseducation and is drawn into a world of rich vicari-ous living. The unspoken relationship between this adolescent and his luminous rock star boyfriend fast becomes the definitive tale of world tours and plush continental hotel rooms. However, as the relationship falters under celebrity's harsh, shape-shifting light, real life fills in the outline of the boy's expectations.'

The 'lover' at the centre of the book is not named, but some have looked in Stipe's direction: the lover is the lead singer of a band in Athens, Georgia. Martin writes that before he meets the 'lover' he buys the special edition of one of his albums in a wooden box (which was the *Automatic for the People* special edition); he watches him walk through the desert in a video ('Man On The Moon'); after they become lovers he writes about visitors to his lover (a man with a baby girl fits in with Kurt Cobain's visit in 1993; Martin mentions that the man dies soon after); next the lover is away working on an album when he sees on the news that one of his celebrity friends has died (River Phoenix); the lover says, 'Don't confuse the singer with the song' (one of Stipe's favourite sayings); the lover takes Martin to Los Angeles to see the spot where the friend died outside a nightclub (Phoenix again); in Switzerland the lover is drinking heavily because another friend is sick while on tour (Bill Berry's aneurysm); during a family meal Martin's grandmother mistakenly refers to the lover as 'Mike' and they all laugh; the list of 'coincidences' goes on and on.

What is supposed to be a novel can be read as a stylishly-written homoerotic kiss-and-tell, naming names without really naming them. The book is also at times quite explicit. Martin gained a minor amount of publicity when the book first came out. 'The fact that he's a rock star has always been more a metaphor for me,' said Martin. 'When I read Duras' *The Lover*, I have to ask myself where the parallel is in my life. I grew up with the radio telling me that [following musicians] was the way to express my passions. Living in Athens, Georgia, writing around Michael – he has also been less of an inspiration and more of a reality. The book takes off as fiction for me, because it was written from a place of mourning. The narrator of the book is no longer me, those are no longer the circumstances of my life, and I wanted to explore what led to creating those circumstances.' The Canadian *Eye Weekly* speculated, '*Outline of My Lover* by Douglas A. Martin is a thinly disguised account of the young blond wastrel's four-year relationship with the famous singer. (Stipe's name is never mentioned, but the details are unmistakable, a fact reviewers were more than eager to reveal.)'

★ ★ ★

In May, Michael Stipe was back in Athens working on his lyrics and seeing some progress on album tracks with Buck and Mills. But just when things seemed to be getting back on track they ground to a halt again. R.E.M. had agreed to play at the 1998 Tibetan Freedom Concert way back before Bill Berry had left the band, and although no one wanted to pull out at the last minute the timing couldn't have been worse, as they had to halt work on the album to rehearse for the upcoming show. The show's importance as a political statement was now matched by its being R.E.M.'s first public show since Berry's departure and the chance to show off some new songs and the band's new electronic direction.

A week of practice drew in Joey Waronker (previously of Beck's backing band), an experienced and inventive drummer/percussionist who fitted perfectly with the style of the new songs, old collaborator Scott McCaughey, who came in to add some depth to the songs on keyboard and guitar, and multi-instrumentalist Barrett Martin to complete the line-up.

At the giant RFK stadium in Washington, DC, R.E.M. were due to play on the afternoon of Saturday 13 June, but part-way through the show a thunderstorm hit the area. Lightning hit the centre of the standing area and 11 people were injured. With further strikes a distinct possibility the organisers had no choice but to abandon the rest of the show on safety grounds. Michael Stipe stepped forward and offered to go and make the announcement to the obviously disappointed crowd. Some shrewd calculations enabled most of the cancelled bands to be fitted in among shortened sets of the Sunday line-up. So a day late the 'new' R.E.M. took to the stage for the first time.

Michael Stipe took most people's attention as he walked out. He was wearing a skin-tight long-sleeved patterned top, which exposed his midriff, and a long see-through sarong that along with his bald head made him look as if he could be a Tibetan monk. As he took the stage, the opening chords of 'Airportman' drifted across the heads of the crowd; they could almost have been some weird Tibetan chants of their own. Stipe would later say that the eight-song performance was 'rattling' and admit that his vocal performance wasn't the greatest it could have been. New songs 'Suspicion', 'Parakeet' and 'Sad Professor' were also débuted – quite a brave thing to attempt with a new line-up and a crowd that weren't necessarily all R.E.M. fans. Radiohead's Thom Yorke joined Stipe to sing 'Be Mine' and 'E-Bow, The Letter' (Stipe also joined Radiohead's set to sing 'Lucky') and R.E.M. came off stage with the confidence that they could go on without Bill Berry.

After a night of celebrating the show's success it was back to business on Monday morning, as Michael Stipe had a meeting scheduled with the Beastie Boys' Adam Yauch, Dave Matthews and President Clinton over the situation in Tibet. R.E.M. were also going to play as a trio on the Capitol lawn as part of a Tibet rally. After complaining that he wasn't usually out of bed at such an early hour, Stipe joined the more conventional R.E.M. line-up of Mills and Buck to run quickly through acoustic versions of 'Fall On Me' and 'Losing My Religion'. Stipe then told the crowd that the meeting with Clinton had been cancelled by the White House.

Now the trio were faced with having to try to finish the album, and keep to a schedule of releasing it in October, while they weren't exactly getting along together. Seeing what was going on, Bertis Downs stepped in as peacemaker and suggested they all get together and talk things through. To cut down on any outside distractions they agreed to go somewhere remote; that place was Idaho. The talks were difficult, but after communal headaches they emerged stronger friends and a stronger band. 'Did we row?' said Peter Buck. 'No. We're not really shouty types. I just tend to get pissed off, then Michael gets upset, and Mike's like, "Well I don't know." We'd just go in circles. We realised that Michael doesn't want all the pressure of us sitting on the couch looking at him, glaring, going, "OK, sing something."'

With problems out in the open it was much easier to get along with finalising the album. This was done in Athens and New York, where Nigel Godrich mixed a handful of songs for the band. The album was named *Up* after Mike Mills saw the instruction 'This way up' on a cardboard box. Finally it was over, and the band was still together, if only just.

★   ★   ★

October saw more charity shows before promotional work for the new album kicked in. There would be no tour, but a handful of shows recorded at TV and radio stations with fan-club members being invited along. On 2 October Stipe joined Patti Smith and Philip Glass in Michigan for an Allen Ginsberg tribute show. Stipe sang 'People Have The Power' with Smith and was accompanied on a delicate new song called 'At My Most Beautiful' by Philip Glass on piano. Stipe also played guitar on stage for the first time as he strummed through 'New Test Leper' and another new tune called 'I'm Not Over You'.

During the third week of October the promotional work really took off. R.E.M. recorded two songs for use on the David Letterman show in New York, 15 years after making their network television début on the same show. Michael Stipe's elevation to pop superstar was evidenced as he sang 'Lotus' with what can only be described as a carpet-underlay rug being worn as a pointy hat, which he stripped off during the song along with his overcoat. He played the front-man routine with panache and confidence, a million miles away from the interview-shy 23-year-old who had been on Letterman's show previously.

'[Letterman] booked us in 1983 with a song that didn't even

have a title yet, which turned into "South Central Rain",' said Stipe. 'I guess, for the time, that was pretty ballsy. You begin to realise how powerful a medium television is, in terms of reaching a large and very diverse audience in a talk-show format. Maybe Letterman, Conan and Leno have a good idea of who they're appealing to, but, if you're just surfing the channels and you see that someone is gonna be on their show, you might plug into it, and step outside that demographic. So, it's kinda interesting in a tentacle way of how it can stretch out to a very diverse audience of people.'

On the eve of the album's release in Europe the band were in London. A busy Sunday saw them at the BBC to record a four-song John Peel radio session, take part in a long interview with Mark Radcliffe for Radio 1 and then play a live radio concert that night in front of a few hundred invited fans.

When *Up* was released almost everyone focused in on the fact that Bill Berry wasn't around any more, and his absence did have a profound effect on the songs. But what was overlooked was the fact that again R.E.M. had changed direction significantly since the last album. The loud pop songs of *Green* had been followed by the acoustic sounds of *Out of Time*. True, that feel had then been slightly repeated for *Automatic for the People*, but then had come the overblown guitars of *Monster* before a switch back to the wide-ranging styles of *New Adventures in Hi-Fi*. The band had been experimenting with more electronic instruments before Berry left, and *Up* is likely the kind of album they would have produced anyway.

The thing that Berry did take with him from the band was his self-patrolled quality control. He'd always focused the band on making things more accessible, and his love of pop music had helped forge some of the band's best work. Now without him there's no doubt that some of the songs drifted along aimlessly, more than they should have. It took Michael Stipe five years finally to tell *Uncut* magazine that *Up* was too long and a couple of songs should have been axed.

Many of the songs were slow- to mid-tempo Kraut rock homages with a couple of piano-led tracks tossed in for good measure. Warner chose 'Daysleeper' to promote the album, a song that gave a wholly unrepresentative take on what else was included. It was straight from the catalogue of typical R.E.M. songs that they could write in their sleep – though Stipe did try to cover new ground with his lyric. Backed with a video of stop-motion colour images Stipe was filmed in a smart business suit and large black-rimmed glasses. Concerning someone who has to work at night, the song touches on commerce, global business and commodity markets. It was perhaps more in touch with late-1990s life, but it was well away from the roots of the band. 'It's like someone who's a soldier ant,' said Stipe. 'They work completely isolated, at night. On something much bigger than maybe even they can grasp. Doing a little job but an important job. It's about what they think about while they're working.'

The second single, 'Lotus', was a labouring rocker that never really got going, and the video featured a topless Michael Stipe reclining on a bed with strange bubbles of light floating out of his chest. 'Hope' was so similar to Leonard Cohen's song 'Suzanne' that he was given a writing credit for the song. 'It just poured out of me,' said Stipe. 'What's on the record is pretty much a first take. I tried to re-sing, I tried and tried to better it and I couldn't, so we just pumped up everything around it and floated the vocal over that.'

Stipe admitted that there was 'whimsy' the album. 'Parakeet' and 'At My Most Beautiful' were probably the songs he meant. He claimed that the former was inspired by Bruno Schulz's *The Street of Crocodiles*, and the latter was a Brian Wilson rip-off, albeit a very good one.

For the first time Stipe allowed all of the album's lyrics to be printed as he was so pleased with them. And after picking up Mike Mills and a bottle of wine he drove out to Bill Berry's farm to play him the album. Despite some good to very good reviews, *Up* managed only half the initial sales of *New Adventures in Hi-Fi* and was the first R.E.M. album in ten years not to reach number 1 in the UK charts, while in the US it peaked at number 3.

With the album in the shops, Stipe was all over the European media. He collected a Lifetime Achievement Award at the Q Awards with R.E.M., though he carefully pointed out that he didn't feel anywhere near the end of his career. Then the band showed up on British TV on Chris Evans's *TFI Friday* along with Larry Hagman, George Wendt and Hootie and the Blowfish. For the R.E.M. performance they were joined on stage by BJ Cole playing lap steel. Stipe wore an open-necked dark blue shirt, black jacket and trousers, with blue eye shadow and copious amounts of pink glitter on his face. With his earpiece, slightly unshaven chin and bald head he cut quite a distinctive figure.

A one-hour special on BBC TV's *Later with Jools Holland* followed. Stipe was in playful mood, trying to get the crowd to scream 'Fuck!' through the encore so it couldn't be broadcast. Shows in Germany, Spain, Austria, Sweden and Italy came next, with the band growing in confidence. Some of the European shows put the band in interesting slots, as Stipe recalled: 'The weirdest foreign TV show we've ever appeared on was in Italy. It was a five-hour television show with no commercials, hosted by an Italian celebrity in his late 60s or 70s and on his third career. He had been, I think, a singer, an actor, and now he was a TV show presenter. His co-presenter was the actress Asia Argento. She was nine months pregnant at the time, and wanted to talk about children's rights with us between songs. We were on a stage that was wheeled out from behind a backdrop by men dressed as Italian policemen, in front of a large studio reconstruction of a desert. There was an actual desert behind us! We were wheeled out on this cart, which took about three minutes, but the whole thing was on live television. We performed "Daysleeper" and then they wheeled us back in. That was kinda crazy.'

After more stops on the US chat-show circuit before Christmas (Conan O'Brien, Jay Leno, Rosie O'Donnell), it was a good end to a difficult year. There was even talk of going back on their decision and touring with *Up*.

Chapter Thirteen

This Is All There Ever Will Be

1999 to 2003

'We're here right now and you're here right now and we're all there is and this is all there ever will be.'

— MICHAEL STIPE

FOR THE LAST YEAR OF THE MILLENNIUM, Michael Stipe was acting out his role of playful pop star, 'media-figure' and all-round arty guy to the full. Early in the year he took part with a female partner in a sexy fashion shoot for *Jane* magazine. The singer was pictured lounging on a bed, and the two of them were photographed watching each other undress and mooching around an apartment in black and white moodiness. To continue the promotion of *Up*, R.E.M. appeared on the teen drama *Party of Five*, Michael Stipe took part in his fifth Tibetan benefit show in two years and then the band departed for Europe, playing mainly for TV shows and at a couple of award ceremonies across Italy, Germany, France and Norway.

With a new tour announced to start in June, the band withdrew to the studio for a new project, writing the musical score for an upcoming biopic of comedian Andy Kaufman. Talented Czech director Milos Forman took the job of bringing the story together, with a cast including Jim Carey and Courtney Love.

The film would be called *Man on the Moon* after the R.E.M. song of that name, which name-checked Kaufman in the lyric. Michael Stipe had been a fan of Andy Kaufman since back in the mid-1970s when Kaufman had been a regular on the long-running TV show *Saturday Night Live*. Stipe homed in on Kaufman's mischievous spirit, as the two shared a similar sense of humour. 'He took the idea of comedy and turned it around so that you couldn't tell what was supposed to be funny and what was not,' said Stipe. 'He was the ultimate prankster.' Jim Carey won a Golden Globe as Best Comedy Actor for his role in the film.

Though the soundtrack album featured only two actual R.E.M. songs, 'Man On The Moon' (not surprisingly) and a new title, 'The Great Beyond', the band scored incidental music for the film as well. 'The Great Beyond' – which earned them a Grammy nomination – was later issued as a single, and the band filmed a video too. The promo clip showed the band performing on a fictional TV talk show, becoming trapped but then managing to escape when Michael Stipe smashes the TV screen from the inside with his mic stand. Director Liz Freidlander skilfully took band footage and worked in clips from the movie. MTV were on hand for the video shoot and interviewed the band between takes. 'It's fun; you get to be a movie star for a day,' beamed Michael Stipe. Later he was spotted hanging out with his friend Cameron Diaz.

During the year Michael Stipe was also involved with the breakthrough movie *Being John Malkovich*, this time as executive producer. The film was an artistic triumph and was nominated for three Golden Globes; Stipe was spotted at the awards ceremony. He was happy to have finally gained some major film success, having had to learn the hard way that the film and music businesses operate in very different ways. One of Stipe's partners at Single Cell Pictures was Sandy Stern. 'It takes months to close a deal, and I think that was difficult for Michael at first,' she says.

'The music world is much more immediate. You put it down, and it's a song. But he has relaxed into the flow of how time travels out here.'

An early attempt to break into Hollywood had been made in the early 1990s with a script called *Desperation Angels* which he was pushing with Jim McKay. For several R.E.M. photo shoots Stipe wore a cap with the title written across the front, but even when Oliver Stone moved in to help gain financing for the project the film still failed to get made. 'Nobody wanted to make it,' says Stipe. 'It was way too political, too dark. The experience pushed Jim [McKay] even more into wanting to do guerrilla independent film, into saying, "I'm not willing to do this dance." But it pushed me a little bit in the other direction, into subverting from within, becoming a tapeworm in Hollywood.'

★　★　★

R.E.M.'s first post-Bill Berry tour opened in Lisbon, Portugal, on 17 June. The band used a tape of 'Airportman' as their entrance music and went on to play six songs from *Up* plus 'The Great Beyond'. The following week, a couple of large indoor shows at Earls Court in London announced the band's arrival in the UK. They dusted off older songs such as 'Gardening At Night', 'Driver 8' and 'Sitting Still' for the first time in what seemed like an age. Stipe was clearly enjoying being back on stage as he wriggled and twisted his way through the shows. The tour used a large-scale set with neon lights, signs and messages that could flash up behind the performers when required. On 25 June R.E.M. finally headlined the Glastonbury Festival after years of rumours that they would appear. In front of almost 100,000 people Stipe put on possibly his best vocal performance of the tour while sporting an overdose of sky-blue eyeliner – a prelude to his later stripes of face paint. The band ploughed through a set of greatest hits, which included 14 singles from their back catalogue. The show boosted their standing in some areas of the music press who had lost the love for the band that had been present three or four years earlier.

Though the very nature of large-scale touring can leave performers aloof, with everyone around the globe wanting a piece of them, Michael Stipe did and does try to keep in touch with the people who matter, be they friends, fans or family members. One example was Keith Leblanc, who had played on one track on *Green* over a decade earlier. In 1999 his secretary was a big R.E.M. fan and he took her along to Earls Court, where he got a message through to Michael Stipe via a roadie. Stipe invited them into the show. 'That guy's got a mind like a steel trap; he doesn't forget anything,' said Leblanc. 'No one's too big or too little for them. They took us backstage, fed us dinner, took time out to talk to my secretary, let us watch the gig from backstage.'

Across Continental Europe Stipe was joined by Patti Smith for a couple of guest spots. During the encores he started coming back on stage alone with a guitar which he would strum through 'Hope', and later in the tour he came out alone for 'Falls To Climb'. Stipe was accompanied on part of the tour by his French artist boyfriend, whom he'd been seeing since 1998. He was also quite open when talking to Q magazine, who asked if he was gay. 'Gay? I don't like that term,' replied Stipe. 'The very concept of gay puts people in categories. "Queer" to me is much broader, the idea that something like sexuality is extremely fluid and not capable of being reduced to a category. Am I queer? Absolutely. I have enjoyed sex with men and women throughout my life. As long as I've been sexually active, I've always been attracted to and slept with men and women. Right now, I've met an incredible man who is an artist, whom I have completely committed myself to.'

Again the spotlight was focused away from R.E.M. the band and shone brightly at Michael Stipe the 'celebrity'. 'Journalists' favourite angle is that I put on this oblique, enigmatic act, and really I'm not like that,' said Stipe. Buck and Mills weren't complaining, though, as they continued to be pretty much left alone.

Unlike previous tours, which had run through the autumn and usually ended in mid- to late November, the *Up* tour ran for the summer only. In amphitheatres across North America R.E.M. played a mix of songs from the last three albums and the occasional old IRS number. At the first of three nights at the Chastain Park Amphitheatre in Atlanta, Bill Berry made a surprise appearance during the encore – but just for a round of applause, not to play anything. After working their way to the north-east, they finished the tour in Mansfield, Massachusetts, on 11 September.

★   ★   ★

Michael Stipe turned 40 in January 2000; as R.E.M. approached their 20th anniversary, the band had taken up exactly half of his life, and all of his adult life. For most of the year Stipe kept a very low profile; it was probably his quietest 12 months since 1979. The band began work on their 12th studio album in May, this time in Vancouver, Canada. Lessons had been learned during the making of *Up*, and after initial demos in Vancouver Stipe and Mills returned alone to Athens to work on some vocal ideas. Then Stipe took off with producer Pat McCarthy to Dublin where he spent the three months from August to October.

The pair rented the Dalkey Lodge, where McCarthy set up equipment to record Stipe's vocals as and when he became inspired. Stipe took the opportunity to fly out from Ireland to the far reaches of Europe looking for ideas. Not surprisingly, a lot of the lyrics he came up with had the themes of summertime and travel running through them. In fact he wrote one song ('I'll Take The Rain') deliberately to get *away* from the summer theme. 'We just sequestered ourselves in a 700-year-old suburb,' Stipe explained. 'I think I went downtown five times in three months. It was really, really under the radar. And I think that benefited the project in a big way. We had an Aga and the whole thing. Did we cook? Of course. Pat McCarthy is a mean cook. He cooks a great omelette, so we had a lot of omelettes. And there's a great restaurant called Thornton's. The chef is an old friend of ours. He'd bring us really good cheese and eggs.'

One of Stipe's field trips took him to see his parents, who were visiting Israel at the time. While there he was spotted by a fan. 'I was at a rave in Tel Aviv,' he said. 'It was four in the morning, I was next to the sea, it was beautiful. Two thousand people jumping up and down, lights, the whole thing. And there I am. And this kid came up to me and he said, "What are you doing here?" And I said, "I came to disappear."'

Back in the US, Stipe did one brief 'show' in Athens – an acoustic run-through of three songs on the steps of the Athens-Clarke County Courthouse in support of Land Aid – and also made a speech supporting groups campaigning for local people to be given more say on Athens land issues and developments. Then he blended back into the ether. The band were, in fact, working on the final mixes for the new album at the Hit Factory in Miami, Florida. Here Stipe had an unexpected meeting on the beach. 'We made part of the record in Miami, and I would go down to the beach,' he explained. 'Not 20 feet from the water I see a fish that is at least seven feet long swimming close to the shore. I did not go back in the ocean the entire month. I was terrified. I called the coastguard. I went online. I was obsessed. I lost two days in the studio over that stupid fish.' Other distractions were more serious, as the presidential election saw the world's eyes turn on Florida: Jeb Bush had a hand in the counting problems throughout the state which eventually handed the presidency to his elder brother George W. Bush. 'We were right there,' recalled Mike Mills. 'Joe Lieberman [Democrat] was in our hotel two days before election day. [Al] Gore was at South Beach the night before. It was amazing: I felt like I was in the vortex of everything.' Unfortunately, as far as R.E.M. were concerned, the vortex spun the way of the Republicans.

The album, entitled *Reveal*, was completed way before the release date of May 2001. With six months to go the band could have been forgiven for taking it easy, but instead they agreed to fly to South America for the first time and play at two massive festivals. On 13 January they headlined the Rock in Rio festival before an estimated 200,000 fans. Four days later they performed a similar feat, in front of fewer fans, in Buenos Aires. Peter Buck went to play a handful of shows with his Minus 5 side-project, but Michael Stipe had little to do for three months apart from a little video work. In late March he flew to Europe with Mike Mills to handle the pre-album interviews and promotional load.

On 20 April Peter Buck set off from Seattle to fly over and join his band mates in London. Exactly what happened during the flight will never be known, but on arrival at Heathrow Buck was arrested and charged with numerous offences, widely reported as 'air rage'. For the first time the band was filling news pages for all the wrong reasons. A court date was eventually set for November 2001, and Buck was released to continue with the band's activities. Stipe and the rest of the R.E.M. camp remained tight-lipped about the whole affair.

In the UK R.E.M. had a heavy schedule ahead of them, with eight events in eight days. Michael Stipe did, however, find the time to go and see the French band Air playing at the Shepherd's Bush Empire, along with members of the band Travis. On 29 April Stipe was centre stage at one of the band's highest-profile UK events of their career: they played as part of the South Africa Day Freedom Concert in front of Nelson Mandela and a TV audience of millions. Their seven-song set was sandwiched between chart bands such as the Corrs, Atomic Kitten and Mel B. Two weeks later, while the band were jetting back and forth across Europe, *Reveal* was released to good reviews.

Reveal was a lush, if slightly over-produced album that proved the band could still write some great music. 'All The Way To Reno', 'I'll Take The Rain' and the surprise hit single 'Imitation Of Life' all hit the spot. In fact this latter song and its catchy chorus propelled the album to number 1 in the UK. The band had also learned lessons from *Up*, and trimmed two takes from the album between promo copies' being sent out and the finished album's going on sale. 'Fascinating' and 'Freeform Jazz Jam' were dropped to give a more satisfying listen.

Meanwhile the press were picking up on stories about Michael Stipe's private affairs and blowing them out of all proportion. After almost a decade of discussing his sexuality Stipe was 'outed' for about the fourth time by the UK press after journalists had picked out comments he made to *Time* magazine.

As they had with *Up* in the months following its release, the band toured *Reveal* mainly for TV and radio shows. A massive outdoor concert in the shadow of Cologne Cathedral was shown live on MTV, and a couple of weeks later they played another *MTV Unplugged* show in New York. The promotional jaunts carried the band to Japan and Australia at the end of July. The rest of 2001 was left for the band to relax. Michael Stipe had bought an apartment in New York at the lower end of Manhattan; he was there on 11 September 2001 as the terrorist attacks were unleashed on the city. He saw the second plane hit the World Trade Center and went out on to the street, where he lent his cell phone to passers-by trying to contact relatives and loved ones. Suddenly 'Everybody Hurts' brought Michael Stipe's voice into homes across the country as the song became one of the most played post-attack songs on US radio. The events shocked Stipe as they did the whole world; they would also infiltrate his writing which would take its most political turn for almost 15 years.

In March 2002 Peter Buck was finally cleared of all charges relating to the 'air rage' in April 2001. The cloud hanging over R.E.M. disappeared and the band lay low for the rest of the year. Stipe did show up at the Kodak Theatre in Los Angeles to sing 'I Got You Babe' with Cher, and later on he added vocals with Coldplay's Chris Martin and the Flaming Lips' Wayne Coyne to electronica outfit Faultline's album.

★ ★ ★

Fast-forward to May 2003: Michael Stipe and R.E.M. had been out of the public eye since Peter Buck's trial and hadn't played any serious shows for almost two years. They met up in Vancouver to rehearse for a new tour and worked up versions of around 75 songs, the equivalent of seven whole albums. The reason for this feverish activity was an upcoming tour to promote a new Warner compilation, *In Time: The Best of R.E.M. 1988–2003*, to celebrate 15 years on the label. Four months before the album was due in the shops, the tour launched at the Tivoli in Utrecht, Holland. Later in the week a pair of shows at London's Brixton Academy showed just what a strong catalogue the band had built up. Hardly any songs were played on both nights. In addition, the first night saw four songs in a row from *Fables of the Reconstruction*, and the second night five songs in a row from *Lifes Rich Pageant*; neither of these albums was on Warner and they had little to do with the forthcoming compilation album.

At the end of the month the band made its second Glastonbury Festival appearance. 'I didn't realize how important Glastonbury is,' said Stipe. 'You can be able to instil memories in people that will live with them for ever and it's a rare feat. To be able to create "a moment".' R.E.M. played the festival circuit across the continent and then returned to North America for an arena tour. When they reached New York in October, Stipe repeated his now usual tour trick of strumming a guitar solo during the encores. This time he did it to cover Interpol's 'NYC'. By now the band had also débuted a new song called 'Final Straw', a thinly veiled political Stipe lyric.

During the month the shows became more TV-show-orientated and the band gave numerous interviews. Stipe was at the centre of these as usual, using his voice – more gravelly than ever after years of smoking, and deeper than his singing voice – to tell of his increasingly political mood after the shock of 9/11. Stipe being

Stipe, he was also happy to chat about art and photography. One subject to come up was the tattoos he's acquired over the years: the cartoon Krazy Kat on his arm and a brick on his hand. The story behind these could well be cryptic, but could equally well just be down to Stipe's love of cartoons. In the cartoon, Krazy Kat was constantly attacked by a character called Ignatz Mouse. The Kat loved the Mouse, but the Mouse hated the Kat. When the Mouse threw a brick at the Kat it was misunderstood by the Kat, who took it as a sign of affection. Did the brick signify a sign of misplaced love in Stipe's life?

In Time: The Best of R.E.M. 1988–2003 did little to boost the band's image in the press. Reviews said that the selection was good, if predictable, while the new songs weren't really worth shelling out for if you had the other albums already. 'Bad Day' was released as a single with an amusing video which spoofed a TV news channel. Michael Stipe played the part of studio anchorman while Buck and Mills doubled as both weathermen and outside reporters.

'CNN loved that they were the ones who premièred "Bad Day", a video that's basically taking a swipe at their medium,' laughed Stipe. 'I thought it was brilliant. I watch both CNN and Fox News. I like to see how people spin things, and it's really different to watch the news on Fox vs. MSNBC vs. CNN vs. CBC. I travel a lot, so this past year I've seen a lot of Canadian TV – which is very different from US coverage of similar events. Impartiality is something that's not shown too much on 24-hour news channels in the US right now, which is what the "Bad Day" video's about. I think one of the main jobs of media in a modern, Western, free democratic country is to question the government and not present something that's just handed to them by whatever administration is in power at the time. They should present things from more than one angle, offering opinions and debating issues that are important to everyone.'

Chapter Fourteen

The Most Open Guy
in the World

2004 to 2007

'I feel like I'm the most open guy in the world, and I don't think I'm any weirder than the next person.'

— MICHAEL STIPE

ROUND THE SUN **TOOK LONGER** than any other R.E.M. album to record. This was partly because they stopped to tour partway through it, but also partly because they just didn't feel the need to rush it. Demos were recorded back in 2002, and further sessions in 2003 and 2004 took them to Vancouver and Compass Point Studios in the Bahamas. In 2003 Stipe described the sessions in Vancouver as 'Very experimental. It's schizophrenic. There's some stuff that's very loud and then some stuff where there's not a lot there, just so quiet it's like a tiny, tiny voice.' Pat McCarthy was producing for the third consecutive R.E.M. album, but evidence of Stipe's early claims of experimentation had all but vanished by the time the album was released. Maybe two years was too long to work on an album. 'We were really able to turn our attention to the new album after the tour when we spent three months writing and recording in the Bahamas,' explained Mike Mills. 'I think what seemed like the interruption of being on the road ultimately helped us in the studio. We had become very focused.'

The lead-off song, 'Leaving New York', was a majestic piece of pop writing. Stipe's vocals were as clear and polished as ever, but while this was probably the best song on the album it was also the most R.E.M.-like and arguably nothing that you hadn't heard from the band before. This was a problem they had to face up to: reviews claimed they had deliberately tried to recreate the style and success of *Automatic for the People*. Certainly 'Leaving New York' would have fitted easily alongside the other tracks on that album. But as Keith Cameron argued in *Mojo*, only two songs from *Around the Sun* would have been seriously considered for inclusion on *Automatic*. It's perhaps a little harsh constantly to be measuring a band against its greatest moment – but it's a standard the band set themselves.

One redeeming feature was Michael Stipe's lyrics, at least on some of the songs, as he returned to some political issues. Ever the mess of contradictions, he then said, 'I consider the three of us to be extremely political, as citizens, and I separate our necessity – who we are as public figures – and what we do as musicians. However there's overlap of course. And so I don't sail out to write as a lyricist, and a front man, I don't sail out to write songs that are political-natured, in fact, with this last record, it was my desire not to, but I couldn't get the events and the aftermath of September 11 out of my head. And I was trying to write songs that would be beautiful songs, and all I could think about is how fucked up the world is. I finally collapsed under the weight, just quit thinking about it, and got advice from a lot of people who do what I do, and moved forward. I don't think politics and art mix very well. I certainly don't think politics and music mix very well.' Despite this the lyrics he penned for 'The Outsiders', 'Final Straw' and 'I Wanted To Be Wrong' all had political overtones.

The album had too much filler and not enough musical bite. Several of the songs are 'nice', but R.E.M. need to be producing more than 'nice'. 'Make It All Okay' and 'Final Straw' stand out, but 'Wanderlust' and 'The Worst Joke Ever' should have been B-sides at best. The closing 'Around The Sun' gives hope that all is not lost for R.E.M. 'It's a song of great hope,' says Stipe. 'The whole record has a theme of ascendancy and velocity and movement and motion. It's about moving from one place to another, from a place where you might be stuck into a place where you're less stuck. I think R.E.M. has always been a great driving band. It's good music to listen to while you're driving. I live a peripatetic life, and I always have. My father was in the military. I was born on an army base, and I've moved around since my first year on this earth. When my father retired, I was 18 years old, and I went to school for a year and then started a band and started moving again. So, from our very first record to this one, there is a feeling of velocity and motion through the music.' Unfortunately, the public and critical perception of three average albums in a row was in danger of colouring the fantastic reputation that they'd worked hard to build over almost 20 years.

R.E.M. spent the second half of 2003 on the road supporting *In Time*, then 12 months from mid-2004 to mid-2005 promoting *Around the Sun*. Just when they'd normally have started working on a tour with the album, they agreed to make their biggest anti-Bush statement to date by joining the 'Vote for Change' tour. During previous presidential election campaigns they had taken out adverts, donated money and made speeches; this tour was aimed directly at persuading undecided voters in important swing states to vote Democrat and possibly tip the election away from George Bush. In short those involved in the tour were trying to bring down the government. 'Five groups wanted to do something in a very important election year,' explained Michael Stipe. 'We realised that we'd have a much stronger and louder voice if we combined our efforts, everyone working together. The idea was that we would swoop down on to a swing state and have everyone play at different venues in different cities on the same night. Then we'd pick up and move on to the next swing state and do the same thing.'

R.E.M. played six shows in 11 days alongside Bruce Springsteen, Dave Matthews, Pearl Jam and others. 'Will it make a difference? I don't know,' said Stipe. 'But I can't just sit back on this one. I think this election is too important, not only because of the different ideologies being projected by the two parties, but also because I think the last election was fraudulent. And a democratic election is part of the foundation of free democracy. You can't have fraudulent presidential elections.'

During these shows R.E.M. played some of their most political songs – as you'd expect. 'Final Straw', 'Begin The Begin', 'World Leader Pretend' and 'Walk Unafraid' formed the backbone of a set that was also sprinkled with new songs and old hits. 'We worked up "Disturbance At The Heron House", which is my take on *Animal Farm*,' said Stipe. 'That song is so fucking political and it's so appropriate to what's going on right now. Like, the kind of arrogance that some of the policy makers and world leaders are carrying with them right now is, I think, reflective of the very worst of the United States. It's that teenage arrogance, as a young country, the know-it-all kind of thing. That makes me crazy.'

R.E.M.'s portion of the show usually ended with 'Man On The Moon', for which they were joined by Bruce Springsteen. Michael Stipe stood back for the second verse, which was sung by Springsteen – after he'd laughed at Stipe's Elvis shimmy just before the chorus. Everyone would pile on stage at the climax of the night, for ensemble versions of 'What's So Funny About Peace, Love and Understanding' and 'People Have The Power'.

The political tour ended on 11 October, leaving the band two months to concentrate on their *Around the Sun* shows before Christmas. On 4 November they played their first show since the election. Despite the publicity surrounding 'Vote for Change' it wasn't enough: George Bush won a second term in office. Michael

Stipe was shattered that the US public had voted in such a way. During the show at Madison Square Garden in New York he said very little, clearly upset by the election result. The band let the music do the talking and played a defiant set, opening for the first time ever with 'It's The End Of The World As We Know It' and continuing with 'Begin The Begin', 'Welcome To The Occupation', 'The Outsiders', 'Cuyahoga', 'I Wanted To Be Wrong', 'Final Straw' and 'Walk Unafraid'. The last show of the year took them to Mexico City for the first time, as the North American portion of the tour was put to bed.

Touring continued for the first half of 2005, progressing through Europe to South Africa, the Far East and Australia. Bertis Downs calculated that by the end of the tour they'd 'played 115 shows of which 46 were in places we never had been'. Michael Stipe was playing the pop-star role even more during 2005. What had started as an expanding array of eye make-up had now been extended to include a wide blue stripe that circled his head and looked like a painted-on Zorro mask. Some people thought he'd stolen the idea from the animated film *The Incredibles*. 'Actually, no, I had the stripe idea before their movie came out,' he said. 'They kind of stole it from me, I believe. I think when people go to see a show they don't really want to see the same person they might see walking down the street. It's a little bit of theatre.'

The tour wasn't without its hiccups. A delay at the Russian–Estonian border meant the planned show in the Estonian capital Tallinn on 26 January was cancelled. In Sheffield on 21 February Mike Mills went down with an ear infection just as the show was about to begin. Michael Stipe came out to apologise to the crowd and sang four acoustic songs, and the show was rescheduled for June. During the European shows the band delved deep into the 75 songs they'd rehearsed ready for the tour. Rarely played songs like 'Seven Chinese Brothers', 'Leave' and 'Me In Honey' were performed. At one show Stipe completely forgot the words to the last of these and just walked to the side of the stage in fits of laughter while the band played on.

Stipe had been involved with some political causes other than the US election at the end of 2004. He joined the Make Trade Fair lobby by taking part in a photo campaign. A number of celebrities were snapped having various commodities tipped on to their heads: Colin Firth was showered with coffee, Thom Yorke with chocolate and Michael Stipe with milk. Then Stipe got a call from Sir Bob Geldof about a concert he was putting together in London. 'The first I heard about Live 8 was eight weeks ago,' explained Michael Stipe. 'I got a call from Bob and he said he was trying to put together this impossible concert and did we feel like playing and I just said yes.'

R.E.M. were one of the biggest bands on the bill and made the cover of the *Radio Times* in the week before the concert. They were also scheduled to play in Switzerland on the same day, so they flew in to London, were introduced by Ricky Gervais, played three hit singles ('Imitation of Life', 'Everybody Hurts' and 'Man On The Moon') and flew out to Switzerland.

R.E.M.'s first show after the London bombings of July 2005 saw them play a large outdoor show at Portman Road, the home of Ipswich Town Football Club. After the band had walked out on stage, Stipe read a prepared statement to the crowd: 'We came here today from London. It's an understatement to say that this has been a difficult couple of days for everyone. Music is, at its best, about catharsis, about epiphany, about feeling, about remembering, about community and about celebration, about celebrating life. The intention here tonight and with this gesture is to honour that, not to forget but to remember and to honour the sanctity of life. Together, tonight, let's raise our voices up in celebration and in remembrance.' The band then opened the show with a poignant rendering of 'Everybody Hurts'.

The last show after almost ten months on the road was on 16 July at London's Hyde Park, a rescheduling of a performance that had been cancelled owing to the London bombs. The tour over, Stipe stayed on in London for a few days, then flew home. He wrote a letter to the R.E.M. website about the tour, and then talked about the difficulties of the 'cold turkey' experienced at the end of any long spell on the road. 'The 15 minutes after I come off stage, I'm incapable of having any kind of normal transaction with anyone. It doesn't matter who it is,' he said. 'The adrenalin jump's so high when [I'm] performing that I have to bring myself back down to earth by doing things like preparing meals for my friends. I became an adrenalin junkie, and that's a much stronger drug than heroin.'

The final event of the year was at a bizarre site in Athens, the Kingpins Bowling Alley. In October this was the location for guitar technician Dewitt Burton's wedding reception, at which the band jumped on stage to play seven songs including 'Wolves, Lower' and 'Permanent Vacation'. The most surprising thing about the evening was that Bill Berry played on all the songs.

Stipe let his inner music fan come to the fore before Christmas as he took in shows by Patti Smith, U2, Dolly Parton and Coldplay. After a solid three years of touring and recording, 2006 was due to be a year off for R.E.M., but Michael Stipe, now 46, was as hyperactive as ever and popping up all over the place. He hit the studio to record with old friend Brian Molko for the next Placebo album, and then after appearing at several Coldplay shows he sang with them at the Austin City Limits Festival, including on the Joseph Arthur song 'In The Sun' and R.E.M.'s 'Nightswimming'. Stipe had bargained with Coldplay that he'd sing with them if Chris Martin would record 'In The Sun' for a charity project Stipe was preparing.

Just as Stipe had taken a lot from seeing Patti Smith perform, it's obvious that that rock lineage has continued with Chris Martin taking a lot from Michael Stipe – from the onstage moves to his having slogans written on the backs of his hands.

The result of their collaboration was a six-track EP featuring different versions of the title song, as an exclusive iTunes download. Stipe set up the In the Sun Foundation to raise funds for Mercy Corps and their programme of disaster relief, specifically along the Gulf Coast in the wake of Hurricane Katrina which had hit Louisiana and beyond in August 2005. 'I had to do something as a public figure,' said Stipe. 'The one thing I can do is sing, and it's probably the best way to get people to pay attention.' James Iha from the Smashing Pumpkins recorded the music, Stipe and Martin sang, and remixes were done by Justin Timberlake and the Black Eyed Peas. 'Everyone who worked on the "In the Sun" project, without exception, was happy to contribute their time, talents, and expertise, free of charge,' said Stipe. 'I realised that so many people wanted to do something, anything, towards helping the Gulf Coast, and this presented them with a way to do just that. The generosity is unparalleled. I was watching the news like everyone, and I saw a pretty pathetic response from the government. I saw people in the most desperate situations. I saw racism, classism. It made me really sad, for how far we've come, how far we've not come from the civil-rights movement. It made me angry that they had no choice.'

From the sublime to the ridiculous, Stipe then hit the news for his attendance at a series of premières and fashion events. In Paris in February he was photographed at a Christian Dior show during Men's Fashion Week. He followed this up with an appearance at the launch of Bono's new ethical-clothing range in New York, where he hobnobbed with likes of Moby and Lou Reed. Whether it was his own fashion statement for the shows or not, Stipe was showing off a pair of large straggly sideburns and wearing a flat cap, which gave an overall impression of Albert Steptoe. However, a week later when he arrived at the première of *Winter Passing* with Zooey Deschanel, the sideburns were gone.

Late in the summer Stipe flew to Europe for a round of press interviews designed to promote yet another upcoming R.E.M.

compilation, this time for IRS Records. The two-CD set, *And I Feel Fine*, was an improvement on the usual 'best of' albums and included the band's singles and hand-picked favourites from the 1982–87 era. On the second disc there was a collector's delight of live tracks, demos, alternate takes and different mixes. A companion DVD, *When the Light Is Mine*, collated the singles from the IRS catalogue plus a host of special extras including MTV's *The Cutting Edge* show from 1984 and appearances on the *Old Grey Whistle Test* and *The Tube*.

After getting back to the States in September, Stipe and the rest of the band began preparing for their induction into the Georgia Music Hall of Fame. Rumours of the possible induction had been brewing for several months – that they'd be placed in the hall alongside such notables as Ray Charles, Otis Redding, James Brown, Gladys Knight, Curtis Mayfield, The Allman Brothers, Gram Parsons, the B-52's, TLC and Kenny Rogers. It had also been hoped that Bill Berry would join the band to play at the ceremony and on September 16 it all came to fruition. The band were inducted at the World Congress Center in Atlanta where the Georgia Senator Max Cleland introduced them to the crowd of 2,000. Stipe made the acceptance speech on behalf of the band before energetic versions of 'Begin the Begin', 'Losing My Religion' and 'Man On The Moon' turned back the clock and made it seem like drummer Bill Berry had never been away, even though it was 11 years since he'd toured as a member of R.E.M. Stipe's speech touched on many topics, including how proud he was to call Georgia his home state and how they had often found themselves the 'unlikely representatives of the American south'. He paid tribute to other Georgian heroes, musical and otherwise: 'Holly Hunter, Isaac Hayes, Little Richard, Otis Redding, Andrew Young, John Lewis, the B-52's, Julia Roberts, James Brown, Peter asked me to say Blind Willie McTell, of course to Ludacris, KRS-One, Chuck D, Outkast, all the way to Danger Mouse. To each of you, we salute you!'

As the lead singer of a band that had been around for over a quarter of a century it was probably expected that Stipe would be viewed as an elder statesman; along with the band he was increasingly seen as someone perhaps reaching the twilight of their creative powers. Certainly in the US the large scale following of the mid-1990s had dwindled, but in Europe he was still seen as an important artist. That autumn, the 20th Anniversary issue of Q magazine was published with 20 different covers featuring 20 different artists and Michael Stipe, not R.E.M., was chosen to grace one of them.

Stipe didn't surface again publicly until well into the new year when he appeared at the Tibet House Benefit in New York at the end of February 2007. It was a cause that he'd supported for over a decade and some high-profile New Yorkers joined him, including Debbie Harry, Lou Reed and Patti Smith.

Earlier in 2007 it had been announced that R.E.M. would be inducted into the Rock and Roll Hall of Fame, open only to acts of at least 25 years standing. The Hall had a love–hate relationship with artists and fans alike. Many wanted Memphis, with it's glorious musical heritage, to be the site of the Hall and the fact that the inductions aren't held in Cleveland further alienate it. Artists too have spoken out about the anti-rock and roll nature of decorating rock's past heroes.

Along with Patti Smith, Grandmaster Flash and the Furious Five, the Ronettes and Van Halen, R.E.M. were honoured on March 12th. The induction took place at the Waldorf Astoria Hotel in New York, although the actual Hall of Fame is based hundreds of miles away. Eddie Vedder of Pearl Jam carried out the induction speech, Michael Stipe made the acceptance speech and the band, again with Bill Berry on drums, played 'Begin the Begin', 'Gardening at Night', 'Man On The Moon', the Stooges' 'I Wanna Be Your Dog' and Patti Smith's 'People Have The Power'. Vedder joined the band for 'Man On The Moon' and the other inductees returned to the stage for 'People Have The Power'.

So after all of the honours coming their way, what was next for R.E.M.? Could they keep things fresh? Their next move was to announce a week's worth of shows at the Olympia Theatre in Dublin. Described as a five-night 'Working Rehearsal' it was placed part way through sessions for the next R.E.M. album that was being produced by Jacknife Lee, best known for his work with Snow Patrol and U2's *How To Dismantle An Atomic Bomb*, which had won a couple of Grammy's.

★ ★ ★

Michael Stipe is in many ways the same as he was in 1980. Even though he isn't married, and doesn't have any children (he has given short shrift to any idea of adopting a child with a partner), he is very much a family man. The close family values instilled in him as a child have remained through his adult life. Even when busy travelling the globe he keeps in close touch with his parents and sisters and uses his rare days off to drive out and visit them.

In other ways, though, Michael Stipe is completely different from the person he was in 1980. Despite his parents' strong Christian beliefs he embodies a patchwork of religious ideas. 'I'm not an intellectual,' he says, 'but I do trust my instincts and that makes me automatically pretty bright.' He contradicts himself often and what he once said in the press he might deny later on. One story he has not altered over the years is that of his sexuality.

Stipe is the only member of the band to be constantly quizzed about his private life. He has stated that he has been tested clear of AIDS numerous times for the benefit of insurance or his partners. He's someone who gathers a crowd wherever he goes. 'Michael is very charismatic and he'll always have a circle of people at least three deep around him,' said Natalie Merchant. 'Later, I came to refer to this as "the 12-headed monster".'

Stipe is a rare commodity in the 21st century: a multi-discipline artist, a celebrity who cares and a real entertainer in the old-fashioned sense of the word. Left-handed people are, according to the old wives' tale, more creative than the rest of the population and Michael Stipe has tried his left hand at everything. Aside from the obvious musical outlets for his creativity, he's read poetry (for a CD of *Pomes All Sizes*, a Jack Kerouac anthology) and published haikus. He's sung of artists (Man Ray in 'Feeling Gravity's Pull'), used artists in videos (see the Caravaggio influence in 'Losing My Religion' or the numerous paintings used in 'Low') and devised stage lighting for concerts.

Away from music, Stipe's natural habitat is the world of photography. He's working on a book of photos about his life and has been a contributing photographer for now defunct *Raygun* magazine. His overall philosophy as regards the creative life is that one shouldn't be afraid of mistakes. He's happy to let them happen because they are the essence of life; he tries to have the ability to recognise them and use them – whether it be the wrong word in a lyric, a bad angle in a film, or a bad photograph. 'A lot of the time I'm grabbing around and bumping into things and I'll throw them together and something will come out.' It's a method he's used in his lyric-writing for years.

'I don't write autobiographically, and I never have, but there's something in there, as an observer, as a voyeur, taking in the world around me, breathing it in and really, really observing, which is what I do best,' he explains. 'If I can just turn off my thinking brain long enough to allow that unconscious voice to do all the work, then I wind up with the 55 minutes of music that comprise a new record. It's OK for them to be nonsensical. You tell me what Bob Dylan is singing about. I don't know. Some of the best songs in the world don't make any linear sense whatsoever. Perhaps the best songs don't. So it doesn't have to have a narrative or follow a train of thought that makes any sense at all. It just has to be good and make you feel something when you hear it.'

Turning off the thinking brain when it comes to lyric-writing has rarely been easy for Michael Stipe. Though he says he can easily take a great photograph he admits it's much, much harder to write a great lyric. 'Taking photographs is really easy for me; it's like breathing,' he says. 'Melody is easy. I can hum along to just about anything. But lyrics and ideas are much more difficult. When I'm able to turn off the thinking brain and let the unconscious voice take over, the best ideas come flying out of me. It's important to note that I've never used the work or interviews as therapy for myself. I don't need the work to be that. But what comes out of me often surprises me in its intensity.'

And it's the intensity of some of Stipe's writing and the elusiveness of the rest of it that make R.E.M.'s catalogue so engaging. An R.E.M. without Michael Stipe would sell only a fraction of the records that they do, even though all the band are brilliant musicians in their own right. For people in a certain age range, Michael Stipe's lyrics have formed the soundtrack to their lives. To many it's shocking to stop and calculate that R.E.M. have been releasing music for over a quarter of a century. 'To be called an elder statesman is so unbelievably insulting,' snaps Stipe. 'Brad Pitt is exactly three years younger than me.'

R.E.M. spent 15 years as what Mike Mills called 'a gang'; now they are more like three individuals who come together once in a while to make music and go on tour. But is it really so surprising that the group dynamic would change after two decades? Now in the 21st century they spend days off alone. 'At this point we love each other very deeply,' Stipe said in 2003. 'There are immense amounts of respect for each other. We also know each other better probably than anyone else on this living earth. What brought us together in the first place was the love of music and that's what has kept us going. We have fights all the time. We have incredible knock-down anxiety-attack kind of fights. It's all the horrible stuff, but it's real.'

Being real is something that Stipe has adhered to throughout his career. The dignity shown by R.E.M. in their slow rise through the ranks to global acclaim is one of their most endearing features. The way they go about their business has garnered fans throughout the industry. Stipe became a friend of many major players during the 1990s – Thom Yorke, Bono, Kurt Cobain – and R.E.M. have influenced the likes of Gene, Coldplay, Pavement and Razorlight, to name just four.

Stipe continues to pursue the complicated balancing act between being a respected artist and, in his own words, a media figure. 'You have to realize there are monumental pressures to being a media figure that people don't really understand,' he says. 'It's not wise and it's not good to gripe about them publicly, and I kind of find that personally offensive as well. But, you have to understand that we're just people like everyone else.' Things he's had to contend with include people tracking him down in Athens. One fan rang his doorbell and then just stood there filming when Stipe opened the door. Someone else took to stealing potted plants from his garden. And it took Stipe quite a while to come to terms with people coming up to him in the street and gushing about how much they loved the last show or album.

He'll do little things to try to deconstruct the walls around him. He rarely signs autographs now, but when he does it's simply 'Michael'. He'd rather pose for photographs with fans (and sometimes take photos of the fans himself) or simply exchange a handshake.

Like everyone else on the planet he can be a bundle of contra-dictions. Some people told Denise Sullivan, for her book *Talk About the Passion*, about his supposed approach to fair-weather friend-ship; others told of him inviting school kids camped outside the R.E.M. office to come in and have a tour around.

Then there's Stipe the activist, who helps organise the Reebok Human Rights Awards alongside Sting, Peter Gabriel and ex-President Carter. He'll be seen as a friend of Bono and Courtney Love but also of Bill Clinton. He's equally at home being photographed with the Dalai Lama or with Jake Gyllenhaal.

One side of Michael Stipe that the public sees less of is the friendly dog-lover who rolls his own cigarettes and still struggles with his own insecurities. 'I always see the one person [at our shows] in the 20,000 who's yawning,' he says. Though not always serious around friends, he is still very serious about his work. In older days he could be flippant in interviews, but he soon learned to rein that side of his personality in. He famously told *Musician* magazine, 'I can't have refrigerators in my house because of the sound they make. It just drives me nuts that that thing operates without me turning it on and off. It just goes. I can't take that.' And he's forever regretted telling *Rolling Stone* that one album sounded like 'two oranges being nailed together'.

During his early years of celebrity and fame, some writers were sceptical that he was working too hard at being misunderstood and was being oblique just for the sake of it. He perhaps encouraged some of this criticism by throwing in comments to interviewers such as that he liked their eyes, or asking them what they had for breakfast.

Stipe gives out an aura of personality that seems to make everyone around want to spend time with him. The paradox here is that he's easily worn down and when he burns out he retreats into himself and has been accused of seeming to brush people off. Now he has learned how to draw the line and not give so much to the general public through his music.

'Michael has always maintained an air of mystery about everything,' says Kate Pierson. 'Sometimes he'll deliberately play the eccentric, come to a party wearing a cape or suddenly throw glitter on you, say things just to see how you react. It's a defence mechanism to keep people from knowing too intimately who he is.'

'I'm not building any mystery,' he said in the 21st century. 'But it's really not important for people to know every little detail. There is always something of the writer in the work but I don't think Melville had to be swallowed by a whale to write a great novel. If I had lived the lives of all the characters of the songs

I've written, that would truly be an extraordinary story. And I'd be a thousand years old. I'm not quite there yet.'

When he was asked in the 1990s what the future held, his whimsical answer was as relevant then as it is today. 'It's all mapped out,' he said, 'on a small piece of paper at the bottom of my bag.' But Stipe knows that one day the band will end. 'It's natural to my personality occasionally to think when I go to our office, "There will be a day when this office will close, because there will be no reason for it to stay open," and it is deeply sad to have that thought,' he admits. 'At the same time, I look at it, and it's this vibrant, incredible place that amazing things are coming out of, and not just music. It's thrilling to me that I'm at the epicentre of that.'

Discography

SINCE AN R.E.M. discography would fill a couple of volumes on its own, to reproduce a complete Michael Stipe discography, including all his collaborations and guest appearances, is just not possible in this book. If you want a thorough breakdown of every commercial release, promo and overseas variation, try to track down a copy of Gary Nabor's book *Remnants*. He managed to fill over 260 pages listing R.E.M. releases issued between 1980 and 1993; an update covering the releases since then would double that book's size. What you will find here is a complete list of R.E.M. albums, singles from the major markets (I haven't included the Polish Postcard singles, for example) and a list of Stipe's guest appearances.

R.E.M. ALBUMS AND EPS

Chronic Town
Wolves, Lower/Gardening At Night/Carnival Of Sorts (Boxcars)/
1,000,000/Stumble

IRS	SP 70502	US	12"	August 1982

Murmur
Radio Free Europe/Pilgrimage/Laughing/Talk About The Passion/Moral
Kiosk/Perfect Circle/Catapult/Sitting Still/9-9/Shaking Through/We
Walk/West Of The Fields

IRS	SP 70604	US	LP	April 1983
IRS	CS 70604	US	Cassette	April 1983
IRS	SP 70604	UK	LP	August 1983
IRS	CD 70014	US	CD	

Reckoning

Harborcoat/Seven Chinese Brothers/South Central Rain/Pretty
Persuasion/Time After Time (Annelise)/Second Guessing/Letter Never
Sent/Camera/(Don't Go Back To) Rockville/Little America

IRS	SP 70044	US	LP	April 1984
IRS	CS 70044	US	Cassette	April 1984
UK	7045	UK	LP	April 1984
IRS	2847	Japan	LP	1985
IRS	CD 70044	US	CD	

Fables of the Reconstruction

Feeling Gravity's Pull/Maps And Legends/Driver 8/Life And How To
Live It/Old Man Kensey/Can't Get There From Here/Green Grow
The Rushes/Kohoutek/Auctioneer (Another Engine)/Good
Advices/Wendell Gee

IRS	IRS-5592	US	LP	June 1985
IRS	IRSC-5592	US	Cassette	June 1985
IRS	MIRF1003	UK	LP	June 1985
IRS	IRSD-5592	US	CD	

Lifes Rich Pageant

Begin The Begin/These Days/Fall On Me/Cuyahoga/Hyena/Underneath
The Bunker/The Flowers Of Guatemala/I Believe/What If We Give It
Away?/Just A Touch/Swan Swan H/Superman

IRS	IRS-5783	US	LP	July 1986
IRS	IRSC-5783	US	Cassette	July 1986
IRS	IRSD-5783	US	CD	July 1986
IRS	MIRG1014	UK	LP	July 1986

| IRS | – | UK | CD | July 1986 |
| IRS | ELPS 4550 | New Zealand | LP | 1986 |

Dead Letter Office

Crazy/There She Goes Again/Burning Down/Voice Of Harold/Burning Hell/White Tornado/Toys In The Attic/Windout/Ages Of You/Pale Blue Eyes/Rotary Ten/Bandwagon/Femme Fatale/Walter's Theme/King Of The Road

IRS	SP 70054	US	LP	April 1987
IRS	–	US	Cassette	April 1987
IRS	CD 70054	US	CD	April 1987
IRS	SP 70054	UK	LP	April 1987

Document

Finest Worksong/Welcome To The Occupation/Exhuming McCarthy/Disturbance At The Heron House/Strange/It's The End Of The World As We Know It (And I Feel Fine)/The One I Love/Fireplace/Lightin' Hopkins/King Of Birds/Oddfellows Local 151

IRS	IRS-42059	US	LP	September 1987
IRS	IRSC-42059	US	Cassette	September 1987
IRS	IRSD-42059	US	CD	September 1987
IRS	MIRG1025	UK	LP	September 1987
IRS	460105 1	Australia	LP	1987
IRS	3382	Japan	LP	1987
IRS	724349946613-4	US	LP 180g	1999
IRS	72435-2127627	US	CD	1999

Eponymous

Radio Free Europe [Hib-Tone]/Gardening At Night/Talk About The Passion/South Central Rain/(Don't Go Back To) Rockville/Can't Get There From Here/Driver 8/Romance/Fall On Me/The One I Love/Finest Worksong/It's The End Of The World As We Know It (And I Feel Fine)

IRS	IRS-6262	US	LP	October 1988
IRS	IRSC-6262	US	Cassette	October 1988
IRS	IRSD-6262	US	CD	October 1988
IRS	MIRG1038	UK	LP	October 1988

Green

Pop Song '89/Get Up/You Are The Everything/Stand/World Leader
Pretend/The Wrong Child/Orange Crush/Turn You Inside-Out/Hairshirt/
I Remember California/Eleventh, Untitled Song

WB	9-25795-1	US	LP	November 1988
WB	9 25795-4	US	Cassette	November 1988
WB	9 25795-2	US	CD	November 1988
WB	WX234	UK	LP	November 1988
WB	9257952	Australia	CD	1995
WB	WEA 80127	Argentina	LP	1988
WB	LXWB-6813	Mexico	LP	1988
(Song titles written in Spanish on the above)				
WB/Tusk	WBC 1654	South Africa	LP	1988
WB/Tusk	WBCD 1654	South Africa	CD	1988

Out of Time

Radio Song/Losing My Religion/Low/Near Wild Heaven/Endgame/Shiny
Happy People/Belong/Half A World Away/Texarkana/Country
Feedback/Me In Honey

WB	9 26496-1	US	LP	March 1991
WB	9 26496-4	US	Cassette	March 1991
WB	9 26496-2	US	CD	March 1991
WB	WPCP 4195	Japan	CD	April 1991
WB	7599264962	Australia	CD	1995
WB/Tusk	WBCD 1701	South Africa	CD	1991

The Best of R.E.M.

Carnival Of Sorts (Boxcars)/Radio Free Europe/Perfect Circle/Talk
About The Passion/South Central Rain/(Don't Go Back To)

Rockville/Pretty Persuasion/Green Grow The Rushes/Can't Get There From Here/Driver 8/Fall On Me/I Believe/Cuyahoga/The One I Love/Finest Worksong/It's The End Of The World As We Know It (And I Feel Fine)

IRS	DMIRH 1	UK	LP	September 1991
IRS	DMIRH 1	UK	CD	September 1991
IRS	DMIRH 1	UK	Cassette	September 1991
IRS	TOCP-7265	Japan	CD	September 1991

Automatic for the People

Drive/Try Not To Breathe/The Sidewinder Sleeps Tonite/Everybody Hurts/New Orleans Instrumental No. 1/Sweetness Follows/Monty Got A Raw Deal/Ignoreland/Star Me Kitten/Man On The Moon/Nightswimming/ Find The River

WB	9 45055-2	US	LP	October 1992
WB	9 45055-4	US	Cassette	October 1992
WB	9 45055-2	US	CD	October 1992
WB	9362-45055-2	Australia	CD	1995
WB	WX-488	UK	LP	October 1992
WB/Tusk	WBCD 1745	South Africa	CD	1992
WB/Tusk	ZWBC 1745	South Africa	Cassette	1992

R.E.M. Singles Collected

Radio Free Europe [edit]/There She Goes Again/South Central Rain/King Of The Road/(Don't Go Back To) Rockville [edit]/Catapult [live]/Can't Get There From Here [edit]/Bandwagon/Wendell Gee/Crazy/Fall On Me/Rotary Ten/Superman/White Tornado/The One I Love/Maps And Legends [live]/It's The End Of The World As We Know It (And I Feel Fine)[edit]/Last Date/Finest Worksong [other mix]/Time After Time Etc.

IRS	7234 8 2964223	Holland	CD	September 1994
IRS	7243 8 296423	Australia	CD	September 1994

Monster

What's The Frequency, Kenneth?/Crush With Eyeliner/King Of Comedy/I Don't Sleep, I Dream/Star 69/Strange Currencies/Tongue/Bang And Blame/I Took Your Name/Let Me In/Circus Envy/You

WB	9 45740-1	US	LP	September 1994
WB	9 45740-4	US	Cassette	September 1994
WB	9 45740-2	US	CD	September 1994
WB	9362-45740-1	Germany	LP	September 1994
WB	WPCR-101	Japan	CD	September 1994
WB	9362457402	Australia	CD	1995
WB/Tusk	WBCD 1802	South Africa	CD	1994

New Adventures in Hi-Fi

How The West Was Won And Where It Got Us/The Wake-Up Bomb/New Test Leper/Undertow/E-Bow, The Letter/Leave/Departure/ Bitter Sweet Me/Be Mine/Binky The Doormat/Zither/So Fast So Numb/ Low Desert/Electrolite

WB	9 46320-1	US	2LP	September 1996
WB	9 46320-4	US	Cassette	September 1996
WB	9 46320-2	US	CD	September 1996
WB	9362-46320-1	UK	2LP	September 1996
WB	9362-46320-2	UK	CD	September 1996
WB	WPCR-801	Japan	CD	1996
WB/Tusk	WBCD 1851	South Africa	CD	1996

In the Attic

Finest Worksong/Driver 8/Gardening At Night/Swan Swan H/Disturbance At The Heron House/Maps And Legends/Tired Of Singing Trouble/Just A Touch/Toys In The Attic/(All I Have To Do Is) Dream/The One I Love/Crazy/Can't Get There From Here/Last Date

| EMI | 72438-2132127 | US | CD | 1997 |

Up

Airportman/Lotus/Hope/At My Most Beautiful/The Apologist/Sad Professor/In The Air/Walk Unafraid/Why Not Smile/Daysleeper/Diminished – I'm Not Over You/Parakeet/Falls To Climb

WB	9 47112-1	US	2LP	October 1998
WB	9 47112-4	US	Cassette	October 1998
WB	9 47112-2	US	CD	October 1998
WB	WPCR-2400	Japan	CD	October 1998
WB	936247112-2	Australia	CD	October 1998

Man On The Moon

WB	9 47483-2	US	CD	February 2000

Reveal

The Lifting/I've Been High/All The Way To Reno (You're Gonna Be A Star)/She Just Wants To Be/Disappear/Saturn Return/Beat A Drum/Imitation Of Life/Summer Turns To High/Chorus And The Ring/I'll Take The Rain/Beachball

WB	9 47946-2	US	CD	May 2001
WB	9 47946-4	US	Cassette	May 2001
WB	9 47946-1	US	LP	May 2001
WB		UK	2LP	May 2001
WB	9362 479462	Australia	CD	May 2001
WB	WPCR-11010	Japan	CD	May 2001
WB/Gallo	WBCD 1994	South Africa	CD	May 2001

In Time: The Best of R.E.M. 1988–2003

Man On The Moon/The Great Beyond/Bad Day/What's The Frequency, Kenneth?/All The Way To Reno (You're Gonna Be a Star)/Losing My Religion/E-Bow, The Letter/Orange Crush/Imitation Of Life/Daysleeper/Animal/The Sidewinder Sleeps Tonite/Stand/Electrolite/All The Right Friends/Everybody Hurts/At My Most Beautiful/Nightswimming

| WB | 9362-48381-2 | US | CD | October 2003 |
| WB | 9362483812 | UK | CD | October 2003 |

Around the Sun

Leaving New York/Electron Blue/The Outsiders/Make It All Okay/Final Straw/I Wanted To Be Wrong/Wander Lust/The Boy In The Well/Aftermath/High Speed Train/Worst Joke Ever/The Ascent Of Man/Around The Sun

WB	9362-48894-2	US	CD	October 2004
WB	9362488942	UK	CD	October 2004
WB	78422	US	2LP	October 2004

R.E.M. SINGLES

Radio Free Europe
w/Sitting Still

| Hib-Tone | HT-0001 | US | 7" | July 1981 |

w/There She Goes Again

| IRS | IR-9916 | US | 7" | May 1983 |
| IRS | PFP-1017 | UK | 7" | August 1983 |

Talk About The Passion
w/Shaking Through/Carnival Of Sorts (Boxcars)/1,000,000l

| RS | PSFX 1026 | UK | 12" | November 1983 |

South Central Rain (I'm Sorry)
w/King Of The Road

IRS	IRS 105	UK	7"	March 1984
IRS	IR-9927	US	7"	March 1984
IRS	IR-9927	Canada	7"	March 1984
IRS	A-4255	Holland	7"	March 1984

w/Voice Of Harold/Pale Blue Eyes

| IRS | IRSX 105 | UK | 12" | March 1984 |
| IRS | A12-4255 | Holland | 12" | March 1984 |

(Don't Go Back To) Rockville
w/Wolves, Lower

| RS | IRS 107 | UK | 7" | June 1984 |

w/Wolves, Lower/9-9 [live]/Gardening At Night [live]

| IRS | IRSX 107 | UK | 12" | June 1984 |

w/Catapult [live]

| IRS | IR-9931 | US | 7" | August 1984 |

Can't Get There From Here
w/Bandwagon

RS	IRS-52642	US	7"	June 1985
IRS	IRS-52642	Canada	7"	July 1985
IRS	IRM 102	UK	7"	July 1985

w/Bandwagon/Burning Hell

| IRS | IRT 102 | UK | 12" | July 1985 |

Driver 8
w/Crazy

| RS | IRS-52678 | US | 7" | September 1985 |

Wendell Gee
w/Crazy

| IRS | IRM 105 | UK | 7" | September 1985 |

w/Crazy/Ages Of You/Burning Down

| IRS | IRMD 105 | UK | 2 x 7" | September 1985 |

w/Crazy/Driver 8 [live]

| IRS | IRT 105 | UK | 12" | October 1985 |

Fall On Me
w/Rotary Ten

IRS	IRS-52883	US	7"	August 1986
IRS	IRS-52883	Canada	7"	August 1986
IRS	IRM 121	UK	7"	September 1986

w/Rotary Ten/Toys In The Attic

IRS	IRMT 121	UK	12"	July 1986

Superman
w/White Tornado

IRS	IRS-52971	US	7"	November 1986
IRS	IRS-52971	Canada	7"	December 1986
IRS	IRM 128	UK	7"	March 1987

w/White Tornado/Femme Fatale

IRS	IRMT 128	UK	12"	March 1987

w/White Tornado/Perfect Circle

IRS	ILS 65025 5 6	Holland	12"	April 1987

It's The End Of The World As We Know It (And I Feel Fine)
w/This One Goes Out [live]

IRS	IRM 145	UK	7"	August 1987

w/This One Goes Out [live]/Maps And Legends [live acoustic]

IRS	IRMT 145	UK	12"	August 1987

w/Last Date

IRS	IRS-53220	US	7"	January 1988

w/Radio Free Europe

IRS	IRM 180	UK	7"	December 1991

w/Radio Free Europe/Time After Time Etc.

IRS	DIRMT 180	UK	CD	December 1991

w/Radio Free Europe [Hib-Tone]/Last Date/White Tornado

| IRS | DIRMX 180 | UK | CD | December 1991 |

The One I Love
w/Maps And Legends [live acoustic]

| IRS | IRS-53171 | US | 7" | August 1987 |
| CBS | SSC 6067 | South Africa | 7" | August 1987 |

w/Last Date

| IRS | IRM 146 | UK | 7" | November 1987 |

w/Fall On Me

| IRS | IRM 173 | UK | 7" | October 1988 |

w/The One I Love [live]/Maps And Legends [live acoustic]

| IRS | IRS-23792 | US | 12" | August 1987 |
| IRS | DIRMT 178 | UK | CD | September 1991 |

w/Last Date/Disturbance At The Heron House [live]

| IRS | IRMT 146 | UK | 12" | November 1987 |
| IRS | DIRM 146 | UK | CD | November 1987 |

w/Fall On Me/South Central Rain

| IRS | IRMT 173 | UK | 12" | October 1988 |
| IRS | DIRM 173 | UK | CD | October 1988 |

w/Crazy

| IRS | IRM 178 | UK | 7" | November 1991 |

w/Driver 8 [live]/Disturbance At The Heron House [live]/Crazy

| IRS | DIRMX 178 | UK | CD | September 1991 |

Finest Worksong
w/Time After Time Etc. [live]

| IRS | IRM 161 | UK | 7" | April 1988 |

w/Finest Worksong [other mix]/Time After Time Etc. [live]

IRS	IRS-23850	US	12"	March 1988
IRS	IRMT 161	UK	12"	April 1988
IRS	ILS 651320	Holland	3"CD	November 1987

w/Time After Time Etc./It's The End Of The World As We Know It (And I Feel Fine)

IRS	DIRM 161	UK	CD	April 1988

Stand
w/Memphis Train Blues

WB	7-27688	US	7"	January 1989
WB	W7577	UK	7"	January 1989
WB	W7577X	UK	7"	January 1989

(above in recycled paper sleeve)

WB	7-27577	Australia	7"	January 1989
WB	7599-27688-2	US	3"CD	February 1989
WB	10P3 6078	Japan	3"CD	February 1989

w/Pop Song '89 [acoustic]

WB	W2833	UK	7"	August 1989
WB	W2833W	UK	7"	August 1989

(above in fold-out stencil sleeve)

w/Memphis Train Blues/Untitled [instrumental]

WB	W7577T	UK	12"	January 1989

w/Pop Song '89 [acoustic]/Skin Tight [live]

WB	W2833T	UK	12"	August 1989
WB	W2833CD	UK	3"CD	August 1989
WB	W2833CDX	UK	3"CD	August 1989

w/Memphis Train Blues/Untitled [instrumental]

WB	W7577CD	UK	3"CD	January 1989

WB	W7577CDX	UK	CD	January 1989

(above in maple-leaf-shaped sleeve)

Orange Crush
w/Ghost Riders

WB	W2960	UK	7"	May 1989
WB	W2960X	UK	7"	May 1989

(above in recycled paper sleeve)

w/Memphis Train Blues

WB	7-27652	Australia	7"	May 1989

w/Ghost Riders/Dark Globe

WB	W2960T	UK	12"	May 1989
WB	W2960CD	UK	3"CD	May 1989

Get Up
w/Funtime

WB	7-22791	US	7"	September 1989

Losing My Religion
w/Rotary Eleven

WB	W0015	UK	7"	February 1991

w/Rotary Eleven/After Hours [live]

WB	W0015T	UK	12"	February 1991
WB	W0015CD	UK	CD	March 1991

w/Stand [live]/Turn You Inside-Out [live]/World Leader Pretend [live]

WB	W0015CDX	UK	CD	March 1991

Shiny Happy People
w/Forty Second Song

WB	W0027	UK	7"	June 1991

w/Forty Second Song/Losing My Religion [live acoustic]

| WB | W0027T | UK | 12" | May 1991 |
| WB | W0027CD | UK | CD | June 1991 |

w/I Remember California [live]/Get Up [live]/Pop Song '89 [live]

| WB | W0027CDX | UK | CD | June 1991 |

Near Wild Heaven
w/Pop Song '89 [live acoustic]

| WB | W0055 | UK | 7" | August 1991 |

w/Pop Song '89 [live acoustic]/Half A World Away [live acoustic]

| WB | W0055T | UK | 12" | August 1991 |

w/Tom's Diner [live]/Low [live]/Endgame [live]

| WB | W0055CDX | UK | CD | August 1991 |

Radio Song
w/Love Is All Around [live acoustic]

WB	7-19246	US	7"	November 1991
WB	W0072	UK	7"	November 1991
WB	5439-19246-7	Germany	7"	November 1991

w/Love Is All Around [live acoustic]/Belong [live]

| WB | 0-40229 | US | 12" | November 1991 |
| WB | 9-40229-2 | US | CD | November 1991 |

w/Love Is All Around [live acoustic]/Shiny Happy People [remix]

| WB | W0072T | UK | 12" | November 1991 |

w/You Are The Everything [live]/Orange Crush [live]/Belong [live]

| WB | W0072CDX | UK | CD | November 1991 |

Drive
w/World Leader Pretend

| WB | W0136 | UK | 7" | September 1992 |

w/Winged Mammal Theme

WB	7-18729	US	7"	October 1992
WB	2-18729	US	CD	October 1992
WB	WPDP-6308	Japan	3"CD	November 1992

w/It's A Free World, Baby/Winged Mammal Theme/First We Take Manhattan

WB	W0136CDX	UK	CD	September 1992

Man On The Moon
w/Turn You Inside-Out

WB	W0143	UK	7"	November 1992
WB	5439-18656-7	Germany	7"	November 1992

w/Fruity Organ/New Orleans Instrumental No. 2/Arms Of Love

WB	W0143CDX	UK	CD	November 1992

w/New Orleans Instrumental No. 2

WB	2-18642	US	CD	January 1993
WB	WPDP-6318	Japan	3"CD	January 1993

The Sidewinder Sleeps Tonite
w/Get Up

WB	W0152	UK	7"	February 1993

w/The Lion Sleeps Tonight/Fretless

WB	W0152CD1	UK	CD	February 1993
WB	9362-40770-2	Australia	CD	February 1993

w/Organ Song/Star Me Kitten [demo]

WB	W0152CD2	UK	CD	February 1993

Everybody Hurts
w/Pop Song '89

WB	W0169	UK	7"	April 1993

w/Mandolin Strum/Belong [live acoustic]/Orange Crush [live]

| WB | 0-40989 | US | 12" | August 1993 |
| WB | 2-40989 | US | CD | August 1993 |

w/Star Me Kitten [demo]/Losing My Religion [live acoustic]/Organ Song

| WB | 0-40992 | US | 12" | August 1993 |
| WB | 2-40992 | US | CD | August 1993 |

w/New Orleans Instrumental No. 1 [long version]/Mandolin Strum

| WB | W0169CD1 | UK | CD | April 1993 |

w/Chance [dub]/Dark Globe

| WB | W0169CD2 | UK | CD | April 1993 |

w/Mandolin Strum/Chance [dub]/Dark Globe

| WB | 9362-40867-9 | France | CD | April 1993 |
| WB | 9362-40867-2 | Australia | CD | April 1993 |

w/Mandolin Strum

| WB | 2-18638 | US | CD | July 1993 |

Nightswimming
W/Losing My Religion [live acoustic]

| WB | W0184 | UK | 7" | July 1993 |

w/World Leader Pretend [live acoustic]/Belong [live acoustic]/Low [live acoustic]

WB	W0184TP	UK	12"	July 1993
WB	W0184CD	UK	CD	July 1993
WB	9362-40976-2	Germany	CD	July 1993
WB	9362-40986-9	France	CD	July 1993
WB	9362-40986-2	Australia	CD	July 1993

Find The River
w/Everybody Hurts [live]

| WB | W0211 | UK | 7" | December 1993 |

What's The Frequency, Kenneth?
w/What's The Frequency, Kenneth? [instrumental]

WB	W0265	UK	7"		September 1994
WB	7-18050-A	US	7"		September 1994

w/Monty Got A Raw Deal [live]/Everybody Hurts [live]/Man On The Moon [live]

WB	0-41760	US	12"		September 1994
WB	W0265CD	Germany	CD		September 1994
WB	9-41760-2	US	CD		September 1994

Bang And Blame
w/Bang And Blame [instrumental]

WB	W0275	UK	7"		November 1994
WB	7-17994	US	7"		January 1995
WB	9-17994-2	US	CD		January 1997

w/Losing My Religion [live]/Country Feedback [live]/Begin The Begin [live]

WB	0-41857	US	12"		January 1995
WB	2-41857	US	CD		January 1995
WB	WPCR 163	Japan	CD		1995

Crush With Eyeliner
w/Crush With Eyeliner [instrumental]

WB	W0281X	UK	7"		January 1995

(above on orange vinyl with free calendar sleeve)

w/Fall On Me [live]/Me In Honey [live]/Finest Worksong [live]

WB	9 41904-0	US	12"		1995
WB	WPCR-2177	Japan	CD		October 1998
WB/Tusk	WBSD 6	South Africa	CD		1995
WB	9-41904-2	US	CD		January 1995

Strange Currencies
w/Strange Currencies [instrumental]

WB	7-17900	US	7"		April 1995

WB	W0290X	UK	7"	April 1995

(above on green vinyl with free pin badge)

WB	2-17900	US	CD	April 1995

w/Drive [live]/Funtime [live]/Radio Free Europe [live]

WB	0-43513	US	12"	April 1995
WB	2-43513	US	CD	April 1995
WB	W0290CD	Germany	CD	April 1995

Tongue
w/Tongue [instrumental]

WB	W0308X	UK	7"	September 1995

(above with tour booklet, limited edition)

w/What's The Frequency, Kenneth? [live]/Bang And Blame [live]/I Don't Sleep, I Dream [live]

WB	W0308CD	UK	CD	October 1995

E-Bow, The Letter
w/Triangle/Departure/Wall Of Death

WB	9 43763-0	US	12"	August 1996
WB	W0369CD	UK	CD	August 1996
WB	9 43763-2	US	CD	August 1996
WB	9362437632	Australia	CD	August 1996
WB	WPCR-2180	Japan	CD	October 1998
WB/Tusk	WBSD 12	South Africa	CD	1998

Bittersweet Me
w/Undertow [live]

WB	7-17490	US	7"	November 1996

w/Undertow [live]/Wichita Lineman [live]/New Test Leper [acoustic]

WB	9 43790-0	US	12"	November 1996
WB	9 43790-2	US	CD	November 1996
WB	2-43790	UK	CD	November 1996

WB	9362437902	Australia	CD	1996
WB	WPCR 922	Japan	CD	1996

Electrolite
w/The Wake-Up Bomb [live]

WB	7-17446	US	7"	1997

w/The Wake-Up Bomb [Atlanta]/Binky The Doormat [Atlanta]/King Of Comedy [808 State remix]

WB	9 43810-0	US	12"	February 1997
WB	W0383CDX	UK	CD	December 1996
WB	9 43810-2	US	CD	February 1997
WB	5439174464	Australia	CD	1997
WB	WPCR 966	Japan	CD	1997

How The West Was Won And Where It Got Us
w/Be Mine [Mike on Bus version]/Love Is All Around/Sponge

WB	9362-43851-2	Germany	CD	April 1997
WB	WPCR-975	Japan	CD	April 1997

Daysleeper
w/Emphysema

WB	7-17129	US	7"	October 1998
WB	W0455LC	UK	7"	October 1998
WB	9 17129-2	US	CD	October 1998

w/Emphysema/Why Not Smile [Oxford American version]

WB	W0455CD	UK	CD	October 1998

w/Emphysema/Sad Professor [live]/Why Not Smile [Oxford American version]

WB	9362-44568-2	Germany	CD	October 1998
WB	WPCR-2249	Japan	CD	October 1998
WB	9362445682	Australia	CD	October 1998
WB/Gallo	WBSD 22	South Africa	CD	1998

Lotus
w/Surfing The Ganges/Lotus [weird mix]

WB	W466CD	UK	CD	December 1998

w/Suspicion [live in the studio]

WB	W466CDX	UK	3"CD	December 1998

w/Surfing The Ganges/Suspicion [live]/Lotus [weird mix]

WB	9362446002	Australia	CD	February 1999
WB/Gallo	WBSD 26	South Africa	CD	1999

At My Most Beautiful
w/The Passenger [live]/Country Feedback [live]

WB	W477CD	UK	CD	March 1999

w/South Central Rain [live]

WB	W477CDX	UK	3"CD	March 1999

w/The Passenger [live]/Country Feedback [live]/South Central Rain [live]

WB	932446272	Australia	CD	March 1999
WB	WPCR-10066	Japan	CD	March 1999

Suspicion
w/Electrolite [live]/Man On The Moon [live]

WB	W488CD	UK	CD	June 1999

w/Perfect Circle [live]

WB	W488CDX	UK	3"CD	June 1999

The Great Beyond
w/Man On The Moon [live]

WB	7-16888	US	7"	February 2000
WB	9 16888-2	US	CD	February 2000

w/The One I Love [live]/Everybody Hurts [live]/Man On The Moon [live]

WB	9362448122	Australia	CD	December 1999

WB	9 44816-2	US	CD	February 2000
WB	WCPR-10638	Japan	CD	February 2000
WB	WBSD-38	South Africa	CD	February 2000
WB	W516CD	UK	CD	March 2000

Imitation Of Life
w/The Lifting [original]/Beat A Drum [Dalkey demo]/2JN

WB	9 42363-0	US	12"	May 2001
WB	9362449942	Australia	CD	April 2001
WB	942363-2	US	CD	May 2001

w/The Lifting [original]/Beat A Drum [Dalkey demo]

| WB | W559CD | UK | CD | April 2001 |

Imitation Of Life [video]/2JN/The Lifting

| WB | W559DVD | UK | CD | April 2001 |

All The Way To Reno (You're Gonna Be A Star)
w/Yellow River/Imitation Of Life [live]/Imitation Of Live [live video]

| WB | 9362423962 | UK | CD | July 2001 |
| WB | 9362423952 | Australia | CD | 2001 |

[video]/Yellow River/165 Hillcrest

| WB | W568DVD | UK | CD | 2001 |

I'll Take The Rain
w/32 Chord Song/I've Been High [live video]

| WB | W573CDX | UK | CD | November 2001 |

w/I've Been High [live video]/She Just Wants To Be [live]

| WB | W573CD | UK | CD | November 2001 |

w/She Just Wants To Be [live]/I've Been High [live]/I've Been High [live video]

| WB | 9362-42416-2 | UK | CD | 2001 |

Bad Day
w/Favorite Writer

WB	W624	US	7"	2003
WB	5439-16533-2	Germany	CD	2003

w/Favorite Writer/Bad Day [video]

WB	W624CD1	UK	CD	2003

w/Out In The Country/Adagio

WB	W624CD2	UK	CD	2003

Animal
w/South Central Rain [live]

WB	CD16489	Canada	CD	2003

w/Pretty Persuasion [live]/Losing My Religion [live video]

WB	W633CD	UK	CD	January 2004

Leaving New York
w/(Don't Go Back To) Rockville [live]

WB	W654	UK	7"	September 2004
WB	W654CD1	UK	CD	September 2004

w/You Are The Everything [live]/These Days [live]

WB	W654CD2	UK	CD	September 2004

Aftermath
w/High Speed Train [live]

WB	W658CD1	UK	CD	November 2004

w/So Fast, So Numb [live]/All The Right Friends [live]

WB	W658CD2	UK	CD	November 2004

Electron Blue
w/What's The Frequency, Kenneth? [live]

| WB | W665 | UK | 7" | February 2005 |
| WB | W665CD1 | UK | CD | February 2005 |

w/Sweetness Follows [live]/Leaving New York [live video]

| WB | W665CD2 | UK | CD | February 2005 |

Wanderlust
w/The Outsiders

| WB | W676 | UK | 7" | July 2005 |

w/Low [alternative version]

| WB | W676CD1 | UK | CD | July 2005 |

w/The Outsiders [alternative version]/Bad Day [live video]

| WB | W676CD2 | UK | CD | July 2005 |

Michael Stipe
Guest Appearances

BILLY BRAGG
Don't Try This at Home (1991)

MICHAEL BROOK
Albino Alligator (1997)

NENEH CHERRY
Homebrew (1992)

VIC CHESNUTT
Little (1990)
West of Rome (1991)

CHICKASAW MUDD PUPPIES
White Dirt (1990) producer
8 Track Stomp (1991)

FAULTLINE
Your Love Means Everything (2002)

THE GOLDEN PALOMINOS
Visions of Excess (1985)
Drunk with Passion (1991)
A History (1982–1985) (1992)

Best of the Golden Palominos (1997)
Run Pony Run (2002)

GRANT LEE BUFFALO
Jubilee (1998)

KRISTIN HERSH
Hips and Makers (1994)

ROBYN HITCHCOCK
Perspex Island (1991)

HUGO LARGO
Drum (1988)

INDIGO GIRLS
Indigo Girls (1989)
Live at the Uptown Lounge (1990)
The Best of the Indigo Girls (1995)

MAGNAPOP
Magnapop (1992)

ONE GIANT LEAP
One Giant Leap (2002)

OUR FAVOURITE BAND
Saturday Nights & Sunday Mornings (1987)

GRANT LEE PHILLIPS
Mobilize (2001)

PATTI SMITH
Peace and Noise (1997)
Patti Smith Gung Ho (2000)

SPACEHOG
Chinese Album (1998)

SYD STRAW
Surprise (1989)

10,000 MANIACS
In My Tribe (1987)

WARREN ZEVON
Sentimental Hygiene (1987)

Filmography

AS PRODUCER

Slo-Mo (2006)

Runner-Up (2005)

Johnny Berlin (2005)

Room (2005)

Saved! (2004))

Everyday People (2004)

Thirteen Conversations About One Thing (2001)

The Sleepy Time Gal (2001)

Stranger Inside (2001)

Our Song (2000)

Olive, the Other Reindeer (1999)

Spring Forward (1999)

Being John Malkovich (1999)

American Movie (1999)

Velvet Goldmine (1998)

AS ACTOR

Olive, the Other Reindeer (1999) as Schnitzel

Color of a Brisk and Leaping Day (1996) as Skeeter

The Adventures of Pete & Pete (TV) as Captain Scrummy
Arena Brains (1988) as the 'watcher'
Anthem (1997) as himself
Space Ghost Coast to Coast (TV) as himself

Bibliography

Brown, Rodger Lyle, *Party Out of Bounds*, Penguin, 1991.

Buckley, David, *R.E.M. Fiction*, Virgin, 2002.

Jovanovic, Rob, and Abbott, Tim, *Adventures in Hi-Fi: The Complete R.E.M.*, Orion, 2001.

Fletcher, Tony, *Remade, The Story of R.E.M.*, Omnibus, 2002.

Gray, Marcus, *It Crawled from the South*, Fourth Estate, 1997.

Platt, John, ed., *The R.E.M. Companion*, Schirmer, 1998.

Platt, John, *Murmur*, Schirmer, 1999.

Sullivan, Denise, *Talk About the Passion*, Da Capo, 1998.

Picture Credits

Index